CW01432165

mastering Raku

mastering Raku

Steven Branfman

- Making Ware
- Glazes
- Building Kilns
- Firing

LARK BOOKS

A Division of Sterling Publishing Co., Inc.
New York / London

Editor: Larry Shea

Text Editor: Chris Rich

Development Editor: Suzanne J. E. Tourtillott

Art Director: Carol Morse

Illustrator: Olivier Rollin

Photographer: Nicki Pardo

Cover Designer: Chris Bryant

Library of Congress Cataloging-in-Publication Data

Branfman, Steven.
    Mastering raku : making ware, glazes, building kilns, firing / Steven
Branfman.—1st ed.
      p. cm.
    Includes index.
    ISBN 978-1-60059-295-9 (hc-plc with jacket : alk. paper)
    1. Pottery craft.   2. Raku pottery.   I. Title.
   TT920.B695 2009
   738.3'7—dc22

                           2009003805

10 9 8 7 6 5 4 3 2 1

First Edition

Published by Lark Books, A Division of Sterling Publishing Co., Inc.
387 Park Avenue South, New York, NY 10016

Text © 2009, Steven Branfman
Photography © 2009, Lark Books, a Division of Sterling Publishing Co., Inc.,
unless otherwise specified
Illustrations © 2009, Lark Books, a Division of Sterling Publishing Co., Inc.

Cover gallery images: back cover: Steven Branfman, *Vessel* (page 66); front flap: Ruth Apter, *White
Buffalo* (page 143); back flap: Kate Jacobson and Will Jacobson, *Auntie's Garden* (page 131).

Distributed in Canada by Sterling Publishing, c/o Canadian Manda Group, 165 Dufferin Street
Toronto, Ontario, Canada M6K 3H6

Distributed in the United Kingdom by GMC Distribution Services, Castle Place, 166 High Street,
Lewes, East Sussex, England BN7 1XU

Distributed in Australia by Capricorn Link (Australia) Pty Ltd., P.O. Box 704,
Windsor, NSW 2756 Australia

The written instructions, photographs, designs, patterns, and projects in this volume are
intended for the personal use of the reader and may be reproduced for that purpose only.
Any other use, especially commercial use, is forbidden under law without written permission
of the copyright holder.

Every effort has been made to ensure that all the information in this book is accurate. However,
due to differing conditions, tools, and individual skills, the publisher cannot be responsible for any
injuries, losses, and other damages that may result from the use of the information in this book.

If you have questions or comments about this book, please contact:
Lark Books
67 Broadway
Asheville, NC 28801
828-253-0467

Manufactured in China
All rights reserved

ISBN-13: 978-1-60059-295-9

For information about custom editions, special sales, premium and corporate purchases, please
contact Sterling Special Sales Department at 800-805-5489 or specialsales@sterlingpub.com.

mastering Raku

STEVEN BRANFMAN
Tea Bowl, 2008
3 x 4 inches (7.6 x 10.2 cm)
Brushed multi layered commercial low fire glaze; pressed surface texture

My introduction to raku came many years ago, when I was a graduate student at the Rhode Island School of Design. While working quietly in the studio, a student burst through the doors from the kiln room, coughing wildly, tears streaming from his eyes. "What are you doing?" I asked. "Raku," he choked out through the cloud of smoke that had followed him. "What's that?" I asked. "Firing technique," he gasped. That's all he said, but it changed the course of my career. My fascination with raku firing hasn't let up since that day.

The first two things I learned about this wonderfully participatory and creative firing technique were: indoors isn't the ideal location for it and billowing clouds of smoke definitely aren't prerequisites for success. *Mastering Raku* is my effort to share with both novice

STEVEN BRANFMAN
Vessel, 2007
21 1/2 x 10 inches (54.6 x 25.4 cm)
Brushed multi layered raku and
commercial low fire glaze; pressed and
combed surface texture

and expert potters the many other lessons I've learned in the years since then.

What is raku? The simplest answer is that raku is a firing technique and a type of ceramic ware that have utterly metamorphosed since their sixteenth-century Japanese origins (see pages 12–17 for more detail). Traditional raku pieces— the exquisitely simple but beautiful earthenware bowls produced for the Japanese tea ceremony—were fired at low temperatures, removed from the kiln while still hot, and either immediately placed in water or cooled in the open air.

The Japanese potters who created this ware might not recognize contemporary Western raku in its many forms, but at its most rudimentary level today's raku does stay close to its origins. It's still a low-fire pottery technique that requires quick heating and quick cooling the ware. Pieces are placed in a kiln, brought up to temperature, and—when the glazes have matured—removed from the kiln, and either cooled quickly in water, in the open air, or—a Western innovation—placed immediately in a container with combustible material, covered, and allowed to smoke for a predetermined length of time. Today's potters practice many variations, of course— and those variations are among the aspects of raku that make it so absorbing.

My intent when I wrote *Mastering Raku* was to create the book that didn't exist when I first tried my hand at this craft—a book that not only walks beginning potters through every step of a basic raku firing, but that also helps experienced potters expand and evolve as artists. Within these pages, I offer readers a brief introduction to the history of raku in its many incarnations, a wealth of practical information, and the encouragement to explore their own aesthetics. I know from experience that the spontaneous processes

and sometimes unpredictable results of raku are well within reach of beginners; I've been teaching raku since 1974. I also know, as an experienced ceramic artist, that raku offers something that few other firing techniques do: a deep and satisfying participation in the firing process itself—and through that involvement, countless opportunities to grow.

For beginners who've only worked with conventional firing before, the book includes easy-to-follow explanations of every basic aspect of raku, from how to choose appropriate commercial clays and glazes (or formulate your own) and how to build raku kilns, to simple firing, post-firing, and finishing techniques. For long-time raku practitioners and teachers, I describe a variety of advanced techniques and offer tips I've gleaned from my own raku experiences, as well as a wide selection of clay and glaze recipes. Critical health and safety issues are covered in a separate chapter, but I address specific health-related concerns throughout the book. And, thanks to the generosity of many of today's finest raku artists, I've been able to include photographs of many truly inspiring works.

My emphasis throughout *Mastering Raku* is on experimentation and creativity. Unlike conventional firing methods, raku invites—and in fact, demands—both. You won't be pressing electronic kiln controls, for example, or waiting for cones to tell you when your glazes are mature. Instead, you'll be active in every aspect of the firing. You'll learn how to control the kiln—which I'll show you how to build yourself—by monitoring the fuel supply and air intake closely, and adjusting them as needed. You'll determine glaze maturity visually by watching the various stages a glaze goes through as it's fired.

STEVEN BRANFMAN
Tea Bowl, 2008
3¹/₂ x 4 inches (8.9 x 10.2 cm)
Brushed raku and commercial low fire glaze; altered shape

You'll (deftly, I hope) unload your ware while it's glowing hot, and quickly transfer it to reduction containers for smoking.

Before you begin, let me offer these words of encouragement: once you understand the processes that make raku what it is, you'll find that the world it inhabits is a remarkably flexible and inviting one. Don't be afraid to experiment. My hope is that you'll treat the information in this book as a starting point for your own expeditions into creativity.

Fine lines exist between technical expertise, unbridled expression, and aesthetic success. Even if you're experienced with other firing techniques, you may sometimes find the raku process unpredictable, seemingly uncontrollable, and possibly frustrating. But I hope you'll also find it refreshing. Allow yourself to grow into raku. With patience and practice, you'll achieve success on all fronts.

what is
Raku?

CHAPTER 1

Raku is often surrounded by
confusion. Is it a pottery-making,
glazing, or firing method? Is it a
philosophy or religion? A family
name or place? A custom, ritual,
or ceremony? Defining raku is
a difficult task, in part because
traditional raku can be viewed
from many different perspectives—
technical, historical, cultural, and
aesthetic—and in part because the
many forms that contemporary raku
takes can be so different from those it
took in the past.

STEVEN BRANFMAN
Vessel, 2008
15 x 8 inches (38.1 x 20.3 cm)
Brushed multi layered commercial low fire glaze;
pressed surface texture

Raku as a Pottery Technique

Raku can be described as a category of pottery, just as one might describe salt or wood firing, maiolica, lusterware, or earthenware. *At its most rudimentary technical level, contemporary raku is differentiated from other pottery protocols by the fact that the ware is fired quickly at low temperatures and cooled quickly as well.* Unlike most conventional methods, in which pots are fired over an 8- to 15-hour cycle and unloaded from the kiln after they've cooled, raku ware is fired in cycles as short as 15 minutes. When the glaze has matured, the hot pieces are removed from the kiln and cooled in the open air, cooled immediately in water, or—a distinctly Western technique—immediately smoked in a combustible material during what's known as a *post-firing reduction phase* (see pages 21 and 108–110).

Traditional Japanese raku, which was much more limited in technical scope, fell into two broad categories: *red raku* and *black raku*. Red raku was made with a red earthenware clay; glazed with a creamy, clear glaze; fired quickly to a low temperature; removed from the kiln while hot; and allowed to cool. (Some historical sources claim that the red color was achieved by covering the clay with an ochre slip prior to glazing.) Black raku, on the other hand, was made with a stoneware clay, decorated with a black glaze, and fired more slowly to stoneware temperatures. Rapid cooling of the ware contributed both to its black color and to its texture. Both types of raku were bisque fired prior to being raku fired.

Most pottery processes limit the creative influence of the potter during the firing. Contemporary raku firing, however, extends our creative involvement as far as we care to go. A raku piece doesn't disappear into a kiln and emerge as finished ware. Our eyes are almost always on it; we're continually judging, determining, deciding, and altering. We end the firing when we see fit, usually without the aid of cones or other temperature-measuring devices, and we alone determine how or whether to carry out the post-firing phase and subsequent steps. The conventions and so-called rules of today's raku are flexible enough to change along with the potter's expectations.

Because traditional and contemporary raku can be so dissimilar, a reasonable case can be made for completely abandoning the word "raku" as a label for today's ware, but I contend that calling our ware by its Japanese name encourages us to connect intellectually and philosophically with raku's beginnings. Our practice of raku, even with its Western innovations and aesthetic principles, is still intimately bound to the spirit and traditional practice of the original technique. Maintaining that connection is as much about respect, remembrance, and gratitude as it is about aesthetic style and technical methods. Today's raku offers us the best of two worlds. While it's deeply rooted in Japanese tradition, its incarnations are very different. We can simultaneously work in a traditional style, with an established protocol, and in a contemporary manner, defining our own rules as our work is in progress.

JOHN MATHIESON
Tea Bowl, 2008
$6^{1}/_{2}$ x $4^{3}/_{4}$ x $3^{15}/_{16}$ inches
(16.5 x 12 x 10 cm)
Thrown, rolled and cut T-Material and Harry Fraser porcelain; dipped glaze; roulette rolled, splash lines; propane fired, 900°C on pyrometer; air cooling, reduction in mixed sawdust
Photo by artist

All of my raku work pictured in this book (such as the piece on the facing page) is wheel thrown Laguna #250; propane fired; post firing with controlled cooling and coarse sawdust, wood shavings, or pine needles.

PATRICK CRABB
Untitled
(Shard Vase Series), 2001
24 x 14 x 6 inches
(61 x 35.6 x 15.2 cm)
Thrown and altered recycled clay;
broken and reassembled with shards
decorated and fired individually
as follows: brushed and sprayed
glaze; brushwork, masking tape
resist, sigillatta burnish; electric and
gas fired; air cooling, smoking for
reduction; cone 05
Photo by artist

The History of Raku

The cultural and historical auras associated with raku—unlike those associated with many other techniques—are unusually strong and have had a great influence on its contemporary practice. When potters want to learn salt firing, for example, they don't often feel impelled to research the entire history and social context of German salt-glazed ware or delve into its origins and development in centuries past. And whether or not they adhere faithfully to the original aesthetics of salt-glazed ware seems unimportant. So why is the opposite true when it comes to raku? I can't offer you a definitive answer, but perhaps one can be found in the word "raku" itself—a Japanese word that never fails to remind us of this technique's beginnings. When those of us who feel that our own pottery roots emanate from Eastern rather than Western civilization lay claim to a process so strongly associated with its founders, perhaps we feel a sense of guilt. For whatever reasons, raku does tend to compel us to connect in some way with its history.

As a modern potter interested in pursuing a contemporary process, why should you bother to consider the origins and historical significance of raku? Because through your practice of raku, you're part of its continuing evolution, one from which you can benefit and to which you may add. The goal of learning anything new should be to amass an inventory of knowledge that you can apply in whole or in part to solving particular problems. Developing an historical perspective, especially in the case of raku, allows us not only to appreciate and learn from the efforts of our predecessors but also to be innovative ourselves.

Japanese Origins

The story of how raku began is fascinating, provocative—and still somewhat mysterious. We know that as a style of pottery, it originated in the Kyoto area of Japan during the Momoyama period (1573–1615). Popular belief, supported by the writings of numerous historians, has held that two men there—Chojiro, a Korean potter and tile maker enslaved by the Japanese, and Sen no Rikyu, a preeminent tea master at that time—were responsible for the creation and popularization of raku, respectively.

According to these accounts, the tea master Rikyu developed and codified the Zen-based aesthetic philosophy known as *Wabi-No-Chado.* To understand this philosophy—one deeply embedded in the Japanese tea ceremony and in traditional raku ware—we must take a look at the tea ceremony (*Cha-no-yu*) itself, a ritual established centuries ago that has been refined through the ages. Its practice is designed to invoke a uniform aesthetic response to the strictly formalized preparation and drinking of tea. Central to the aesthetic established by Rikyu are the Zen Buddhist concepts of *wabi* and *shibui.* Wabi encompasses the Zen principles of austerity, transience, seclusion, and tranquility and is the intangible essence of the tea ceremony—its simplicity, harmony, and restraint. Shibui encompasses the same attributes but in a more concrete way; it's the visible beauty in objects—in fact, the ultimate beauty in them.

How does this philosophy relate to raku? Rikyu sought out and patronized craftspeople whose work reflected the qualities of wabi, and Chojiro was one of those craftspeople. Rikyu brought Chojiro's unique raku ware to the attention of both the emperor and Rikyu's *daimyo* (feudal lord) and tea student Hideyoshi. The emperor's patronage and Hideyoshi's influence with other tea practitioners made the ware popular. It was greatly prized by Japanese tea masters because it was unpretentious but aesthetically pleasing, and it embodied the wabi ideal. On a more practical level, the porous clay body from which raku ware was made acted as insulation between the hot tea and the hand and produced a pleasantly dull, gentle sound when it came in contact with utensils and tabletops.

In this version of raku's origins, Hideyoshi, in memory of Chojiro, bestowed a gold seal on Chojiro's son Jokei, who had continued to produce the ware. The word "raku"—loosely translated to mean enjoyment, pleasure, comfort, happiness, or contentment—is believed to have come from the ideograph engraved on that gold seal. Chojiro's descendants, the "Raku Family," still practice raku today. In fact, many people still believe that only the Raku Family can produce true raku. The title of the head of that family in any generation is *Kichizaemon* or *Raku-san*.

While this account of raku's beginnings is tidy, it appears to be more myth than truth. Building on the work of Japanese archaeologists, Morgan Pitelka, a professor of Asian Studies, published research in his 2005 book *Handmade Culture* that points to a different story. Chojiro was not an enslaved Korean but more likely one of a group of Chinese potters who had immigrated to Kyoto, bringing with them a low-fire, lead-glazed technique from Fujian, China—a technique derived from an ancient Chinese style known as "three color ware." Supporting Pitelka's view is the fact that numerous examples of tea ware and other pottery forms similar to Chojiro's, made during the same time but clearly from different kilns, have been found in many Japanese cities. Furthermore, the word "raku" probably didn't originate with Chojiro's gold seal; it's more likely an abbreviation of Jurakudai, an area of Kyoto where some of these early raku potters dug their clay. Pitelka's perspective has influenced the long-standing view of the contemporary Raku Family. Kichizaemon XV, the current head of that family, continues the raku tradition, but the family is no longer universally thought of as "sole proprietor" of the traditional raku technique.

RAKU TAN'NYU (1795–1854)
Red Raku Tea Bowl
3¼ x 4½ inches (8.3 x 11.4 cm)
Photo by Lance Keimig
Courtesy of the Art Complex Museum, Duxbury, MA

WALLY ASSELBERGHS
UCO (Unidentified Ceramic Object), 2007
10⅝ x 10⅝ x 4⁵⁄₁₆ inches
(27 x 27 x 11 cm)
Press molded and slab built Westerwald Clay; splashed glaze; burnished; gas fired; smoking for reduction
Photo by Lucille Feremans

The details of the raku firing process in those early days have been difficult to unearth, but archaeological records indicate that one or two pots at a time were placed in a small indoor kiln, quickly brought up to temperature (black raku was fired more slowly than red), removed from the kiln with tongs, and allowed to cool in the open air. Just how this method of firing developed is a matter of speculation. One explanation is that in an effort to speed up the firing process during the production of clay roof tiles, impatient potters removed the still-hot tiles from the kiln. Most likely to their surprise, the tiles remained intact despite the rapid cooling. Supporting this theory are two facts: Chojiro was a maker of roof tiles, and the oldest existing example of his work was probably fired in this way.

JAMES C. WATKINS
Raku Tea Pot, 2007
15 x 13 inches (38.1 x 33 cm)
Hand built and wheel thrown
personal clay; brushed glaze; carved;
gas fired; smoking for reduction
Photo by Jon Thompson

Raku Moves West

Bernard Leach, a painter who had no experience with pottery, was the person who first brought raku to the attention of the Western world. In 1911, while living in Japan, Leach attended the same kind of *raku party* (a group-firing experience) that has introduced many of today's potters to raku. According to Leach, he and the other guests—painters, writers, and actors among them— were invited to decorate bisque ware with strange pigments using "queer long brushes." The pots were then dipped into a thick glaze and placed in a preheated kiln. Much to Leach's surprise, the pots didn't break. After half an hour or so, he could see the melted and glossy glaze through the spyhole in the kiln. The hot pots were then removed from the kiln and allowed to cool, and again Leach was amazed that the pots didn't break during the rapid cooling.

Although this was the experience that inspired Leach to study pottery in the first place, he felt that raku as a technique had limited creative possibilities for the contemporary studio potter who wanted to develop a personal style and make an artistic statement through clay. He viewed raku as a way to have fun and entertain his friends and customers. By the way, a common misconception, probably contributed to by Leach's account of his first raku experience, is that the raku firing itself is part of the Japanese tea ceremony. It isn't!

Warren Gilbertson, who lived and worked in Japan from 1938 to 1940, is credited as being the first American potter to study raku seriously in that country. When he returned home, the Art Institute of Chicago held a major exhibition of his work. While no written account of that show exists today, some raku pieces were undoubtedly among the several hundred exhibited. In 1942, Gilbertson presented a paper at the annual meeting of the American Ceramic Society titled "Making of Raku Ware and Its Value in the Teaching of Beginner's Pottery in America," in which he described the raku process, glazes, decoration, and types of kilns. As the title of his paper implies, he viewed the technique merely as a curiosity that could be used to introduce pottery making to beginners; he made only cursory note of any cultural significance that raku may have had. Gilbertson was at the forefront of the newly emerging studio pottery movement in America. Tragically, he died in an automobile crash in 1954 before the movement was fully underway.

Exactly when the American raku movement started, beyond Gilbertson's introduction of the technique, is difficult to ascertain. Perhaps its earliest pioneer was Hal Riegger, who was already experimenting with raku in the late 1940s. Riegger had a strong interest in Zen studies and maintained a steadfast commitment to a traditional and spiritual involvement with the raku technique. He advocated both the use of standard hand-building methods to make the ware and the traditional use of wood- and coal-burning kilns to fire it. He presented raku through primitive-firing workshops and demonstrations, and in 1958, he taught raku at the Haystack Mountain School of Crafts. A three-part article Riegger wrote and published in *Ceramics Monthly* in 1965 appears to be the first major writing on the subject, and his book *Raku Art and Technique* (Van Nostrand, 1970)

was the first to bring both the history of raku and instruction in the new Western variation of this technique to a wide audience.

A raku bowl Riegger made in 1948 (right) shows a beautifully crackled copper glaze. It is possibly the earliest example of what we have come to call "post-firing reduction." In June, 2000, Riegger wrote, "I really don't remember where I picked up the idea of 'post-glaze reduction.' Other than reading Leach and Gilbertson, my first instruction was from a Japanese student at CCAC (California College of Arts and Crafts) in Oakland named Kaz Hirai, who loaned me a department store catalog of an exhibit of raku tea bowls ... Of course traditionally the Japanese did not reduce pots after the glaze firing but rather before, so I must have misinterpreted that. It's the only explanation I can think of."

HAL RIEGGER
Tea Bowl, 1948
3½ x 4 inches (8.9 x 10.2 cm)
Thrown and carved; copper glaze; reduction in sawdust
Photo by artist

A common misconception is that the raku firing itself is part of the Japanese tea ceremony. It isn't!

At about the same time, Jean Griffith and some fellow graduate students at the University of Washington were also experimenting with the raku process. Using Leach as a guide, they held raku parties and presented demonstrations. They, too, included a post-firing reduction phase as part of their technique, but as Griffith once related, they didn't know who had first incorporated that phase.

RAKU SONYU (1664–1716)
Black Raku Tea Bowl "Eboshi"
3³⁄₈ x 4⁵⁄₈ inches (8.6 x 11.7 cm)
Photo by Lance Keimig
*Courtesy of the Art Complex Museum,
Duxbury, MA*

Paul Soldner is the potter most responsible for establishing raku as a popular, creative method of pottery making in the West. He began his raku experiments around 1960 with information gathered only from Leach's *A Potter's Book* (Faber and Faber, 1940). Because Soldner was dissatisfied with the bland nature of the color development in his raku pots, he spontaneously placed a still-hot, fired piece in some leaves and allowed the leaves to burn. He thus made another "discovery" of post-firing reduction. When he found out that other American potters were also smoking their ware, he assumed this post-firing process must be a traditional part of raku. Not until he visited Japan in the early 1970s did it become clear to him that it wasn't.

Neither Riegger nor Soldner knew it then, but both were working with raku and post-firing reduction during roughly the same time period. Although Riegger began to experiment with raku in 1948, as many as 12 years before Soldner, he has never been fully credited with this innovation (perhaps because of his quiet, reserved approach to his work).

Leaders in the early development of the Western-style raku technique also

PAUL SOLDNER
Vessel, 1972
10¹⁄₂ x 12¹⁄₂ x 6¹⁄₂ inches (26.7 x 31.8 x 16.5 cm)
Thrown and altered; brushed and dipped glaze; smoking for reduction
Photo by Nicole Frazer
Courtesy of David Armstrong

include Bill Abright, Nancy Baldwin, Jamie Davis, Rick Dillingham, Angelo Garzio, Wayne Higby, Rick Hirsch, Anne Hyland, Susan and Steven Kemenyffy, David Kuraoka, David Middlebrook, Robert Piepenburg, Jim Romberg, Harvey Sadow, Howard-Yana Shapiro, Kit-Yin Snyder, Dave Tell, Billy Waters, and Sue Wechsler. These potters, with others, have contributed stimulating perspectives and notable variations to this exciting process. Soldner, Riegger, Griffith, and these many pioneers were truly breaking new creative ground. They had no experts to guide them or answer questions. They carried out their experiments by trial and error and tried to make their "accidents" work aesthetically.

Western raku is still evolving. It survived the raku mania of the 1970s and 1980s, when raku had fad-like appeal, and has now settled as a mainstream process that exists from coast to coast. Of course, raku has also continued to develop in Japan, where there are four basic raku "camps." One is still loyal to the concept that only the Raku Family can and should make raku ware. Closely aligned to that group is another that accepts as legitimate and authentic the ware made by a few other families with historical connections to the Raku Family. Then there are the potters who have no connection to the Raku Family at all but who do create traditional-style raku ware. Not surprisingly, the fourth camp is the generation of new young potters who work within the Western raku style and its influences.

Here's a story that illustrates the difficulty of defining raku in an objective way. In 1978, Rick Hirsch, an early innovator in contemporary Western raku, demonstrated the technique to an audience in Kyoto that included the Prince and Princess of Japan, as well as the fourteenth-generation Kichizaemon. Raku-san was extremely impressed by Hirsch's demonstration of firing, post-firing reduction, and fuming. He praised Hirsch's technique by describing his own work as a "butterfly" and this new American method as a "bird."

But Raku-san was clearly confused by Hirsch's calling his technique "raku." He hadn't realized that raku was known, appreciated, and possibly even understood outside Japan—or that what Hirsch was demonstrating was a version of it. In his eyes, American potters had simply taken his style of quick firing beyond its traditional boundaries.

During the ensuing panel discussion, in which both Hirsch and Paul Soldner were participants, Tadanari Mitsuoka, a prominent Japanese art historian, adamantly refused to recognize Hirsch's process as raku, thus deepening Raku-san's confusion. The possibility that anyone other than the Raku Family could produce raku was inconceivable to him.

Soldner, who realized that Japanese and Westerners did many things in opposite ways, responded to the differences between raku as practiced by Raku-san and his family and the raku practiced by himself and other American potters by declaring that he would call his own work "ukar"—raku spelled backwards.

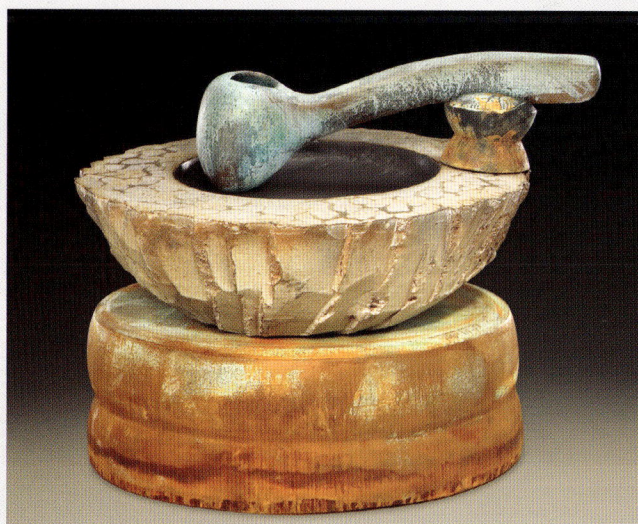

RICHARD HIRSCH
Altar Bowl with Ladle #1, 2007
19 x 24 x 24 inches (48.3 x 61 x 61 cm)
Relief sculpted, wheel thrown, and thrown and altered clay; sprayed and sponged glaze; gas fired; selective smoking for reduction; cone 04
Photo by Geoff Tesh

The Aesthetics of Raku

BILL ABRIGHT
Birdland, 2007
20 x 16 x 7 inches
(50.8 x 40.6 x 17.8 cm)
Big Red clay; poured glaze;
paint/non-ceramic/non-
fired; gas fired; selective
smoking for reduction
Photo by Jay Graham

The aesthetics of raku originated in Zen Buddhism and the Japanese tea ceremony. Tea masters deliberately attempted to incorporate the ideals of wabi and shibui, along with the principles of Zen, into the ceremony by demanding that tea ware have a humble, spontaneous, and innocent appearance and that it encourage a physical and emotional connection between human beings and nature. Potters who make raku ware for the tea ceremony continue to express these ideals in their work by using conventions of asymmetry: soft, undulating rims and surfaces, spontaneous drips and impressions, irregular hand-carved feet, and a general unevenness—all intentional and controlled, although the results appear completely uncontrived. Although the Zen concepts embedded in traditional raku are subtle and sometimes difficult to understand, when we're in the presence of—and even have the opportunity to hold, as I have—a raku tea bowl of the seventeenth or eighteenth century, our appreciation of them can elicit an intensely moving emotional experience. I had a similar response when I stood in front of Michelangelo's *David*; it brought me to tears.

Just as a grasp of the Japanese underpinnings of the tea ceremony is important to our understanding of raku, so are the aesthetic boundaries that we may find ourselves working with today. Most of us who now do raku aren't doing it under the umbrella of the tea ceremony, so which, if any, aesthetic rules apply to us?

Pottery originated as functional ware. The potter of old infused all of his or her creative energies into the object itself and how it would be used, without regard for that object's eventual audience. For the Chinese folk potter throwing rice bowls on a kick wheel, the East African potter coil-building storage containers on a tree stump, and the nineteenth-century American in Bennington, Vermont, turning a molasses jug on a treadle wheel—their efforts to achieve a pleasing aesthetic and functional success were essentially the same. This function-based tradition forms the foundation of our aesthetics today, but what we build on that foundation is up to us.

To be successful, our creations must be governed by a sense of organization that brings together material, method, and design—components that are often seen as disparate—into a harmonious and satisfying package. Just as we no longer automatically refer to ourselves as "potters," but as ceramists, clay workers, ceramic sculptors, craftspeople, artists, artist-potters, and artist-craftspeople, so too have our aesthetic concepts been broadened and redefined—to such an extent that they have sometimes polarized the ceramics community.

How does raku fit into this complicated picture? If you're new to raku, you may find that the process places you in unfamiliar territory. Ware that's been successful for you in the past may suddenly prove uninspiring as raku. Glaze applications, brush strokes, and textures that rendered strong statements of color and design in your previous work may prove weak. Likewise, the subtle effects you obtained through well-practiced techniques may appear crude and uncontrolled in raku—or they may not appear at all.

Periods of adjustment are inevitable when you're exploring any unfamiliar area, so let me encourage you to persevere until you come to grips with the raku technique and its idiosyncrasies. Embrace the aesthetic tenets I've described, even though they may seem difficult to understand at first. Learn the origins of raku, and become familiar with its traditional practice. Recognize the ways in which raku has evolved and branched off to embrace the modern methods that Western potters have applied to it.

Successful work comes from a combination of aesthetic sophistication and technical expertise in which neither is sacrificed in favor of the other. The more raku you produce, the finer your control becomes and the more the nuances make themselves apparent. As your skills develop through practice and perseverance, you'll define raku for yourself. That process of evolution is precisely what makes raku so special. In an address to the International Ceramics Symposium, Paul Soldner described a spirit of "rakuness" that we can strive for in our work—a state that transcends any one pottery-making technique or any individual kind of creative act—in which our work appears to be effortless and has no ties to any one form of expression, culture, or religion. Perhaps that is the true definition of raku.

There are those who still maintain that only the raku created for the traditional Japanese tea ceremony, using traditional techniques and established aesthetic

pedagogy, is "real" raku. Others regard raku as nothing more than an enjoyable hobby. But for many potters, raku is a creative and evolving technique with undeniable connections to a rich spiritual and cultural heritage—one in which much still remains to be discovered, experienced, and shared. I believe that our practice of raku today, with all its technical and aesthetic innovations, is connected to the past through a transcendental quality but shouldn't compete with it. Our work must be able to stand alone aesthetically. While my work, like that of many potters, doesn't pay exclusive homage to the ideals of raku's origins, I never forget them. I hope that you find, as I have, that raku allows you a combination of exciting technique and satisfying aesthetics—both a contemporary style and a rich historical tradition.

My dear Japanese friend, Makoto Yabe, who passed away in 2005, first learned pottery in a traditional apprenticeship in his homeland. He would often tell me, with pride, about the first six months he spent doing nothing but sweeping up after the master. He spent the next six months learning how to wedge, another six months learning how to center clay on the wheel—and so on. When he shared this story with participants at his workshops, their faces would fall and a few would even ask why he stood for that kind of abuse. "Abuse?" he'd say, shaking his head with surprise at the word choice. "To learn," Makoto explained, "to learn."

EXTERIOR/INTERIOR OF
***SHOFUAN* (PINE WIND HUT)**
FOR THE TEA CEREMONY
Photo by Lance Keimig
Courtesy of the Art Complex Museum,
Duxbury, MA

Frequently Asked Questions about Raku

ATTRIBUTED TO RAKU KEINYU (1817–1902)
Black Raku Tea Bowl
3 x 3¾ inches (7.6 x 9.5 cm)
Photo by Lance Keimig
Courtesy of the Art Complex Museum, Duxbury, MA

RAKU KONYU (1857–1932)
Raku with Black Glaze Tea Bowl "Seppo" (Snowy Peak)
4¼ x 3⅞ inches
(10.8 x 9.8 cm)
Photo by Lance Keimig
Courtesy of the Art Complex Museum, Duxbury, MA

Q: *Is raku a philosophy, religion, Buddhist ceremony, or pottery technique?*
A: Any or all of the above can be true, depending on the potter. (See pages 11 and 18–19.)

Q: *Isn't raku when you fire your pots in a pit instead of a kiln?*
A: Pit firing, smoke firing, and sawdust firing are not the same as raku firing, although the contemporary raku potter sometimes borrows methods from them. Raku ware is fired in a more or less conventional kiln, using standard glaze technology. Pit firing is a primitive technique in which the ware is loaded into a shallow pit and surrounded by the fuel (usually wood). The maturing temperatures are generally lower for pit-fired ware, and glazes aren't usually used on it. (See pages 133–135.)

Q: *Didn't Paul Soldner invent raku?*
A: The raku technique was first developed in sixteenth-century Japan. Soldner was (and is) an innovator in Western raku. He was one of a few people responsible for popularizing it in the United States during the 1950s and 1960s. (See page 16.)

Q: *Is raku suitable for functional work?*
A: No. Traditional use of raku ware in the Japanese tea ceremony has contributed to confusion regarding this issue. All raku-fired ware is fragile, porous, and generally unsuitable for functional use. Think of raku as decorative. (See page 26.)

Q: *My kiln won't reach temperature, no matter how much gas I use. Why?*
A: Chances are that your air-gas mixture is too low on air. One result of insufficient air is a reduction atmosphere in the kiln. Increase your primary and secondary air sources. (See pages 56 and 100–103.)

Q: *Isn't raku a once-fire process in which you don't have to bisque fire your ware first?*
A: Although raku-firing green ware is possible and some potters do fire this way, it's a sure way to line the bottom of your kiln with shards. Resist the temptation. (See pages 34–35.)

Q: *Which cones do I use in a raku firing?*
A: The only cones that should be used near a raku firing are ice cream cones! Due to the fast firing of raku, the varying kiln atmospheres during firing, the firing of multiple loads, and other factors, cones aren't as reliable in raku firings as they are in conventional ones. In raku, visual observation is the best way to determine glaze maturity. In a few situations, such as firing a load of unglazed ware for matte and smoke effects or when your maturing temperature is so fixed and consistent that monitoring the glaze melt is unnecessary, you may find cones or a pyrometer useful. (See pages 103–104 and 122–123.)

Q: *What's the difference between raku firing and salt firing?*
A: Salt firing, soda firing, and other forms of vapor glazing are occasionally confused with raku because adaptations and variations of these techniques are sometimes incorporated in raku firing and post-firing. (See pages 118–121 and 126.)

Q: *Can I fire raku in an electric kiln?*
A: Most certainly. (See pages 53–55.)

Q: *Don't the tongs used to remove hot pots from the kiln leave marks on the ware?*
A: Sometimes. Usually, though, the glaze is still molten enough to melt over the point of contact. Tong marks shouldn't be treated as defects anyway but as characteristics of raku. Historically, they were accepted as a natural part of the raku process and were an indication of how deftly the potter handled the tongs.

Q: *How do you get those bright metallic effects? Sometimes my glazes don't crackle as much as I like. What can I do?*
A: Let's assume that you're using the right glazes and have applied them correctly. Keep in mind that both metallic effects and dark crackle lines result from a fast post-firing reduction technique. You must move your pot quickly from the kiln to the reduction container and cover the container before the pot has a chance to reoxidize. (See pages 108–110.)

Q: *I'm confused about the term "reduction" in raku firing. Isn't reduction a high-fire technique?*
A: In its simplest form, reduction is a method of reducing the amount of free oxygen available for combustion. You can accomplish it at any temperature and in any type of kiln. In raku, it's most often carried out in the post-firing step, though it can also be done during firing. Depending on the glazes and firing method, reduction can have many different effects. (See pages 57–58 and pages 108–110.)

Q: *I understand that I need a special clay to do raku. What is a raku clay?*
A: A raku clay is any clay you can successfully raku fire—in other words, any clay that can withstand the fast firing and fast cooling of the raku process. Many clays are suitable, without alteration or special formulation. (See pages 29–35 and 159–162.)

Q: *How much experience do I need to do raku on my own? I've seen it done a few times, but it looks complicated. Can I really build my own kiln? What do I need to get started? Help!*
A: Before tackling raku on your own, you do need to be familiar with basic pottery-making and firing techniques. Take a class at a local pottery or craft center or through an adult education program. I also recommend reading a good general pottery handbook. Yes, you can build your own kiln. What do you need to get started? A willingness to learn and to be frustrated at times—and this book. Good luck!

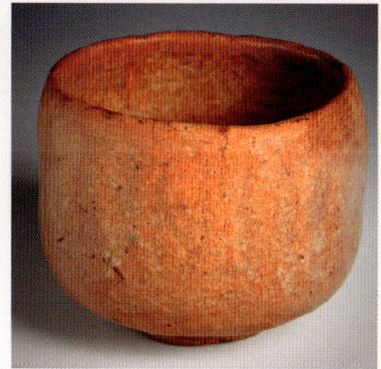

CHOJIRO (1516–1592)
Red Raku Tea Bowl "Nokitsuni"
(Wild Fox)
3⁵⁄₁₆ x 3¹¹⁄₁₆ inches
(8.4 x 9.4 cm)
Red earthenware; clear glaze
Photo by Lance Keimig
Courtesy of the Art Complex
Museum, Duxbury, MA

**ATTRIBUTED TO RAKU
DONYU (1599–1656)**
Black Raku Tea Bowl "Tsutsu"
3³⁄₄ x 4 inches (9.5 x 10.2 cm)
Photo by Lance Keimig
Courtesy of the Art Complex Museum,
Duxbury, MA

health and
Safety

CHAPTER 2

While I'm not about to break new ground on this front, it's impossible to stress safety too much. That's why I address safety issues throughout this book. Far too many people suffer from the "it won't happen to me" syndrome. Whether they're professionals, hobbyists, or students, all potters must realize that their materials and equipment, as well as their surroundings, have the potential to cause, at best, short-term injuries (such as burns, strains, and irritations) and, at worst, chronic physiological conditions. Now that I've issued that grim warning, let me add that staying safe isn't that difficult!

STEVEN BRANFMAN
Vessel, 2007
13½ x 10 inches (34.3 x 25.4 cm)
Brushed and splattered multi layered
stoneware and commercial low fire glaze;
combed and impressed surface texture

Studio Design and Maintenance

Safety begins in the studio. Whether your workspace is small and humble or enviably large, its layout is critical. You'll find in-depth information on designing a space for maximum efficiency and production in my book *The Potter's Professional Handbook* (The American Ceramic Society, 1999). Meanwhile, let me offer some safety-related tips here.

To reduce the likelihood of tripping over your own pots, keep objects off the floor and up on tabletops, countertops, and shelves (see photo 1). Also, keep stairways and doorways clear. The first thing I hear from visitors to my studio is: "I've never seen so many shelves!"

Design and lay out spaces that minimize the need to reach for supplies and tools. Organize your clay and materials storage areas close to entrances or loading docks. Your back will thank you.

Every studio requires general ventilation to keep the atmosphere in it and in separate work spaces safe. Studios also require task-specific ventilation to prevent particular hazards, such as those that arise from air brushing, sanding, kiln emissions, and—for those of you who haven't switched to safer wax emulsions—melting wax. For a complete treatment of ventilation in your studio, I recommend *Ventilation* by Nancy Clark, Thomas Cutter, and Jean-Ann McGrane (Lyons Press, 1987).

Keep your studio immaculately clean. Never dry-sweep it. Instead, wet-clean or use a vacuum cleaner equipped with a *high efficiency particulate air* (HEPA) filter. These filters trap 99.97 percent of airborne particles that are 0.3 micrometers in diameter or larger. Never, under any circumstances, use a home or shop vacuum cleaner unless it's equipped with this type of filter. Standard filter systems aren't designed to trap the fine dust that potters produce; they just re-circulate silica and other types of dust that you generate. Avoid sweeping compounds, too.

DAVID ROBERTS
Counterpoint Vessel, 2008
13 x 11 13/16 x 11 13/16 inches
(33 x 30 x 30 cm)
Hand built T material; poured glaze; sgraffito, marking with latex resist; gas fired; smoking for reduction
Photo by Jerry Hardman-Jones

1

DAPHNE CORREGAN
Pichets Sur Socles, 2003
44$\frac{1}{16}$ x 44$\frac{1}{16}$ x 7$\frac{7}{8}$ inches
(112 x 112 x 20 cm)
Slab built Solargil clay; brushed
glaze; sgraffito, engobes; gas fired;
controlled cooling,
smoking for reduction
Photo by Jean-Marc Pharisien

Kiln Placement and Use

As you identify a suitable location for your firing facilities, you must consider many aspects of raku firing. Is your outdoor kiln as close as possible to the studio door so that you can carry pots and equipment to it easily? Do you want to be able to see the kiln from your studio window? Will you need electricity at the kiln site to feed lighting or a power burner? Do you have a handy water source nearby? Is the kiln sheltered, or can you erect a temporary shelter easily in the event you want to work in the rain or snow? Does the ground offer sure footing? Is the kiln site secure from curious passersby and onlookers?

The single most important factor in kiln placement is safety. You must stay alert to—and be able to prevent—a fire during the raku processes, and your freedom of movement should be completely unencumbered. Locating your kiln and post-firing facilities outdoors lends itself naturally and easily to the raku process. While you might be tempted to place your kiln on a porch, in a vestibule, or under an existing roof of some kind, make absolutely sure these structures are fire resistant. Don't place the kiln near any low-hanging tree limbs, and make sure there are no physical obstacles around the kiln that could impede motion and activity.

If you aren't able to perform either the firing or smoking phase outdoors, you aren't necessarily out of luck. Although not all indoor conditions are adaptable to raku—and the problems related to locating a raku facility indoors are many—with a little ingenuity, you can adapt some indoor spaces for safe use. Following are two examples. Neither is ideal, but each permits raku facilities to exist where none could otherwise.

Photos 2 and 3 show the kiln room and adjacent outdoor area at Thayer Academy where I teach. The concrete-block room has a cement floor and a high, cast-concrete ceiling. The electric kilns are close to a wide double door that opens to the outside, with no obstructions in the way. After we fire indoors, we remove the ware to reduction containers, which we carry outdoors, where

the post-firing phase takes place. Smoke from that phase sometimes circulates through the building and is a nuisance, for sure, but it's tolerable because the room is so well ventilated.

The Harvard/Radcliffe Pottery Studio faced a more complex situation because there was no access to the outdoors. Their ingenious facility, designed by director Nancy Selvage, is shown in photo 4. To the right is the front-loading kiln. On the left is the reduction chamber, which is constructed of galvanized sheet metal and features two acrylic plastic sliding doors fashioned from stock sliding window frames. Note the venting ducts from both the kiln and the reduction chamber. Not only is the natural-gas-fired kiln vented to the outdoors, as it must be, but the post-firing reduction is carried out in an enclosed chamber that is also vented to the outside, so the room is kept free of smoke and fumes.

In chapter 6, Building Your Own Kiln (see pages 66–89), you'll find tips on designing your kiln. You want the chamber to be easily accessible while requiring a minimum of awkward heavy lifting. You also want to secure the burners so they can't be jarred out of position easily. Chapter 6 also includes a section on the building codes that pertain to kiln building and combustion equipment. Safety issues related to preparations for firing and the firing process itself are covered on pages 91–93.

I once saw a shocking ad for a kiln that read: "Made for indoor firing by the raku method … Uses natural gas, propane, or butane." Natural-gas-fired kilns are routinely housed indoors, but those fueled by *liquefied petroleum gas* (LPG), made up of propane and butane, should always be located outdoors. LPG used indoors can have truly tragic results. LPG gases are heavier than air; if there's a leak in the system or if you have difficulty lighting your burner, the escaped gas gathers in low-lying areas and, unlike natural gas, doesn't dissipate quickly. Attempts to relight the burner can cause this accumulated gas to ignite or explode.

4

Not all glazes in the potter's arsenal are appropriate for use on functional ware, but apart from the United States Food and Drug Administration (FDA) standards for the use of lead and cadmium on utilitarian pottery, no regulations on the production of functional pottery exist. Unfortunately, the FDA considers all pottery—raku ware included—to be "food-safe" if it doesn't contain lead or cadmium, or if it conforms to the FDA leaching values for lead and cadmium.

For the raku potter concerned about the safe use of their ware, this approach simply isn't adequate. Stable glazes—a term coined by John Hesselberth and Ron Roy in their book *Mastering Cone 6 Glazes: Improving Durability, Fit and Aesthetics* (Glaze Master Press, 2002)—is a much stricter guideline and is quickly becoming accepted within the pottery community. This standard doesn't consider any raku glaze to be stable.

DAVID JONES
Folded
$12^{9}/_{16}$ x $8^{5}/_{8}$ x $10^{5}/_{8}$ inches
(32 x 22 x 27 cm)
Thrown and altered T material and porcelain; sprayed glaze; gas fired
Photo by Rod Dorling

The Functional Use of Raku Ware

Uncertainty often arises regarding whether or not to use raku ware for functional purposes, no doubt because traditional raku ware was used in the Japanese tea ceremony. The potentially harmful effects of lead toxicity and fired-glaze solubility weren't known at the time. However, because the tea-ceremony ritual wasn't an everyday practice and raku ware was only one of several types of ware used, exposure to the consequent health risks were diminished.

Today, some people consider raku ware with lead-free glazes to be safe for functional use, depending on three factors: the nature of the foods or liquids placed in it, whether the glaze meets chemical release standards, and how frequently the ware is used. At best, these proponents of functional raku ware are treading on the thinnest of ice, especially regarding chemical release standards. Due to its very nature, raku ware is fragile and has a soft, crazed glaze that results in a nondurable, unsanitary, unstable, and ultimately non-food-safe surface. I strongly advise you to regard raku ware of all types as decorative. Don't use it for food or drink.

Protective Wear

Gloves are the most important pieces of protective wear you'll own. If you have an old pair of asbestos ones, don't use them! Although the new high-tech gloves (like ones made of Kevlar) are more expensive than the traditional asbestos versions, they're just as heat-resistant and even more durable. Plus, they eliminate the risks associated with asbestos exposure.

For high-heat exposure, such as removing pots from the kiln, or for any direct or close contact with the kiln or pots, wear gloves that extend above your wrists. These are available in different lengths, either unlined or lined with cotton or wool. The lined gloves afford slightly more protection but can be uncomfortably warm during the hottest months of the year. I wear 23-inch (58.4 cm) lined gloves that come up to my biceps.

Gloves made of newer fabrics, like Zetex and Zetex Plus, offer more protection than those made of Kevlar when you're in direct contact with hot objects. The primary reason for wearing gloves, however, is to protect you from radiant heat, so for most of us, the hot-contact advantages of the new material don't justify its higher cost. If your raku technique involves direct handling of hot ware, however, you might want to spring for the newer fabrics. Even though these new gloves appear heavy and formidable, handle them with care and don't get them wet if you want to protect your investment.

For moderate heat conditions, such as handling reduction containers, applying reduction materials, and removing warm pots after reduction, high-quality, heavy leather work gloves, welding gloves, or fireplace gloves will suffice. The best leather gloves are dry-tanned to minimize the stiffening of the leather when it's exposed to high heat. Photo 5 shows, from left to right, leather welding gloves, 23-inch-long (58.4 cm) Zetex gloves, and shorter Kevlar gloves with a cover mitt made of the same material.

"Ah ha!" you say. "Why not combine the refractory protection of Kevlar with the durability of leather?" It's already been done in the form of leather-palmed Kevlar gloves, but I can't recommend them. The leather eventually hardens, making the gloves uncomfortable. Use Kevlar gloves for high heat, rubber gloves to protect your skin when you're mixing or applying corrosive or otherwise dangerous materials, and leather gloves for everything else.

Face and eye protection are also crucial. The safety standard for eye protection from the ultraviolet rays produced by

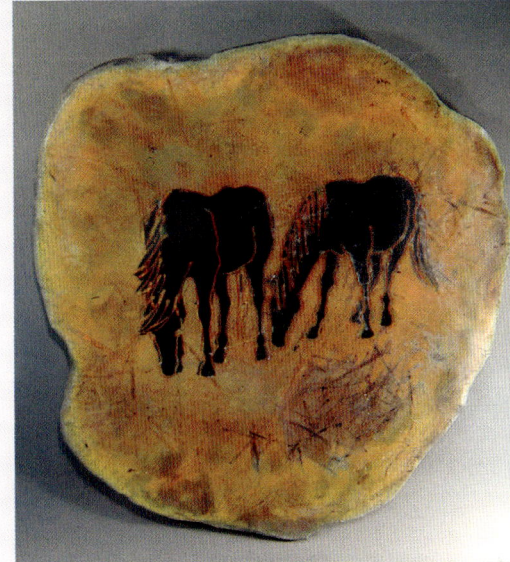

MARCIA SELSOR
In the Wind, 2006
$21\frac{1}{2}$ x $19\frac{1}{2}$ x 1 inches
(54.6 x 49.5 x 2.5 cm)
Slab built Raku Smooth Alligator
Clay MC117
Photo by artist

5

27

high-fire kilns is a C-4 lens, but in the low temperatures of raku, we're more concerned with protection from heat and particles. For this purpose, a lightweight mask of clear plastic—the kind designed for protection from flying particles during grinding—works well.

A common misfortune among beginners is having their pots break during the heating cycle. If you're looking into a kiln from close range and a pot blows up, you can be hit by a shard flying out of the flue or peephole. Use the mask by wearing it! Avoid holding it up in front of the flue at arm's length; it may melt.

For protection during fuming, salting, and other processes that produce dangerous fumes or vapors, you need an appropriate respirator. High-quality respirators accommodate interchangeable filters. A respirator, a typical mask, and heavy rubber gloves, all adequate for your purposes, are shown in photo 6.

I once received some literature advertising a kiln that "trapped the heat in the kiln away from the operator" and eliminated "the need for expensive protective clothing while rakuing."

Both of these statements are misleading and dangerous. No raku kiln, no matter how it's designed, can completely trap the heat when it's opened to expose the ware. Always wear appropriate clothing! Long pants, long-sleeved shirts, and footwear are important; those pots, tongs, and reduction containers are extremely hot.

If you have long hair, tie it back to keep it out of the kiln and away from the flames of reduction materials. And while we're on the subject of hair, even arm hair, facial hair, eyebrows, and eyelashes can be singed by close contact with the heat from a kiln, so be careful.

Always err on the side of caution and overprotect yourself. At a recent workshop I conducted, a participant was outfitted in a fully aluminized suit. Was it overkill? For her, not at all. While an expert might think her costume excessive, it made her comfortable and confident—and kept her safe. Above all, think clearly, use common sense, and let caution govern your behavior in all situations.

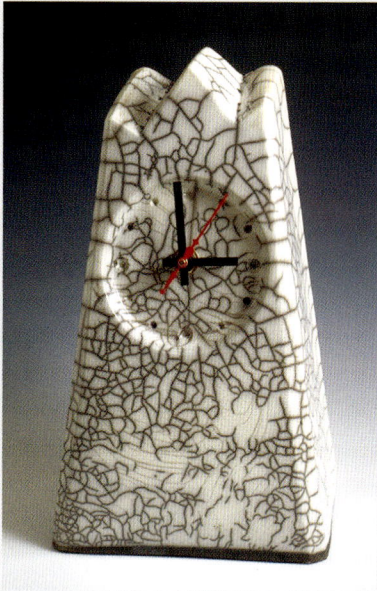

ROBERT COMPTON
Empire Clock, 2006
12 x 6 inches (30.5 x 15.2 cm)
Slip cast; dipped glaze; gas fired;
smoking for reduction
Photo by artist

6

Any study of the raku technique must begin with an understanding of the types of clay bodies suitable for raku. First, let me debunk two myths: you don't have to use so-called raku clay for raku firing, and you don't have to use low-fire clay just because raku is a low-temperature technique. A raku clay is any clay that we can successfully raku fire. The only thing that differentiates "raku clay" from any other is its refractory nature; due to careful formulation, it can withstand the extremely rapid heating and cooling of the raku process.

STEVEN BRANFMAN
Vessel, 2008
16½ x 8 inches (41.9 x 20.3 cm)
Brushed multi layered raku and commercial
low fire glaze; dry clay application and
combed surface texture

Throughout this book, you'll come across words and phrases from "the language of clay." Knowing this language is essential to your understanding of processes, methods, and materials and to your ability to communicate with suppliers, manufacturers, and other potters. Here are a few definitions:

Density refers to the porosity of a clay body. Generally speaking, the less dense and more porous a clay, the more thermal shock it can withstand. Greater porosity also allows the bisque-fired clay to absorb more glaze.

Thermal shock is the stress induced in clay when it undergoes rapid heating and cooling.

Plasticity is the capacity of a clay to be molded, stretched, and successfully formed. The greater the plasticity, the easier the clay is to work with; a plastic clay will show very little stress. Less plastic clays tend to be difficult to join, show stretch marks on their surfaces, and crack.

Suitable Clays

While almost any clay can be raku fired, you should begin with one that will give you the most consistent and easily reproducible results—in other words, less breakage. To achieve this, choose or formulate a clay that has certain characteristics.

First, the clay should have an open, porous structure that doesn't vitrify at either the bisque- or raku-firing temperature. You achieve this structure through the liberal use of grog, silica sand, stoneware clay, or fillers such as sawdust or beach sand that are mixed or wedged into the clay body. Second, the clay should be plastic enough and have the right surface characteristics for the type of forming you want to do—throwing or hand building, for example. Third, if you plan to apply glazes or slips to your pots, they must be compatible with your clay. (*Compatibility* refers here to the capacity of a glaze or slip to adhere to a particular clay through the drying, firing, and post-firing stages.) Finally, your clay should be the lightest color you want on your pots. If you're aiming for fired pots with white areas, choosing a red or buff clay will make your job difficult.

JOHN MATHIESON
People, 2008
Tallest: 6^{11}/$_{16}$ inches (17 cm)
Wheel thrown and rolled
T-Material and Harry Fraser
porcelain; dipped and
sponged glaze; impressing
of wooden stamps; propane
fired, 900°C on pyrometer;
air cooling, reduction in
mixed sawdust
Photo by artist

Selecting Commercial Clay Bodies

Most potters—and certainly those just starting out—are limited to commercially formulated and prepared clay bodies; mixing their own clays simply isn't practical. I use a commercial clay body as a practical matter. I don't care to include clay-mixing facilities in my studio, and I'd rather spend the time in other ways. I could have my own clay body prepared for me, and for many potters that process makes sense, but I came across the commercial clay that I now use more than 30 years ago, quite by accident, and it's served me well ever since. It has every characteristic that I look for: extreme plasticity, a very white color, a somewhat smooth texture, and a cone 8–10 vitrification point.

Clay bodies for raku are readily available; almost every supplier has at least one in its catalog. They're generally less expensive than custom mixes, too. On page 159, you'll find a list of the ones that I've had opportunities to use and

that work well in raku. You'll notice that they have a lot in common, but they're by no means the only suitable clays available, and your taste in clay may be different from mine. Remember that there's no such thing as a universal raku body; clays designed for raku can vary to extreme degrees. Try clay bodies from different suppliers until you find one that meets all of your own requirements.

Essentially, any type of commercially available stoneware body is suitable for raku, provided it's not too dense and it contains the other characteristics you desire. In fact, some suppliers simply take one of their stoneware bodies, alter it slightly, and label it "raku." If you need to make minor alterations to your clay, wedge in a handful of fine to medium grog or stoneware clay for each 10 pounds (4.54 kg) of your raku clay. Add more as needed.

Formulating Clay Bodies

If you'd like to formulate your own clay body, start with a stoneware recipe that you've been using, and try it, unaltered, in raku. If repeated cracking in your raku firing makes you think the clay may be too dense, add about 10 percent medium grog. For added refractory qualities, try kyanite in place of or in addition to grog. Other common materials found in raku clays are the ones you would normally associate with stoneware bodies. These include spodumene, talc, flint, feldspar, and fireclay. When using fireclay, you may have to add ball clay and small amounts (1 percent) of bentonite or macaloid to improve the overall plasticity.

The color of the body is a matter of personal taste. I prefer a white body because glazes on it appear brightest and offer the most contrast. Formulating a white or nearly white raku body requires care; the purer your materials, the whiter the body. The popular clays used in formulation—such as Cedar Heights Redart, Jordan Clay, and Calvert Clay—contain minerals that darken and otherwise color them. Unless your clay includes an ingredient with a high iron content or other naturally occurring impurities it, it should be mostly tan or buff toward white. If you're tempted to affect the feel and texture of your clay by adding garden dirt (no kidding; potters do), beach sand, or a material you find in your studio, just remember that these will affect the clay's color.

WAYNE HIGBY
Disciple's Bay, 1999
8½ x 9 x 4½ inches (21.6 x 22.9 x 11.4 cm)
Hand built; brushed glaze; gas fired; controlled cooling, smoking for reduction
Photo by Brian Oglesbee

T-Material—a clay of great use to the raku potter—is a commercially prepared, white-firing body with great refractory qualities. It does lack plasticity and strength, however, so it's best used in combination with other clays. Y-Material is a similar and less expensive alternative that's manufactured England. Both T-Material and Y-Material are widely available in the United Kingdom and throughout Europe but have yet to find a home in the United States. Keep an eye out for future availability.

Now, what about the rumors you may have heard regarding raku firing porcelain? Doesn't porcelain fail to meet all the technical requirements of a raku clay body? I meant it when I said that almost any clay can be raku fired, but porcelain does require very slow and careful heating and cooling. Your success rate will be greatly diminished if you try to preheat your pots and then place them in a hot kiln. Instead, fire them slowly from a cold kiln.

If you wonder why you should even bother to try using porcelain in raku firing, you have a point! However, if your objective is the whitest, smoothest, most elegant surface possible, porcelain may be the right choice. (You'll find a recommended porcelain clay body in the list of commercial clay bodies on page 159.) Very small porcelain pieces and jewelry pose fewer problems than large pieces. Macaloid, kyanite, silica sand, and T- or Y-Material can all be added to a porcelain body to increase its resistance to thermal shock, and although the addition of these materials compromises the "porcelain" qualities, experimenting with them can be worthwhile.

An alternative to using a porcelain clay body is to apply a layer of porcelain slip to the surface of your piece while the clay is wet (see pages 47–48). Doing so often yields the desired whiteness without the uncertainties of raku firing a porcelain body, and the slip can add a textural quality to the surface of your ware as well.

A sampling of clay-body recipes that I've collected over the years, all suitable for raku, is provided on pages 160–162.

Forming Methods for Raku

The three principle methods for forming clay into objects that are suitable for raku are hand building, throwing, and using molds. Each has its potential raku-related hazards, but they're avoidable if you know what they are and follow simple, logical rules as you work.

Hand Building

Traditional raku ware was hand built in a deliberate attempt to produce pieces that looked natural, unassuming, spontaneous, and humble. This aesthetic, so unlike European standards, is sometimes difficult for Westerners to incorporate into their own sensibilities.

Pinching was probably the most widely used method for making Japanese tea bowls, though many historical accounts, including that by Warren Gilbertson in his written observations of raku production in Japan (see page 14), indicate that coiling was also common. Dishes and other objects were slab built—and I wouldn't assume that Japanese potters never took stabs at raku firing pieces they'd thrown on the wheel. During and after forming, the work was carved with simple bamboo tools. Carving a tea bowl from a solid piece of clay is still a traditional forming method (see photo 1).

1

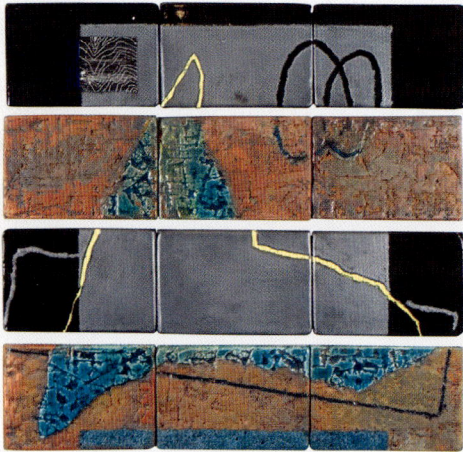

GEOFFREY PAGEN
Detrital, 2007
41 x 43 x 2 inches
(104.1 x 109.2 x 5.1 cm)
Slab built clay; brushed glaze; stamped, sgraffito; gas fired, forced air raku kiln; smoked for reduction
Photo by Stephen Cridland

For your purposes, hand building is a perfectly acceptable method, but keep in mind that any ware for raku must be able to withstand the extreme stress put on the work by the rapid firing. Imagine a perfect, bisque-fired load of coil pots. You glaze them, put them in the raku kiln—and watch with horror as the coils separate. The moral of this story is that bisque firing is *not* raku firing; a pot fired without any problems in a conventional firing may not survive the rigors of a raku firing. Whether your work is made out of coils, slabs, or any combination of applied clay, take care to score and slip all joints in order to create strong bonds that won't be susceptible to expansion and separation during the firing (see photo 2).

Appendages such as handles, spouts, or any protruding elements should also be well attached. Consider the situations you may encounter with these elements during all parts of the raku process— removing the hot piece from the kiln, placing it in the reduction container, and cleaning it after cooling. Don't hesitate to hand build; just anticipate potential problems, think a few steps ahead, and treat the pieces with care.

Throwing

Thrown ware is perfectly fine for raku firing. In fact, it's the safest of all forming methods because the ware is generally made of a single piece of well-prepared clay. Your goal is to shape pieces that will expand and contract evenly during the heating and cooling cycles. To that end, wedge your clay carefully in order to make it compact and to free it of lumps, air bubbles, and air trapped between clay particles. Let me debunk another pottery misconception here: although air bubbles do contribute to uneven expansion and contraction, pots don't usually crack and explode because of them. Cracking that takes place during bisque firing can more often be traced to clay that was still wet when fired.

Make the walls of your ware even in thickness and throw them perhaps a little on the thick side, using the least amount of water necessary (see photo 3). Compressing the bottoms well, trimming evenly, and drying your ware slowly will all help ensure even expansion and contraction—and fewer cracks and breakage—in both the bisque and raku firing.

MARK EINHORN
Untitled, 2002
9 x 8½ x 6 inches
(22.9 x 21.6 x 15.2 cm)
Thrown and altered Laguna Clay;
brushed glaze; stamped, underglaze
brushwork; gas fired, smoked for
reduction, sawdust and newspaper
Photo by artist

4

Take extra care if you're attaching appendages or working with specialized techniques such as coil-and-throw that require joining multiple sections. When attaching a coil to a thrown form, for example, score and slip only the rim of the piece and round the ends of the coil so you don't trap any air bubbles between the coil and rim or between the two ends of the coil (see photo 4).

For two reasons, wide-bottomed forms, particularly platters, are constant sources of headaches for raku potters. Heating those expanses evenly during the raku firing (and even the bisque) is difficult; as pieces expand and contract, wide bottoms can drag on the kiln shelf, causing cracking. Before placing your platter in the kiln, sprinkle some fine grog on the shelf. It will act as ball bearings would, reducing the amount of drag.

Using Molds

Molds fall into two categories: those for use with conventional clay, such as press molds and drape molds, and molds for slip casting. The former pose no pitfalls in raku other than the ones already described. Slip casting, however, is a different ball game altogether.

The slip-cast form isn't the issue; it's the makeup of the slip itself. The potential danger here is that slip for casting is often fine—that is, smooth, dense, nonporous, and generally non-raku-like. If you can formulate a slip that will withstand the raku torture of rapid heating and cooling, you're all set. And again, remember that most clays (even slip for casting) can be successfully raku fired if you're patient and careful during the process.

Bisque Firing

The raku technique isn't a once-fire or raw glazing process. The purposes of bisque firing are twofold: to strengthen the ware so you can handle it safely during glazing and kiln loading, and to develop a clay porosity adequate for correct absorption of the glaze (see photo 5). And in the case of raku, of course you want to render the clay more resistant to thermal shock.

Some practitioners of raku contend that ware should be bisqued anywhere from one to three cones lower than the conventional bisque-firing temperature recommended by the clay manufacturer. Others insist that the work has a much higher survival rate if it's fired one to three cones higher. Some advocate a "normal" (whatever that is) bisque firing, while others don't bisque fire at all.

So where do I stand? If you bisque too low, the clay may be too absorbent, soak up too much glaze, and either crack in the raku firing or give you undesirable glaze results. You may even render the clay too fragile to allow for glazing at all. Bisque firing too high, on the other hand, may make the clay too dense and nonporous and bring it too close to vitrification, which makes proper glaze absorption impossible and which may also cause cracking due to the clay's inability to expand and contract quickly enough during the raku firing.

I bisque my commercial raku body (see page 159) to cone 08. The combination of my chosen clay body and this bisque temperature gives me consistently successful results in the raku firing. If you're trying raku for the first time and are using your own clay body, bisque as you have been doing and adjust ac-

MARVIN SWEET
*Tree of Life Series:
Arrangement 22*, 2008
27 x 17 x 15 inches
(68.6 x 43.2 x 38.1 cm)
Hand built commercial clay;
sprayed glaze; gas fired;
smoking for reduction
Photo by Lisa Nugent

cordingly if your raku-fired results are unacceptable. In all other cases, bisque to cone 08 over a seven- or eight-hour cycle. If your pots are very large or have particularly thick walls, lengthen the firing but don't change the cone.

Which is better: to bisque in an electric kiln or in a fuel-burning kiln? The answer is whichever is easier and more convenient; the end results remain the same.

What if you don't bisque at all? Well, you open yourself up to all kinds of unnecessary dangers and disasters. For one thing, you'd have to raku fire green ware considerably more slowly, and it's much more prone to cracking if you try to preheat your next load on top of the kiln. Both factors detract from two of the main attractions of the raku process: speed and spontaneity. Some potters maintain that green ware is more susceptible than bisque ware to the desirable effects of atmospheric changes and smoking. Potters at workshops have presented pieces to me that they've single fired and have touted the practice, but I've painstakingly raku fired green ware on several occasions and haven't recognized any differences in the final

results—except in the state of my nerves. I therefore recommend bisquing your ware prior to raku firing it.

Yet another approach is the wet-firing raku technique, in which drying and bisque firing are omitted entirely. The theory behind wet firing is that as the ware is fired and the water in it evaporates, an envelope of steam surrounds the piece, thereby creating an equilibrium of pressure that prevents cracking. Yes, this technique works, but frankly, I see no reason to use it. For successful wet firing, a piece must be fresh off the wheel, so there's no time for trimming. Except for small pinch pots, most hand-built pieces would already be too dry by the time you were finished forming them. And loading a wet, soft piece into the kiln successfully is a feat in itself. Basically, you're no longer in the realm of raku—you're into something else entirely!

STEVE MATTISON
Sky Series, 2008
25⁹⁄₁₆ x 23⁵⁄₈ inches
(65 x 60 cm)
Press molded Westerwald Stoneware; brushed glaze; colored and laminated clays; gas fired; smoking for reduction, selective smoking; 1000°C
Photo by artist

PATRICK CRABB
Untitled (Shard Plate Series), 2004
22 x 18 x 3 inches (55.9 x 45.7 x 7.6 cm)
Drape molded and slab built recycled clay; broken and reassembled with shards decorated and fired individually as follows: brushed glaze; brushwork, sigillata slip burnished, masking tape resist; electric and gas fired; air cooling, quick cooling, smoked for reduction, sawdust fired, propane torch halo
Photo by artist

5

glazes, slips, and other coloring agents

"Ah," you say, "here come the secrets of the raku masters—those beautiful coppers, purples, and iridescent effects." Well, not yet. First, we must return to the basics—by understanding the nature of a raku glaze. Think of a raku glaze as any glaze that can be raku fired. Unlike other glaze and firing methods, which often demand exacting control over factors such as application, temperature, cooling, surface integrity, and leaching of materials, raku glazes and firing enjoy wide variations. Results that would ordinarily be categorized as defects can be perfectly acceptable in raku and, in fact, are often sought after.

STEVEN BRANFMAN
Vessel, 2005
13½ x 9½ inches (34.3 x 24.1 cm)
Brushed multi layered commercial low fire glaze;
pressed surface texture

Two common ones are *crazing* (or *crackling*) and *crawling*; depending on your aesthetic, there can be others as well. The pot shown in photo 1, made by Debbie Winnick, is a great example of crazing, which results from a poor glaze/clay body fit. It would be unacceptable for functional ware, but it's desirable (and often uncontrollable) in raku. Crawling (very evident on the pot of mine that's shown in photo 2) is characterized by bare areas on the ware after firing—areas that were previously glazed.

Although traditional raku incorporated both low- and high-fire methods, and contemporary practitioners of both methods exist, Western raku developed as a low-fire technique. Most raku today is fired in the cone 011–06 range. As you hone in on your desired glazes, whether you purchase or formulate them, keep in mind that a glaze-maturing range of two, three, or four cones isn't unusual in the low temperatures of raku, and a wider range certainly gives you more latitude.

I fire my own work in the cone 09–07 range. You may certainly stray from this range if you wish, but your glazes should be compatible with your clay body and within firing range of one another. If you use glazes with maturing temperatures that are too disparate, you won't be able to achieve uniform glaze melting on your pieces. In most cases, you'll either have to pull your pots out of the kiln at different times—a cumbersome task at best—or sacrifice pots to the kiln god by over-firing or under-firing some in order for others to come out "right." Having the flexibility to control the maturing of all of your glazes simultaneously is a worthy goal! (For an exception to this rule, see page 47.)

1

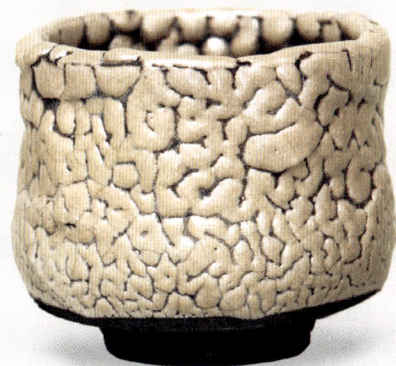

2

KEVIN NIERMAN
132 Pots, 2007
Largest: 15 x 12 x 12 inches (38.1 x 30.5 x 30.5 cm)
Smallest: 4 x 4 x 4 inches (10.2 x 10.2 x 10.2 cm)
Sculpture 412 clay body; brushed glaze;
propane fired, cone 09
Photo by Dave Larson

Selecting Commercial Glazes

Just as commercial raku clays have become more readily available and of better quality over time, commercially prepared raku glazes have proliferated. The advantage to using them is that they eliminate the variables of potential inconsistency in glaze mixing and changes in materials from batch to batch.

I have two objections to using commercial glazes exclusively, however. First, relying on any commercial material puts you at the mercy of the manufacturer. Will the price go up? Will the glaze continue to be available? Second, and much more important, when you don't mix your own glazes, you give up the most basic connection with your work—an intimate knowledge of your material. The time and effort that mixing glazes takes is well worth the freedom and knowledge gained from the practice. Knowing the contents of your clay body and glazes enables you to adapt a glaze for a better fit more easily. (Clay and glaze manufacturers usually provide a list of ingredients when requested. If your supplier won't, it's time to find a new one.)

I do use commercial low-fire glazes; they're a very important part of my palette. In liquid form, they offer a variety of colors and textures that would be difficult to achieve in any other way. I often select jars of commercial glaze randomly to use either by themselves or with my own raku glazes. Sometimes I purposely choose certain colors by particular manufacturers.

Remember that raku is just another type of low-temperature firing; you can use any glaze that matures in the firing range of your clay. Try enamels, underglazes, overglazes, commercial slips—anything that looks interesting. Just pay attention to maturing ranges when selecting commercial glazes to fire with your own.

Formulating Glazes

Arriving at a desirable selection of personal homemade glazes begins with choosing simple recipes—ones that yield basic clear glazes—and then experimenting by making simple additions or subtractions of any number of oxides, stains, salts, and opacifiers. For a slightly lower-firing glaze, for example, add a bit more flux or substitute a lower-melting flux such as borax. To raise the maturing temperature, reduce the amount of flux or add a bit more clay.

As long as you don't stray too far from the base glaze, you don't need to be an expert in glaze formulation or chemistry to come up with successful glazes of your own.

MARVIN SWEET
Tree of Life Series:
Turtles All the Way Down, 2006
14 x 8 x 7½ inches (35.6 x 20.3 x 19.1 cm)
Hand built commercial clay; brushed and sprayed glaze; paint/non-ceramic/non-fired; gas fired; smoking for reduction
Photo by Lisa Nugent

EDUARDO LAZO
Patch Raku, 2008
10 x 11 x 11 inches (25.4 x 27.9 x 27.9 cm)
Wheel thrown Soldate 60; brushed glaze; raku fired; smoking for reduction
Photo by David Lazo

Leaving Out the Lead

In the descriptions of glaze recipes that follow, you'll find a conspicuously absent low-fire ingredient: lead. Why expose yourself to a danger that's avoidable? Although traditional raku glazes—and many low-fire glazes, for that matter—include lead as the basic flux, I don't see any reason to use this dangerous substance. Pottery is a craft laden with enough other risks.

From an aesthetic point of view, lead-based glazes don't generally work well in reducing atmospheres anyway, especially the ones encountered in the raku process. Reduction, a process described on page 57, often causes lead glazes to become bubbly and muddy, and to display gunmetal-type surfaces. It doesn't foster the development of the deep, rich, sometimes metallic and lustrous effects that you can obtain with lead-free glazes.

Of course, intriguing surfaces are possible with lead glazes—you can find them in the myriad lead-based raku glazes floating around in books, glaze notes, and on people's pots. Lead-based glazes do in fact offer some advantages: a high index of refraction that results in more brilliant surfaces, low surface tension that gives the glaze the ability to smooth out and cover potential defects, and a wide firing range.

Even taking these advantages into account, however, I would argue that the health risks outweigh the benefits. While I recognize and respect the desire of some potters to maintain a more traditional approach to raku, I feel the need to caution you: if you insist on using lead glazes, observe strict and careful handling methods, and under no circumstances use your fired ware as food or beverage containers.

In place of lead, the most popular low-fire fluxes for raku potters are borax, colemanite, and gerstley borate (GB). All three of these naturally occurring materials offer strong and reliable fluxing action. Of the three, borax is the strongest and is typically used in glazes with the lowest melting points. GB and colemanite are different materials with similar characteristics, but for our purposes, they're interchangeable. Both have been so useful to raku potters that either often accounts for up to 80 percent of the total glaze ingredients. Colemanite as a potter's material predates GB, but GB supplanted it during the 1970s due to cost and availability. Now colemanite is difficult to obtain. As a stable, reliable, and predictable material, colemanite is more desirable, but in the context of the variegated and mottled surface effects desired in raku, either material is acceptable. If you find a recipe calling for colemanite, a one-to-one substitution of GB usually works fine.

Remember that raku is just another type of low-temperature firing; you can use any glaze that matures in the firing range of your clay. Try enamels, underglazes, overglazes, commercial slips—anything that looks interesting.

WAYNE HIGBY
Cloud Bank Bay, 1991
12 x 20½ x 14½ inches
(30.5 x 52.1 x 36.8 cm)
Thrown and altered; brushed glaze; gas fired;
controlled cooling, smoking for reduction
Photo by Brian Oglesbee

WAYNE HIGBY
Midsummer's Bay, 1991
13 x 18½ x 16¾ inches
(33 x 47 x 42.5 cm)
Hand built; brushed glaze; gas fired;
controlled cooling, smoking for reduction
Photo by Brian Oglesbee

As you encounter and collect raku glaze recipes, you'll find glazes labeled as white that in fact are transparent. This common error is due to the widespread use of white raku clay bodies. These glazes work well on white clays, but when they're used on clays that fire to a color other than white, the final color is that of the clay. A true white raku glaze includes one of the opacifiers mentioned in this chapter.

Although GB is readily available at this time (and promises to be for a long time to come), alternatives are available. The most popular are Laguna Borate, Murray's Borate, Gillespie Borate, Cadycal, and Frit CC 289-C. The glaze recipes I've provided in this book (see pages 162–165) have been successfully tested with a one-to-one substitution of Murray's Borate. Other viable substitutes for GB are Ferro Frits #3195 and #3134 and frits by other manufacturers. On page 162, you'll find Tom Buck's recipe for his own synthetic GB mix.

One of the common shortcomings of GB substitutes is their inability to keep glazes well suspended, which results in hard-settling mixtures. To aid suspension, add a handful of Epsom salts (magnesium sulfate) to a 5-gallon (18.93 L) bucket of glaze after screening. A lack of clay in the GB substitutes can also make glazes crawl. Small additions (1 to 2 percent) of bentonite help combat this problem.

Coloring Glazes with Oxides, Opacifiers, and Stains

All the standard coloring oxides and carbonates of those oxides are fair game for experimentation. The oxides are generally twice as strong as the carbonates, though the colors produced by carbonates tend to be a bit more variegated and mottled and are more popular. (By the way, if you run across recipes that simply list "copper" or "cobalt," you can assume they're calling for the carbonate.)

For various luster effects, try different combinations of copper with cobalt, manganese, or iron. When using cobalt, a sneeze-full (¼ to ½ percent) is enough to give you a blue with sub-

stantial presence. You may use copper in amounts up to 5 percent or even more, although 2 percent usually does the trick. Iron, manganese, nickel, and rutile are effective in amounts as little as 1 percent. Chrome is a rather strong colorant in raku and should be tried in small amounts (½ to 1 percent). Keep in mind, though, that the lusters of copper and silver so sought after during an initial encounter with raku—and indeed, in glaze effects of all kinds— result from the combined effects of glazing, firing, and post-firing techniques. The phenomenon of post-firing reduction is what makes American raku unique.

Having both a transparent and a white glaze in your palette expands your ability to affect other glazes and slips. A transparent glaze will tend to brighten glazes and slips, while the opacity of a white glaze will soften and tone down colors. A transparent glaze results in white when you're working with a truly white clay, but a true white glaze is one that contains an opacifier such as tin oxide, Opax, Superpax, or Zircopax. A 5 to 10 percent addition of tin oxide to a transparent glaze gives a very nice white. The other opacifiers mentioned are considerably weaker in strength, so when you substitute one for tin, double the amount called for in the recipe. For example, if the recipe indicates 5 percent tin, use 10 percent Zircopax. If you use any more than that, you'll run the risk of ending up with a thick, milky appearance.

Commercial stains, such as Mason stains, are also good sources of color in glazes. Begin with a 5 percent addition, and then adjust the amount as desired.

Copper Matte and Patina Glazes

Copper matte is a highly saturated copper mixture with just enough flux to fuse it onto the surface of the clay. (See page 169–170 for a few recipes.) Its effect—characterized by a very iridescent, often inconsistent, velvet-like surface—is achieved by applying the glaze in the correct thickness, firing it at an optimum temperature, and carrying out the appropriate post-firing reduction. Laden with personal nuance, copper matte is more about firing and post-firing than about glaze application, so it's covered at greater length in chapter 8, Advanced Firing Techniques (see pages 116–127).

Somewhere between copper matte and the more standard fluxing glazes are patina glazes. Recipes for them (see pages 166–167) include strong metallic components and enough fluxing agents to produce melted and fused—yet often crusty—surfaces with rich variations of color and texture. Glazes with names such as "Alligator," "Lizard Skin," "Lava Rock," "Lichen," "Moss," and the like conjure up appropriate images. Some potters describe the patina glaze effect as similar in appearance to a dried lake bed.

Thick applications are more textured than thinner ones, which tend to look more like copper matte glazes. Recipes are usually (but not always) presented in volume measurements, as opposed to measurements by weight. Firing temperatures vary but are generally in the cone 08 range. However, as with all raku firing, temperature has much to do with the ultimate effect; whether a glaze is described as glossy, semi-matte, matte, or totally dry, the final result is up to you. For more information on glaze maturity, see pages 103–105.

RICK FORIS
Untitled, 2007
25 x 11½ x 11½ inches
(63.5 x 29.2 x 29.2 cm)
Hand built and wheel thrown Paoli Raku; brushed glaze; carved, slip trailing, paint, glazes; gas fired; smoking for reduction, selective smoking for reduction
Photo by Bill Lemke

Preventing Fading and Color Changes

"First you see it—then you don't." For anyone with more than an elementary knowledge of and experience with raku glazes, that sentence needs no clarification. For those of you new to raku, we're talking about the occasional tendency for raku lusters to fade and change color over time. This phenomenon does happen, but not to all pots and not always. As raku has grown more popular, however, and as raku-fired work has become more widely collected and circulated, the problem has been noticed more often and is now of greater concern.

A recipe is nothing more than a tool, like a knife or brush. The tool doesn't determine the result; it's what you're able to do with it that does.

Glazes designed for raku tend to be "unstable"; that is, their chemical makeup tends to be out of balance. Typically, their deficiencies are a lack of sufficient silica to form a durable glass, a lack of alumina to harden the glass and make the surface durable, or both. The resulting glazes are soft, and the firing process renders them fragile. (Glazes that have frit components do tend to be less fragile and more durable.) Raku glazes are therefore susceptible to attack by atmospheric and environmental conditions, particularly oxygen, moisture, and sulfur compounds. Ware subjected to salt air and direct sunlight appears to be the most vulnerable. This kind of imbalance would never be tolerated in glazes used on functional, food-bearing ware, but for purely decorative work, imbalanced glaze recipes are common and acceptable.

Enough technical talk. The question is what to do about this problem. On pages 165–166, Tom Buck, a chemical engineer and potter who has researched this subject extensively and explained the chemistry of it in an in-depth article for *Ceramic Review* (#159, May/June 1996), shares some of his glaze recipes that promise to be more stable over time. (With Tom's permission, I've borrowed the title of his article to start out this section.) For tips on applying protective finishes to your fired ware, see page 140.

Sharing Glaze Recipes

The glaze recipes listed on pages 162–168 start with my own and are followed by ones I've collected over the years. Some of the latter I've used, and others I haven't, but I've seen the results of them all. I've added comments to most of them regarding their possible effects, and I've offered application suggestions where appropriate.

Will you achieve the same results as I have with these recipes? Yes, no, or maybe. If you're already an experienced potter, you know that using the same glaze recipe is only one step in an often futile—and ultimately meaningless—attempt to achieve another person's results. Even if you duplicate all the ingredients, there are innumerable reasons why your glaze may not come out like mine: idiosyncrasies in mixing styles; methods of glaze application; the clay bodies, firing rates, and atmospheric conditions in the kiln; and even the chemical makeup of your local water, to name just a few.

Glaze-Application and Decoration Techniques

But whether a certain glaze performs the same for me as it does for you isn't the issue, nor should it be. The ultimate effect is what you're after. Use these glaze recipes as jumping-off points. Your goal should be to develop a palette and vocabulary of your own. Only then will you know that your work is evolving and mandating your technique—that the technique isn't controlling your work instead.

I'm often taken aback by potters who refuse to share recipes, techniques, ideas, or observations for fear that others will copy or steal their originality, thus diminishing the appeal of their work. I'm also surprised by potters who feel that they've worked too hard formulating a glaze to give it to anyone else. Potters who are willing to take but not give eventually hinder the growth of their own work. Often, "their" recipes originally came from books, friends, or workshops anyway.

I prefer a different approach. At The Potters Shop and in my workshop presentations, I routinely share my recipes in the hope that other potters will reciprocate so that we can all expand our creative horizons. A recipe is nothing more than a tool, like a knife or brush. The tool doesn't determine the result; it's what you're able to do with it that does. Having faith and confidence in your own work and going through your own creative evolution allow you the freedom to share. So be generous with your knowledge. We can all benefit.

Novices unleashed into the excitement of the raku technique are often tempted to over-glaze: they use too much glaze, too many different glazes, and/or enough copper luster to blind you. I'm always amused when my students, like clockwork, begin to complain about the lack of interesting glazes on hand, as well as the fact that we don't have enough glazes to choose from. "Why can't we use the same glazes that you use?" is their cry. When I tell them that they *are* using the same glazes and that I've been using the same basic palette of five glazes throughout my entire career, their laments are at least quieted, if not silenced.

Limit yourself to two or three glazes, and go for simplicity, spontaneity, and sophistication. The wide variety of effects obtainable with a limited palette, the black unglazed areas of a piece, and overlapping glazes should keep you busy for a few years. You can try many glazes, of course—but not all on the same pot!

Always take a patient, deliberate approach to the study of raku glaze effects. In raku, as in any glazing and firing method, intelligent experimentation and comparison of results require some degree of consistency of technique. However, so many variables are integral to the raku process that complete consistency is difficult, to say the least. Indeed, inconsistency and a lack of total control are two of the main attractions of raku.

RICK BERMAN
Raku Bottle, 2008
9 x 7 x 7 inches (22.9 x 17.8 x 17.8 cm)
Wheel thrown Standard 239; dipped glaze; overglaze; gas fired; quick water cooling, smoking for reduction
Photo by Erik Haagensen

Commercial, non-raku-specific glazes come with instructions on their labels. "Apply three even coats with a brush, allowing the glaze to dry between coats" is one example. And one of my favorites is: "Not for spraying." Ignore these instructions; they're not for you! Go ahead and apply the glaze any way you want. Be cautious, though, when you use blues, reds, oranges, dark greens, and purples, as these tend to be strong and can be harsh. Dilute these colors and apply them in thin coats.

To help you arrive at desirable glaze results—and preserve your sanity at the same time—keep a record of all your experiments. Write down all your recipes, as well as variations, permutations, and the results of your attempts. And write them down as you work! Do this even if you change only one ingredient, alter only one percentage, or add only one new material. And remember to label your glazes and slips. While accidents can result in interesting effects and new directions (see page 47), forgetting to label your glazes and slips is definitely not recommended!

Many potters think that in raku, the glazing process immediately precedes the loading and firing of the ware. While this is frequently true, it's often at the expense of controlled and successful results. Glaze that's still wet when you position a piece to preheat it or load it into a hot kiln will crack and flake off. Allow the glaze to dry on the piece, preferably overnight, before commencing with the firing. (This isn't to say that intentional cracking and peeling is off limits!)

Applying Color

The rules of application in raku are generally the same as those of all pottery-making techniques. Glazes can be poured (see photo 3), sprayed, brushed, sponged, and dipped (see photo 4). Raku beginners learning the basics of glaze melt and firing control should apply glazes on the thick side so that they're more easily observable as they melt during firing (see pages 103–104).

4

Glazes tend to drip and run more than usual in raku due to their thick application, the rapidity of the firing, and the ease of slightly over-firing. Be careful with your glazing toward the bottoms of your pots. The danger isn't that the pots will stick to the kiln shelf (they're removed while the glaze is still molten), but that dripping glaze will make a mess of your shelf and kiln.

There are several ways to apply glaze thickly and still avoid drips, so don't think that you're caught in a catch-22 situation. One method is to thin out your glaze application as you approach the bottom of the pot. Alternatively, you can leave liberal unglazed areas near the bottom and sponge the glaze off in that area in a way that complements the overall design. Some raku potters simply load their pots onto old kiln-shelf scraps—and to heck with the glaze drips. As you gain firing experience and learn how to recognize a mature glaze melt, you'll be able to glaze all the way down to the foot. Let your own aesthetic guide you.

Copper matte mixtures, which don't melt like glazes, can be applied with less concern about dripping and sticking. They're usually more effective when applied thinly anyway—often in a coat so thin that you're sure they won't work. This is just one potter's opinion, but

3

5

from my aesthetic point of view, copper matte is effective in isolated sections on the surface or by itself on a piece, without overlapping glazed areas.

Applying glaze with a brush can yield interesting effects, providing you use a high-quality brush that allows you to control the glaze thickness. I frequently hear students say they're sure they brushed on a glaze, but there's little evidence of any on their fired work. More often than not, their application was too thin. Inexpensive, throwaway brushes work, as long as you recognize their limitations and advantages.

My own glazing process is always specific to the size of the ware and the effects I seek to achieve. It can also seem very unconventional, flying in the face of common practice. My primary method centers around brushing on multiple, thin layers of repeatedly over-lapped colors. Although the application appears to be random, I plan and execute it carefully. I may use a single glaze or as many as 15 different ones on a single piece. The throwaway-quality brushes I use are perfectly suited, as they don't hold much glaze and transfer it very unevenly. I draw the brush light-ly over the surface of the pot to deposit glaze coats of varying thicknesses. With each successive layer, the surface gets deeper and the glaze coating more and more variegated (see photo 5).

Did I say "unconventional"? Even a rank beginner knows not to con-taminate his or her glazes. Because my glazing method is quick, as my brush deposits glaze on the pot, it invariably picks up some of the wet glaze already on the surface. When I dip this brush

into the glaze again, it contaminates the color. I do this purposely, knowing that my glazes aren't pure, but I don't recom-mend this practice in a studio situation where glazes are shared.

Other methods of application that add movement and contrast to the somewhat static effect of brushing are splattering, dripping, spraying, and very controlled pouring (see photo 6). Experimenting with the thickness of a glaze for pouring will give you different results, depending on the way the glaze runs, drips, and melts. And although we all know to thoroughly mix a glaze before using it, there are times when I either don't bother or purposely gather glaze from the inside wall or lid of the bucket or jar. Doing this often gives an "incomplete" glaze that may offer unusual and unpredictable results.

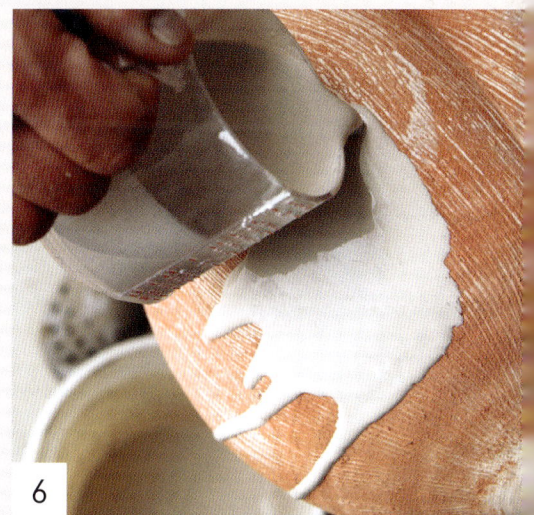

6

For a low-tech approach, try spraying glaze or oxides on your piece with a spray bottle or atomizer. To do this, you'll have to dilute your glaze considerably, which will affect the outcome. Of course, spraying with a compressor and spray gun or airbrush is the approach to take if you're serious about this process (see photo 7).

The use of resists—such as wax, oil, tape, and stencils—is a common decorative approach. Depending on the type of resist, you can brush, dip, pour, or spray your glazes over it. To vary the areas affected, remove the resist after glazing and add another glaze over the previously taped area, or use handheld acetate or cardboard stencils that you can move around while you spray. For more on resist techniques, see pages 129–133.

Creating Textured Clay Surfaces

The surface of your clay can also have an effect on the final outcome. Clay can be textured while wet, leather hard, dry, or after firing, depending on the desired effect. You can glaze heavily textured surfaces and then wash them, leaving glaze in the crevices of carved designs. Alternatively, by using a wide brush, you can apply the glaze only to the raised portions of a design. In certain areas, the thickness and the unevenness of the glaze become a texture in and of itself; it can exhibit nuances of color and appearance. Most of my pots have deeply textured surfaces to begin with, and my color application is intended to accentuate that texture.

Carving, pressing, paddling, and many other methods all produce textures. A more unusual approach is sandblasting with a compressor and the required attachments, available at most home centers. Sandblasting is effective at any stage after leather hard, including after glaze firing.

Other surface-alteration methods include cutting and scratching bisque-fired pieces with a masonry blade, file, or sanding tool. You can also apply dry mixtures of clay, grog, sand, and glaze to wet clay or bisque ware. Because these mixtures are dry and won't adhere to bisqued surfaces, you must load the work into the kiln carefully so you don't disturb the placement. Upon maturity, the glaze, with the other materials embedded in it, fuses to the ware, producing an appearance that bridges that of a glazed surface and an unglazed one. Results vary depending on the glaze you use and the extent of the post-firing.

Combining High- and Low-Fire Glazes

For the sake of efficiency in managing your firings, it's easy to understand why using glazes with the same maturing temperatures is important, but how might you use glazes of different temperatures simultaneously? The only rules are the ones you want to follow!

Commercial low-fire glazes usually fire in the cone 06–04 range, which is considerably higher than the cone 011–08 range common to most raku glazes. If you're using these glazes by themselves, then desired maturity is easy to determine. However, a creative approach is to use them with lower melting ones on the same pot. The different melting degrees can offer an interesting combination of textures and colors that you couldn't achieve otherwise. An extreme example—and a frequent part of my glaze repertoire—is the use of stoneware glazes in order to achieve certain color and texture effects.

Stoneware glazes, you say? This idea came to me accidentally. Years ago, while I was firing some ware and waiting for the pots to heat and the glazes to melt, something didn't seem quite right. On one of the three pots I was firing, only some of the glazed areas were melting, while other areas remained unaffected by the heat. As a raku novice, I didn't have the confidence to trust my instinct about firing time, temperature, glaze maturity, and what the kiln chamber should look like. The firing progressed, and while the glaze was melting on the two other pots, most of the glaze on this particular pot was still as dry and cold looking as it was when it went into the kiln.

When the two pots were ready to pull, I went ahead and took all three out of the kiln, proceeded with my post-firing phase, and waited for them all to cool. To my delight, the "odd" piece with the dry glaze was wonderfully pastel, had a subtle, slightly rough surface, and was very different from any raku results I'd ever seen. What had happened?

I discovered that my assistant had recently mixed some new batches of both raku glaze and cone 8 stoneware glaze but had forgotten to label the buckets as well as the lids (a *big* no–no!). Some of the lids were switched, and I ended up using both stoneware and raku glazes on the same piece. Thus some of the glaze melted, and some areas stayed dry. There were problems linked to the under fired surface: some of the glaze was apt to flake, and some was completely blackened by the smoking phase. I was curious, though, and began to experiment with using high-fire glazes in the low temperatures of raku. For interesting variations on stoneware glazes, see Mark Lancet's recipes on page 167–168.

Applying Slips

Glazes aren't the only means of including color and surface decoration on your pots. Slips can provide texture, and in some ways, color development as well. Generally, though, combining slips with glazes that you apply over them produces the best color results (see photo 8). An applied slip, regardless of its color, is simply an unglazed surface, and in heavy post-firing reduction, most unglazed surfaces blacken, obliterating the color.

Firing a high-fire glaze at a temperature significantly lower than its maturing temperature is counterintuitive; it doesn't seem to make much sense. Do it anyway! Use the high-fire glazes as you might use slips. Apply them in thin layers; thick applications tend to flake because high-fire glazes don't get hot enough to fuse completely to the surface of the pot.

Experiment by applying thin washes of clear raku glaze (or try any raku glaze) as a sealer over the high-fire glaze. Or apply the stoneware glaze over a thin wash of raku glaze. I've achieved interesting results with glazes in the cone 8–10 range that contain copper, rutile, cobalt, and iron. Heavy post-firing reduction makes the high-fire glazes dark and muddy, but don't hesitate to go ahead and try them for yourself.

8

Applying white slips allows you to use a particular clay body that works well in raku but that may have an undesirable buff or tan color.

Although slips can be formulated for application to clay in the wet, green-ware, leather-hard, or bisque state, formulating a foolproof slip for wet clay is easiest. From a design point of view, I like to decorate with slips while I throw. The most sure-fire way to formulate a slip for wet clay—the method I prefer—is to use your clay body as the base. Dry out some clay, pulverize it, and add colorants to it by dry-weight percentages. If you begin with clay that fires to white, any colors are possible. If your clay is buff, tan, or darker, your slip may be limited in tonal range, but it's worth a try. You'll find several slip recipes formulated for application to clay in different stages of dryness on page 168.

White porcelain slips can produce a very white surface on your ware without the breakage risk you'd run by using porcelain clay (see page 32). Applying white slips also allows you to use a particular clay body that works well in raku but that may have an undesirable buff or tan color. The white, clean surface enables brighter colors and often a wider color palette. Try any porcelain slip, and apply it when your piece is wet (see photo 9).

Another use of slips in raku is the *slip resist* (or *naked raku*) technique—a decorative method and firing procedure with many variations and approaches. The basic concept centers around the application of a slip formulated to come off the pot after firing. See page 129 for more information on this technique.

Decorating with Terra Sigillata

Terra sigillata (or *earth seal*) is another form of slip decoration, most recognizable on ancient red and black Greek wares, as well as red Roman wares. Traditionally, terra sigillata is a slip comprised of only the finest particles of an iron-bearing clay that fires red in oxidation and black in reduction. Due to its fine particle size, the slip serves to seal the clay surface and acts almost as a glaze. As would be expected, contemporary potters have embraced this technique while adding their own variations, using other clays and oxides to produce various colors. For the raku potter, terra sigillata offers further possibilities for surface decoration and enhancement; it can stand alone, or you can apply glazes over it.

To make a terra sigillata, mix a slip with an added deflocculant (such as Calgon or Darvon 7) that renders the mixture very fluid. After a period of settling, three layers emerge: heavier particles sink to the bottom, water remains on the top, and the finest particles settle in the middle. Siphon off the water with a syringe or turkey baster to expose the middle layer, which you can then apply in thin layers to green ware. Recipes abound; you'll find some on page 168.

You can burnish terra sigillata surfaces to further accentuate their sheen, but take care not to rub the slip off. Instead, many potters use a soft cloth to polish the leather-hard surface to the desired

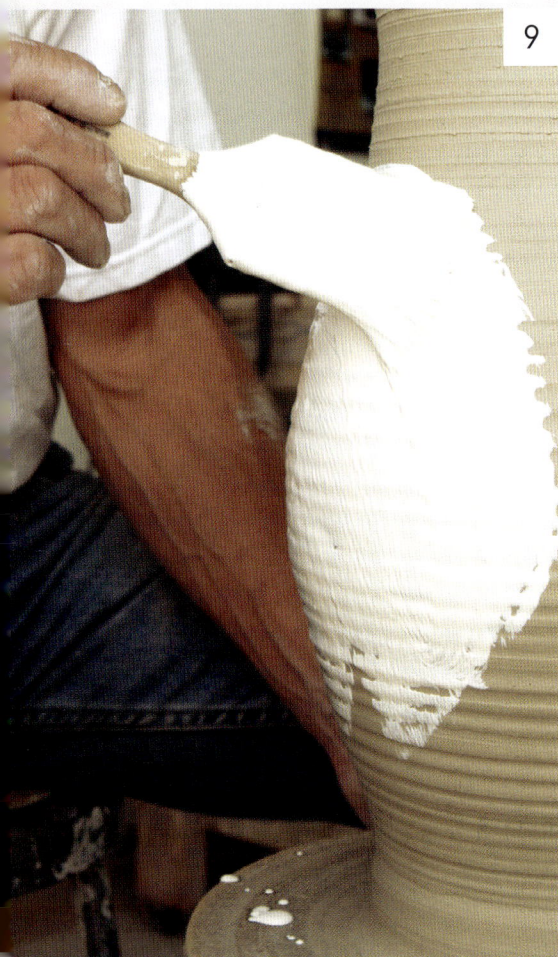

sheen. Fire only to the recommended temperatures for the recipe you're using; as with any burnished or polished surface, if terra sigillata is fired too high, the sheen dulls.

Applying Oxides and Stains

You can use oxides alone as brushed-on washes, as well as in combination with glazes. You can spray on oxides and stains with an atomizer or spray bottle. Oxide-wash recipes, measured by volume, are most easily arrived at through experimentation. Try any oxides you have on hand, using the following measurements as a guide and keeping in mind that the final result depends on your application technique, the clay body, and other decorative materials you may be using.

Per pint (.47 L) of water:

$\frac{1}{2}$ tsp. (2.46 ml) copper carbonate: *light green, turquoise*
$\frac{1}{4}$ tsp. (1.23 ml) copper oxide: *darker greens, blacks*
$\frac{1}{8}$–$\frac{1}{4}$ tsp. (.62–1.23 ml) chrome oxide: *leaf green, opaque*
$\frac{1}{8}$–$\frac{1}{4}$ tsp. (.62–1.23 ml) cobalt carbonate: *light blue, transparent*
$\frac{1}{8}$ tsp. (.62 ml) or less cobalt oxide: *dark blue, black*
$\frac{1}{2}$–1 tsp. (2.46–4.93 ml) red iron oxide: *tan, brick red, brown*
$\frac{1}{4}$–$\frac{1}{2}$ tsp. (1.23–2.46 ml) black iron oxide: *opaque tan, brick red, brown*
$\frac{1}{8}$–$\frac{1}{2}$ tsp. (.62–2.46 ml) manganese dioxide: *brown toward purple*

Commercial stains, such as Mason stains and Cerdec, are also excellent materials to include in washes, glazes, and slips. The number of different stains produced now is daunting; almost every ceramics supplier carries them and can help you choose colors based on how you plan to fire. Mason stains are common; potters have used them for many years. Encapsulated stains, available in the past only to industry and large commercial ceramics operations, are now available to potters. As with all materials you use for the first time, make sure you learn how to handle them safely.

You can also apply oxides and stains in their powdered state to the surface of your freshly formed piece. Combine some of the material with dry ball clay, apply it to the surface with your hand, and then paddle or otherwise force the material into the soft clay. Be very careful to observe health and safety precautions, as the dust that's generated is dangerous to breathe. Wear an appropriate respirator!

Using Salt, Soda, and Soluble Salts

Salt (sodium), soda, and soluble salts further enhance luster effects and, indeed, are effects unto themselves. Salt has a long history of use as a glaze former; using soda ash in its place is a more recent development. Some examples of soluble salts (not to be confused with sodium) are bismuth subnitrate, copper sulfate, stannous chloride, barium sulfate, barium chloride, strontium nitrate, iron sulfate, and silver nitrate.

Before firing, mix the crystals or powders into a glaze, dissolve them in water, and use them as washes or sprays. You can even apply them directly to the ware. During firing, salts—or the soluble salts or soda ash—are introduced into the firing chamber. You can also spray them on or fume them during a post-firing phase. See pages 118–120 for a full description of raku salt/soda firing.

BILL ABRIGHT
Traveler, 1989
71 x 31 x 22 inches
(180.3 x 78.7 x 55.9 cm)
Soldate clay; poured glaze; pre-textured slabs;
quick water cooling, smoking for reduction
Photo by artist

Never use any material before learning about all possible hazards or adverse reactions caused by use of or exposure to it. Manufacturers often provide what are known as Material Safety Data Sheets with the materials when you buy them; these include safe handling requirements. Request these sheets if they're not offered to you. You can also find some online. For other useful information, look through scientific materials catalogs. Try your local high school or college chemistry lab, too; if you introduce yourself and explain what you're looking for, someone there might help you out.

A common misconception is that soluble salts become chemically altered and lose their strength in solution. In fact, *solubility* refers to the capacity of a salt to be dissolved in water *without* inducing an adverse reaction or chemical change. To prepare soluble salts for use as a spray or wash, begin your experiments with 5 grams per cup (237 ml) of hot water. Mix the solution with a wooden stick, spoon, or old brush, as these materials—especially bismuth subnitrate and silver nitrate (the reactant in photography printing)—are highly corrosive.

No glazing method should be excluded from your raku repertoire; explore any means of personalizing your glazing and decorating style that you like. It's all about experimenting!

Silver nitrate is light sensitive; it breaks down and loses strength when exposed to light. Combined with its high cost, you have two good reasons for preparing only what you need to use at the time. When you use it in a glaze, first prepare a large batch of the glaze in a dry mix without the silver nitrate. Next, weigh out only as much glaze as you need, mix it with water, and screen it. Then dissolve the silver nitrate in hot water, and mix it into the glaze. Apply the glaze or wash just before firing to take full advantage of its potency.

If you have any mixture left over, store it in an opaque container out of the light. If the mixture turns a dark color, you'll know that the potency of the silver nitrate has been compromised. Wear rubber gloves when handling silver nitrate; it stains your skin if you don't wash it off immediately. The stains are extremely difficult to remove (try an abrasive soap), although they'll eventually wear away with no ill effects. The pre-wash sprays available at grocery stores usually remove the stains from clothing.

Using silver carbonate as a substitute for silver nitrate has gained some followers. Silver carbonate is safer, doesn't stain or lose its strength, and is apparently easier to use. Availability of this material is so recent that I haven't tried it yet.

Do avoid solutions that combine bismuth and sodium. When you mix the two together, the chemical reaction hardens the resulting solution. Also, stannous chloride is moisture and oxygen sensitive. Open any container of it only briefly, and keep the container tightly sealed to prevent this material from breaking down and losing strength.

You can mix copper, barium, and iron sulfate in solutions of $^1/_2$ to 2 or more cups (118 to 473 ml) per gallon (3.79 L) of water. Spray or brush the solution onto the surface of your ware, or try soaking the ware in it and leaving it unglazed.

Multi-Firing

You may have come across the term *multi-firing* in reference to color and surface development. This is the process of glazing and firing the same piece several times. A high-temperature firing may be followed by a low-fire and then by a luster or enamel firing at even lower temperatures. Sometimes, firing the same piece more than once at the same cone alters the final effect. Depending on your approach, you can do multiple firings independently or during the same firing session.

Multi-firing techniques certainly work with the raku process. For example, you can raku fire a porcelain piece that's been glazed and fired to cone 9 (with or without the addition of raku glaze) for interesting color, crackle, and smoke effects. See page 118 for more information on this topic.

While successful raku work is always the result of the combined effects of forming, decorating (if applicable), and firing, don't restrict your approach to traditional glazing and surface embellishment. No glazing method should be excluded from your raku repertoire; explore any means of personalizing your glazing and decorating style that you like. It's all about experimenting!

HARVEY SADOW
Liang's Garden #2005-16, 2005
8½ x 12 x 12 inches (21.6 x 30.5 x 30.5 cm)
Wheel thrown Laguna "Sadow blend"; brushed and dipped glaze;
wax resist over fired glaze, reglazed with slip; raku fired in gas kiln;
smoking for fast heavy reduction, slow cool, multi fired
Photo by artist

Kilns

CHAPTER 5

Raku is a technique that's flexible and, to a certain degree, accommodating, in the sense that it extends many of the parameters that ordinarily confine us in conventional pottery making, glazing, and firing. We've seen how suitable glazes and clays for raku, for instance, can span a rather wide range. You'll soon learn that appropriate kiln designs include an equally wide variety. Just about any fuel, including electricity, can power your kiln. The size and shape of the kiln can also vary tremendously, as can the refractory material used in its construction.

STEVEN BRANFMAN
Vessel, 2005
14 x 8½ inches (35.6 x 21.6 cm)
Sprayed stoneware and raku
glaze; impressed texture

Kiln Designs

Manufacturers of pottery equipment place great emphasis on simplicity of kiln design and ease of control. This is a good thing! Because the operation of their equipment is handed to the consumer on a silver platter, however, many potters operate their commercial kilns—whether electric or gas, large or small, low-fire or high-fire—without any understanding of how or why their kilns work. This often leads to a standstill when something goes awry, which is not a good thing. As we begin our foray into kiln theory, design, and construction, we must start by taking a look at the different types of kilns, their heat sources, and the combustion theory that allows them to operate.

Although we tend to classify or label kilns according to the type of fuel they use and their construction style (wood-fired, catenary arch, sprung arch, downdraft, and so on), the fundamental difference between kilns is whether they run on electricity or burn fuel. The reason potters often separate electric kilns from the other types is that all the factors that go into designing, powering, and controlling a fuel-burning kiln are essentially similar, whether the kiln burns gas, wood, oil, or any other fossil fuel. Electric kilns, on the other hand, are quite different.

Electric Kilns

The most commonly available kilns in use by studio potters are electric. If you're under the impression that these kilns aren't suitable for raku, let me be the first to dispel this notion by telling you that you *can* fire raku in an electric kiln. While it isn't the best or most versatile of kilns for this purpose, it's clean, relatively safe, and in many ways, the easiest and most convenient to use, depending on your studio situation. If you already have some raku experience—if you've attended group firings, for example—you may wonder how firing in an electric kiln allows you to experience the wonderful spectacle for which raku is known. To put it briefly: raku doesn't have to be a community-rousing event!

KATHI TIGHE
Raku Bowl, 2006
9$\frac{1}{2}$ x 9$\frac{1}{2}$ x 3$\frac{1}{4}$ inches
(24.1 x 24.1 x 8.3 cm)
Thrown and altered Deco Porcelain with molochite and kyanite; sprayed glaze; carving, stains; gas fired; smoking for reduction; cone 05
Photo by Monica Ripley

1

2

All electric kilns are basically the same. An electrical current causes resistance wires (referred to *elements* or *coils*) in them to heat up, and the heat is transferred to the firing chamber to raise the temperatures inside it. Switches either control the amount of current that passes through the elements or how often the current passes through them. Either method allows the operator to control the rate of temperature rise and the ultimate temperature reached.

The most familiar studio-pottery electric kilns are top-loading or front-loading (see photos 1 and 2). These can range in size from small kilns designed for enameling or jewelry work, about ½ cubic foot (14.2 cu. dm) in volume, up to 12 cubic feet (339.8 cu. dm) for larger work. Electric kilns made specifically for raku, such as the Olympic Kiln shown below, are also available.

An electric kiln is well insulated, vents a minimum of hot exhaust gases, and heats up and cools down slowly. Unfortunately, these inherent advantages prevent the raku potter from firing multiple loads—one of the attractions of raku firing. Successfully firing multiple loads requires being able to preheat the next load of ware, usually by placing it on top of the kiln, to warm in the escaping heat and exhaust from the load being fired. You must also have immediate temperature control so that you can raise the kiln temperature slowly or quickly. This isn't possible with an electric kiln.

Other aspects to consider when using electric kilns for raku are the cumulative effects of exposing the kiln's heating elements and bricks to the rapid heating and cooling required; the harsh use of kiln hardware, such as lids, handles, and hinges; and the exposure of the hot interior face of the kiln lid to room temperatures. All of these will shorten the life of the kiln. By how much? Certainly not enough to discourage you from doing raku if the only kiln you have is electric. Renowned raku artist Hal Riegger routinely used his homebuilt electric kiln to fire his ware (see photo 3). To minimize the harsh effects of raku on the kiln, see the tips on page 55.

I've raku fired in an electric kiln for years, with minimal damage to it. In fact, using an electric kiln for raku has some clear advantages. Most cracking occurs during the heating cycle because the temperature has been raised too quickly; the slow, even temperature rise of an electric kiln automatically solves this problem. It's a slow solution, for sure, but essentially foolproof! Tending to the firing is also minimized: turn an electric kiln on high, and after one firing, you'll know exactly how long that kiln takes to reach temperature—usually two to three hours in a typical electric kiln. And if you *soak* your glazes at the end of the firing to achieve particular effects, an electric kiln is ideal. (Soaking is the process of holding the kiln at a constant temperature for a predetermined period of time.) Simply turn the switches down to medium, and soak to your heart's content.

If you use an electric kiln at all, you should learn how to do basic kiln repair and maintenance—that is, change the coils and switches as well as replace crumbled bricks and worn-out hardware. Potters should strive for as much self-reliance as possible. The goal isn't to become completely self-sustaining

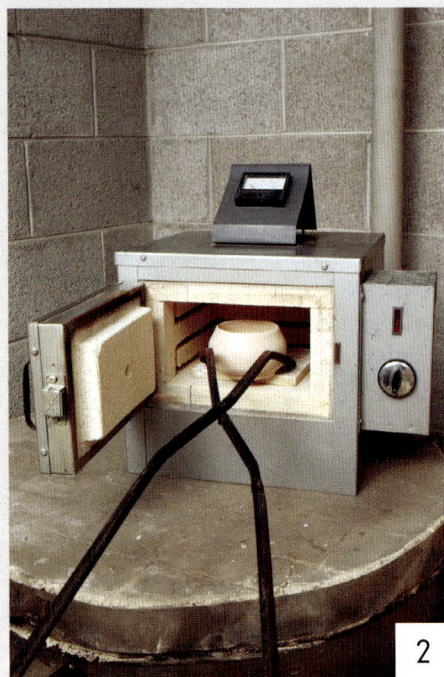

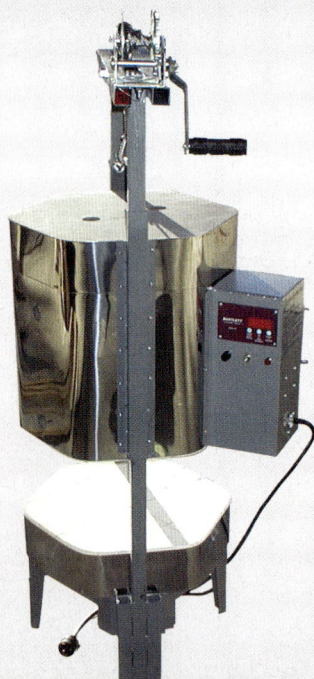

or isolated but to achieve a degree of independence from otherwise uncontrollable situations that might affect your work. You don't want to have to reschedule a firing and disturb a work plan while waiting for a kiln-repair service to replace a burnt-out coil or a bent lid hinge.

An electric kiln requires little by way of special preparation. If you purchase a small one that operates on standard 100- to 120-volt household current (240 volts in the United Kingdom), you don't even need special electrical service. If you maintain the kiln yourself and don't plan on doing raku every day of the year, an electric kiln used for raku will live a long, productive life without being much worse for the wear.

Fuel-Burning Kilns

Fuel-burning kilns can be fired with natural gas, LPG (liquefied petroleum gas—a mixture of propane and butane that's often referred to as propane), wood, oil, coal, or charcoal. Although kilns designed for each type of fuel differ somewhat, their basic operations are similar. The process of selecting a fuel can be almost philosophical in nature. Propane is a plentiful fuel that's simple to use. Wood is the preferred fuel of the purist; some potters insist on using it in order to keep modern technology at arm's length. Wood is certainly the most traditional fuel and has an appealing purity and romanticism associated with it. Similar sentiments exist about coal and charcoal, though charcoal is easier to obtain and use.

Oil used to be the potter's fuel of choice, but with the near-universal availability of both natural gas service and LPG as well as the simple, efficient, commercial combustion systems available today, gas has replaced all other fuels. For the raku potter who's looking for convenience, nothing beats it. Gas is clean, efficient, and easy to master and control. In addition, dismantling the kiln (or at least the burner system) for storage, which raku potters often need to do after each firing, is an easy process with a gas system.

To extend the life of your electric kiln, follow these simple guidelines:

▪ Use a gentle touch when opening and closing the kiln lid or door so you don't inadvertently subject the interior bricks to treatment that's rougher than necessary.

▪ When opening the lid of a top-loader, use tongs to grab the handle, being careful not to bend or otherwise mangle it.

▪ Stack your pots no closer than 2 inches (5.1 cm) from the interior walls of the kiln. This will help prevent molten glaze from touching the brick as it drips or when you lift out your fired pieces.

▪ Stack your ware as close to the top of the kiln as possible by using a kiln shelf. The closer your pieces are to the top, the less likely you'll be to touch an interior surface with a tong or pot when you remove the ware.

▪ Minimize temperature shock to the hot kiln bricks when removing your pots by opening the kiln only as much as necessary.

ANDREW M. DENNEY
Sangam Cup, 2007
6 x 6 x 6 inches
(15.2 x 15.2 x 15.2 cm)
Hand built stoneware; brushed
glaze; carved, terra sigillata; gas
fired; smoking for reduction
Photo by Christa Denney

Combustion

Combustion in fuel-burning kilns—the process that occurs when fuel is ignited and burns—depends on the fuel used, the structure of the kiln, and the way in which you operate that kiln. An understanding of combustion theory and the terms associated with it is important for two reasons: because your goal during firing is to control combustion and because when you learn how to build your own kiln (see the next chapter), you'll need to know how certain kiln dimensions and other kiln-design considerations affect it. Although I focus primarily on propane-fueled kilns here, the theory behind their operation is similar from one fuel-burning kiln to another.

The Relationship of Air and Fuel

Understanding the relationship between air and fuel during combustion is critical. Unfortunately, it's a relationship that's frequently misunderstood by novice potters.

Different labels are used to describe the air that mixes with the fuel during the firing. *Primary air* enters the burner and mixes with the fuel prior to ignition. It's the easiest air to control. *Secondary air* is all the air that mixes with the fuel after ignition. The kiln's *burner port* (the inlet for the burner), even though it's a fixed opening, and flue (see the next section) are sources of secondary air that you can manipulate during the firing. What I call *incidental air*—the air that enters the firing chamber through cracks in the walls, spaces between the bricks, and/or through a loose-fitting lid—is also secondary air. Although eliminating these openings is impossible, a well-designed kiln minimizes them, and you can stuff any openings that develop once a firing

is underway—due to expansion or a loose brick, for example—with small pieces of refractory fiber. (But watch your fingers!)

Up to a certain point, the more air that enters the kiln, the richer the air-fuel mixture and the more efficient the combustion. (You'll find more information on controlling and adjusting air sources on pages 100–102.)

Basic Kiln Structure

Before I continue, let me define the terms *draft*, *flue*, *stack*, and *damper*. All four kiln features work together to control the operation and efficiency of your combustion system.

The *draft* is the rate of flow of gas, air, and heat through the kiln and out the stack. It's akin to the sucking action of a vacuum cleaner and affects the *atmosphere* (see the next section) within the kiln. The greater the draft, the greater is the sucking action or "breathing" of the kiln through all of its openings, especially the secondary air sources.

The *flue* is the passageway that connects the kiln's combustion source, firing chamber, and *stack* (or *chimney*). Its purposes are to provide for and facilitate the circulation of heat, to help control the atmosphere, to allow for sufficient draft, and to provide an exit for the exhaust.

The *damper* opens and closes the connection between the flue and the stack and controls how they operate. It allows you to adjust the gases and heat entering the stack, as well as the amount of draft.

Take a look at figure 1, which shows a typical downdraft kiln. The *bagwall*, which consists of bricks with spaces between them, protects the pots from direct contact with the flame from the burner. The damper is a kiln shelf that slides open or closed to control the strength of the draft. The simplest raku kilns, including the ones you'll learn how to build in the next chapter, have no formal flue feature or chimney of any sort, and the damper is often just a piece of kiln shelf or brick placed over an opening in the top of the kiln (see photo 4). In these basic kilns, the flue, damper, and stack details are effectively combined with—and are inside—the kiln chamber itself. (When I use the term *flue* in this book, I'm referring to the opening at the top of this type of kiln.)

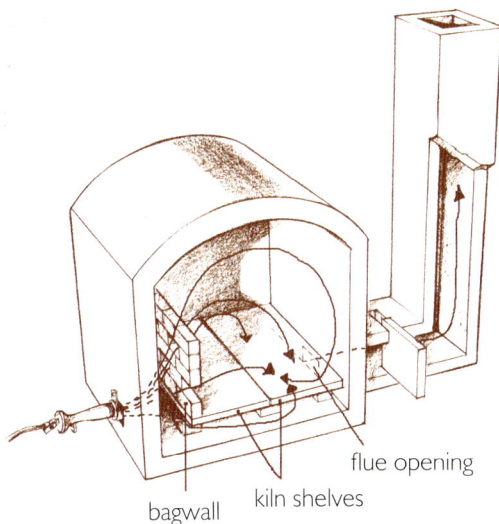

flue opening

kiln shelves

bagwall

FIGURE I

Other kiln components that influence combustion include the type and size of burner, the burner *orifice* (the opening through which the natural gas or propane passes prior to ignition), the dimensions of the flue opening and burner port (or ports), and the size of the *firebox*. Yes, even gas kilns have a firebox; it's the space between the floor of the kiln and the kiln shelf above.

Atmosphere

Now let's add another variable: atmosphere. The atmosphere in a kiln is the result of the ratio of air and fuel inside it and is characterized by the quality of the flame. Changing that ratio affects the temperature, heat, and atmosphere.

An *oxidizing* atmosphere is one in which plenty of air is mixed with the fuel. An oxidizing flame, which is blue, indicates that the fuel is burning efficiently. (An electric kiln, although it produces no flame, provides an oxidizing atmosphere.) An ideal oxidizing atmosphere isn't possible—the imperfect combustion in any fuel-burning system produces some carbon—but for all practical purposes, an effective oxidizing atmosphere doesn't have to be an ideal one.

A *reduction* atmosphere, characterized by a yellow flame, results when you reduce the amount of oxygen, both primary and secondary, that's available to the fuel. Combustion in this atmosphere is inefficient. Because the fuel in a kiln that's in heavy reduction mode must search elsewhere for oxygen, flames emanate from the flue and, depending on the intensity of combustion, even from the peepholes and burner port or, in the case of a wood-fired kiln, the firebox. For the potter, a reduction atmosphere can be a wonderfully creative tool: the fuel looks to glazes for the oxygen it needs and can alter glaze effects in desirable ways. Hence the term *reduction glazes*.

You can create a reduction atmosphere in an electric kiln by introducing organic materials such as wood or coal or by introducing propane into the chamber with a small burner or torch. Electric

4

The terms "temperature" and "heat" are often misunderstood, and, ironically, the use of cones as temperature-measuring devices contributes to this misunderstanding. Temperature is a measurement of heat at a certain instant. However, achieving a prescribed temperature won't necessarily give you the firing results you expect. Heat is an amount of energy produced and is a factor of temperature and time. It's the correct heat, not the temperature, that's needed to melt and mature your glazes. Although cones have equivalent temperatures, these temperatures are comparative only.

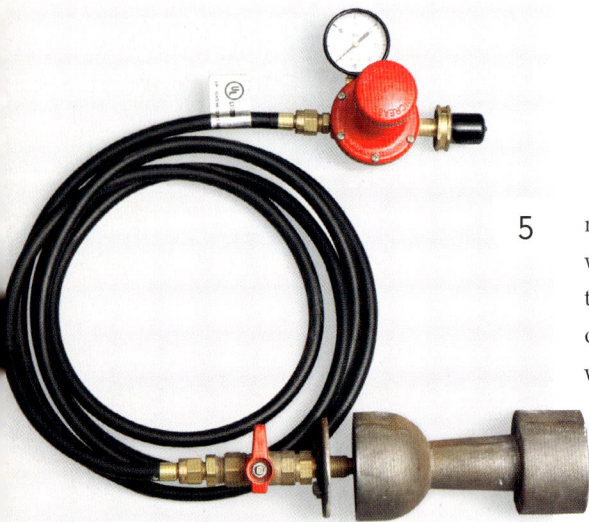

5

reduction firing must be carried out in a well-ventilated kiln area, however, and the kiln must be fitted with a drawer or opening towards the bottom through which you can introduce the reduction material. Although many potters have successfully used electric kilns in this way, some have reported premature coil failure as a result. If you're restricted to the use of an electric kiln, reduction firing should be an occasional practice only and not your usual firing mode.

In raku, as in other types of firing, you want to be able to achieve oxidation and reduction atmospheres at the appropriate times. An oxidizing flame and atmosphere are necessary for temperature advance; a reduction atmosphere is necessary if you want particular glaze effects. The goal is to create the most efficient operating system you can while still allowing yourself the greatest flexibility and amount of control.

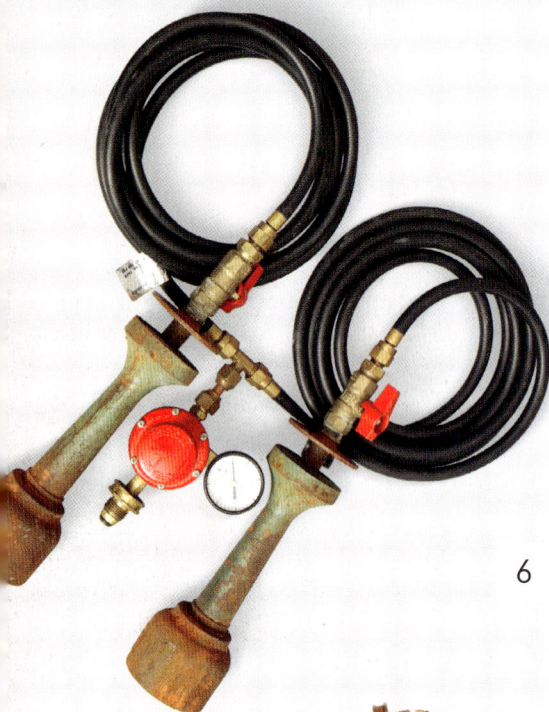

6

To summarize, combustion is achieved through an efficient combination of air and fuel. Introducing too much air can cool a kiln, but you must welcome air into your system. I've seen well-designed, well-built kilns—with more than adequate burners, good fuel supplies, and a fine fuel pressure—fail to melt glazes no matter how long they're fired. Novice raku firers sometimes think the problem is heat escaping through the peepholes or flue, so they all but close these openings down. In most cases, though, the problem is just the opposite: not enough air is entering the kiln. Fuel needs air to burn; without enough air, the flame only gets so hot. Although widening the kiln openings may seem

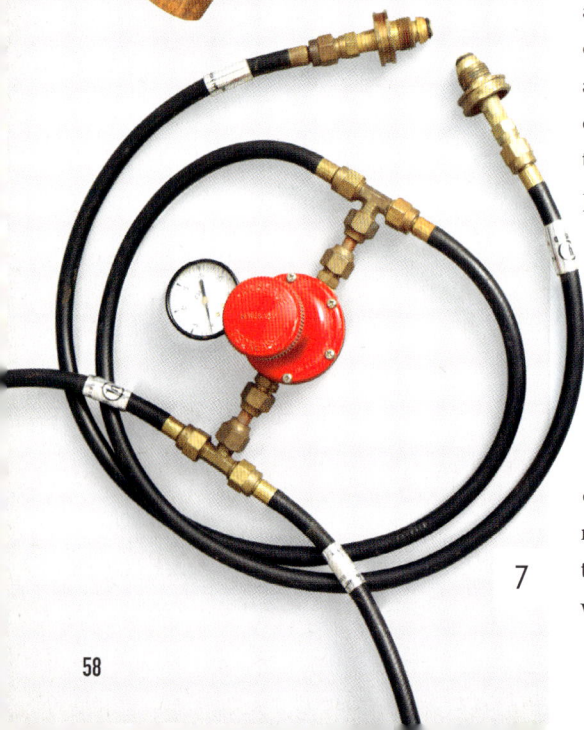

7

counterintuitive, allowing more air to enter through the primary and secondary sources causes the temperature to rise. For more detailed information on this topic, turn to pages 100–102.

Gas-Fueled Kilns

Photo 5 shows all the parts of a complete combustion system for a gas-fueled kiln except for the fuel source itself: a pressure regulator (the round red component at the top); a gauge above the regulator; a hose or, in the case of natural gas, a rigid gas line to carry the gas to the burner; a gas valve (the red handle-like switch at the bottom); and a burner (shown just beyond the valve). Systems can be set up for single (photo 5) or multiple (photo 6) burners, and, if you use bottled gas, it can be attached to one or more fuel tanks (photo 7).

Burners

Generally, burners fall into two categories: *atmospheric burners* and *forced-air* (or *power*) burners. Atmospheric burners, of which the most common are *Venturi burners*, are designed to facilitate control of the air-fuel mixture by virtue of their shape (see figure 2). The term *venturi* refers to the constriction (or narrowing) that draws air into this type of burner by creating a slight vacuum. Forced-air burners have built-in blowers or fans that force air into them instead (see photo 8). They're most commonly used with natural gas, although they can be used with LPG as well. In the realm of raku kilns, you're most likely to encounter the venturi-style burner. It's simple in design and, unlike a forced-air system, doesn't require electricity. Which do I prefer? I've used both, and they work equally well.

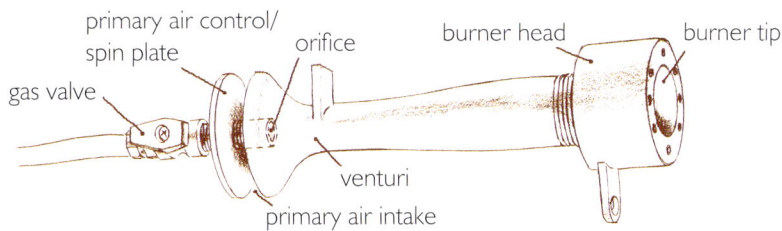

primary air control/
spin plate

gas valve

orifice

burner head

burner tip

venturi

primary air intake

FIGURE 2

In both types of systems, primary air enters the burner before combustion and mixes directly with the fuel, which is emitted through the orifice. On an atmospheric burner, a spin plate on a threaded post at the open end of the burner opens and closes to control the primary air intake. Secondary air enters the kiln through the burner port and through open peepholes. With a gas-fired kiln, as long as the burner is large enough and you provide for adequate secondary air sources, control of the kiln is always in your hands.

Whether you purchase your kiln or build your own, two factors are crucial when choosing the correct burner system for it: the kiln's interior volume and the material from which the kiln is made. These factors determine the approximate heat input (measured in Btu's or joules) that the kiln requires per hour and cubic foot (or cubic decimeter). (See pages 69–70 for an explanation of how to calculate the necessary heat input.) The more energy-efficient your kiln-construction materials, the smaller your burner system needs to be, the less gas it'll use, and the faster the kiln will reach the desired temperature for both the first firing of the day and for multiple loads thereafter. Keeping fuel expenses down should be a good incentive for buying or building an efficient kiln. The more firings you can do before having your propane tanks refilled, the better.

Depending on the shape and design of your kiln, a dual burner system may be more appropriate and efficient than a single burner, but because most raku kilns are in the 10-cubic-foot (283 cu. dm) range or smaller, a single system is usually sufficient. The propane pressure should be set at approximately 7 to 10 psi (48.3 to 68.9 kPa) and adjusted for maximum efficiency. (See pages 99–105 for more information on regulators, pressure, and combustion.)

Gas combustion systems set up for larger, traditional-style kilns routinely include safety systems to guard against the accidental extinguishing of a flame. If the flame goes out, these systems terminate the gas flow in a matter of seconds. Typically, though, because raku kilns are small, located outdoors, and usually monitored throughout the firing, these safety systems are abandoned due to cost. If you decide not to include a safety system, remember that you're choosing to take on a role that would otherwise be controlled automatically. Don't take this responsibility lightly!

8

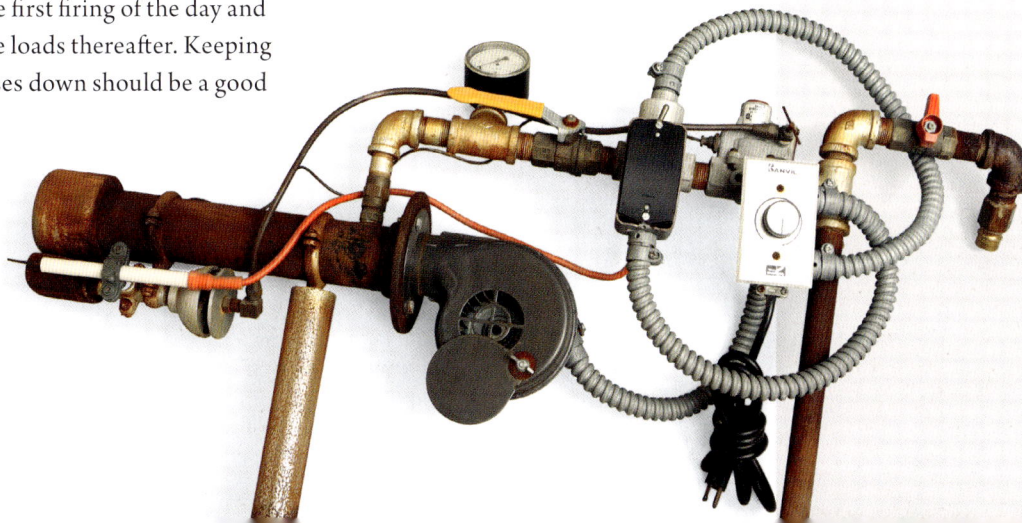

Propane Gas

Propane (LPG) is available in different sized tanks. The 20-pound (9.1 kg) tank used with outdoor gas grills is the most common. Photo 9 shows a 20-pound, a 30-pound, and a 100-pound (9.1, 13.6, and 45.4 kg) tank. Other readily available sizes are 40- and 60-pound (18.1 and 27.2 kg) tanks and 250- and 500-gallon (946 and 1893 L) tanks. Why are some tanks sized in pounds and others in gallons? Tanks up to and including 100 pounds (45.4 kg) are considered portable; the *tare weight* (or weight of the empty tank) in pounds is stamped on the tank collar. In photo 10, for example, the tare weight—70.2 pounds (31.8 kg)—is stamped at the lower right.

Propane tanks are filled to capacity less about 20 percent to allow for expansion. Exact tank weights vary according to the manufacturer, but in general an empty 20-pound (9.1 kg) tank weighs about 18½ pounds (8.4 kg). Add that to the weight of the gas, and you have the total full weight. An empty 30-pound (13.6 kg) tank weighs about 25 pounds (11.3 kg) and a 40-pound tank (18.1 kg), about 30 pounds (13.6 kg). A full 100-pound (45.4 kg) tank weighs approximately 150 pounds (68 kg). Larger tanks are stationary and are labeled by their capacity in gallons. For volume comparison, 4.84 pounds (2.2 kg) equal 1 gallon (3.8 L) of gas.

For a small kiln—up to 3 or 4 cubic feet (85 or 113.3 cu. dm)—when you plan to fire no more than three loads in succession and when the weather is warm, a 20-pound (9.1 kg) tank is adequate. What does warm weather have to do with raku firing? I'll explain shortly!

9

The collar on a propane tank contains important information. In addition to the tare (or empty) weight of the tank, the serial number and expiration date of the tank are also listed. Tanks are certified for 12 years and must be replaced after that.

10

I recommend using 40- or 60-pound (18.1 or 27.2 kg) tanks; they hold reasonably high volumes of gas and are still portable. If you work on a large scale that requires a larger kiln, if you need to fire four or more loads in succession, or if you want to fire two kilns simultaneously, ganging or manifolding two or more tanks together is easy. Your combustion equipment provider or local gas supplier should be able to outfit you with the proper hoses and fittings to accomplish this. Of course, manifolding small tanks together still may not give you a sufficient fuel supply. At this point, you'll need a larger tank.

Large 100-pound (45.4 kg) tanks are great because they seem bottomless, but although they're considered portable, they aren't easy to transport. A filled tank this size is very heavy, requires a truck for transportation, and can be dangerous to move. Many gas suppliers will deliver full tanks in exchange for the empties. Some will even pick up your empty tanks and refill them at little or no charge other than the cost of the gas. Regardless of the capacity of your fuel supply, keep a few 20- or 30-pound (9.1 or 13.6 kg) tanks around as spares. While 20-pound (9.1 kg) tanks are readily available at hardware stores, lumberyards, discount stores, and even some supermarkets, you will usually have to order 100-pound (45.4 kg) tanks from a bottled gas company.

Now what about this warm weather issue I hinted at earlier? Propane in a tank is under pressure, and a percentage of it is in vapor form. The vast majority of LPG burners and combustion systems operate via vapor withdrawal. As the vapor is withdrawn from the tank, the pressure drops, and the tank starts to freeze. As this continues, the ability of the propane to remain in the vapor state decreases and can halt the flow of fuel to the burner. Firing in warm weather lengthens the time that freezing takes. One way to avoid this freezing predicament is to use the largest tank possible. Manifolding tanks together is another solution. Even after taking these precautions, however, freeze-ups can happen, especially if you're firing in cold weather. Remedies include pouring water over the tank and fittings or setting the tank in a basin of water until the firing is finished.

In situations where freeze-ups are unavoidable and problematic, the best solution is to install a liquid withdrawal system such as the one shown in photo 11, which comes complete with a specially designed burner, high-pressure liquid/vapor withdrawal regulator, liquid withdrawal valve, and dip tube. This system withdraws and volatilizes liquid propane, thereby eliminating the freezing stage. The regulator can be attached either to a conventional propane tank with a stock vapor valve, requiring the tank to be inverted or turned on its side, or to a liquid withdrawal valve that

has a dip tube, in which case the tank must be used in its upright position. A knowledgeable LPG supplier can fit a standard tank with a liquid withdrawal valve and dip tube. Detailed instructions for installing and using the system shown below are included with the commercial package.

Either method works safely if you're careful, but never confuse a conventional (vapor) burner system with a liquid system. Drawing liquid propane through a vapor regulator to a standard vapor burner creates a very dangerous and explosive situation. And never invert or lay a propane tank on its side unless you're using a liquid withdrawal system.

Propane tank valves are equipped with an automatic pressure-release mechanism in the event the tank is overfilled or warm weather causes the gas to expand. If the mechanism is activated while your tank is in storage, you'll hear a hiss or see gas being emitted. Open the valve for a few seconds to relieve the pressure by releasing some gas. Use common sense: do this only outdoors, in an open area that's well away from any fire or flame.

Industrial or commercial (non-pottery-related) suppliers of gas, tanks, and accessories differ greatly in what they offer and in their knowledge about bottled gas. Shop for the best value, and make sure your supplier knows what he's doing before you allow him to fill your tanks. Most lumberyards and hardware stores are only familiar with 20-pound (9.1 kg) tanks and may not know what to do with larger ones. To avoid a potentially dangerous situation, make sure you know the capacities of your tanks. Some suppliers charge a set price per tank/per fill-up, regardless of whether the tank is empty. Others charge you only for the amount of gas you buy.

11

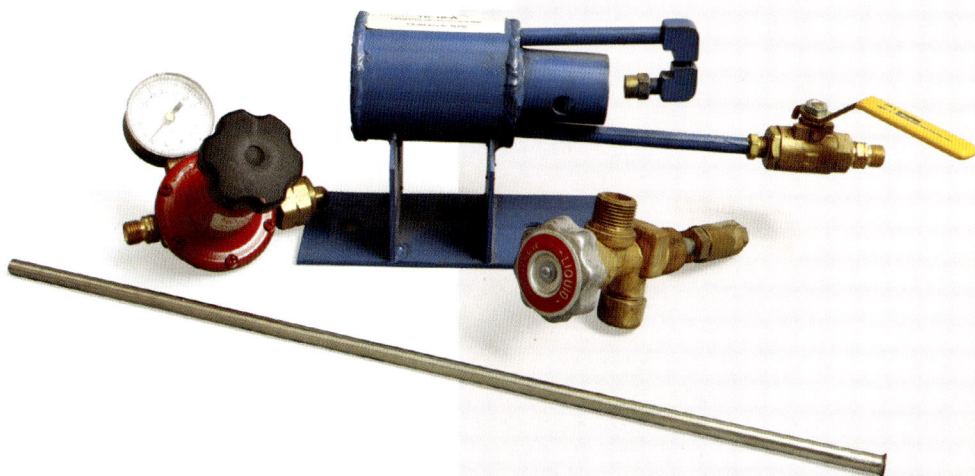

Natural Gas

The ultimate solution to the inconveniences of LPG systems is the use of natural gas. If you sometimes operate on a moment's notice, the "bottomless tank" of natural gas can be a real lifesaver. Tank storage isn't an issue either, and provided that you're equipped with the proper safety devices, using natural gas indoors is safe. Keep in mind, however, that the permanent, rigid plumbing connections for gas must be installed by a licensed plumber, so the cost of getting set up is higher than if you use LPG. These connections also reduce your flexibility if you want to move, rebuild, or alter your kiln—processes that are often as much a part of raku as making and firing the pots.

To use natural gas, the gas pressure must be adequate, and your kiln must be close enough to the gas meter to avoid the pressure drop that occurs when the gas has to travel too far from the meter to the kiln. Have a gas-company representative come out and give you the specifications of your gas service. You'll need this information when you order your combustion system.

If you sometimes operate on a moment's notice, the "bottomless tank" of natural gas can be a real lifesaver.

Because natural gas pressure is lower than that of LPG, power burners—that is, burners with electric blowers attached—are preferable to venturi-type burners and are more expensive.

The burners must be set up with the correct orifice size for natural gas and for the pressure at which you'll be firing. Weigh these advantages and disadvantages, and then make your decision. I'll tell you, though: it's hard to beat not having to worry about a frozen system or running out of fuel.

Other Equipment

Your best source for hoses, fittings, pressure regulators, and other specialized components is someone who speaks your language—either a specialist in gas kilns and firing systems or someone at a pottery supply company that carries combustion equipment. Local gas companies can also be rich sources of equipment and information. Look for companies that supply hospitals and other high-tech environments; they tend to have more experience with a wider range of gases and related paraphernalia. You'll know quickly whether your source is knowledgeable, understands your needs, and is interested in helping you. The simple fact that you're a potter often intrigues people enough to make them willing to help.

Commercial plumbing-supply houses can also be good sources of equipment, but in my experience, employees at them tend to have little patience with people not in the trade. If they've posted a sign saying "Homeowners: Go to the back of the line," you probably won't get the help you need finding the correct hose for ganging your tanks. The more you know about what you need, the wider your range of sources becomes.

Wood-Fired Kilns

Wood is an elemental fuel that needs little by way of equipment in order to burn—no electricity, burners, tanks, or hoses. All you need is a kiln with an ample firebox and an ash pit, an ax and wood supply, plenty of stamina and brawn, and an unwavering dedication to the firing process!

Wood-fired kilns are sometimes quite primitive. You can build one with common (and even found) materials such as common red bricks, clay, and gravel. If you have the opportunity, give wood a try. Remember that although wood firing may save you some expense, you'll more than make up for it in the time you spend preparing the wood and firing the kiln.

For proper combustion, wood requires a large firebox, one that exposes the wood to maximum oxygen to ignite it and allows it to give off its energy quickly. Like any solid fuel, wood burns from the surface; smaller pieces therefore fire hotter and give off more heat than larger ones. Therefore, use large pieces of wood when the firing begins and smaller pieces as the firing progresses. The wood should be thoroughly dried for about a year to prevent the release of steam into the chamber. Steam has a cooling effect on the firing and may prevent the kiln from reaching temperature.

Softwood is preferable to hardwood; it's less dense and thus burns faster. For more information on building and firing wood kilns, turn to pages 83–85 and 99–100.

Coal-Fired Kilns

Several different types of coal can fuel a kiln. *Anthracite*, the coal used for home heating, is hard, burns slowly, has little-to-no sulfur content, and creates few emissions. It's available in approximately 10 different graded sizes and looks like random-sized rocks. *Bituminous coal*, of which there are several varieties, is used in industry and is the coal that's traditionally been used to fire kilns. It's softer than anthracite and is available in graded sizes, as well as in dust and powder forms.

True *charcoal* is an all-wood product, and although it isn't related to coal at all, it's placed in the same category.

DON ELLIS
Raku Vessel, Copper Matte Luster, 2008
18 x 22 inches (45.7 x 55.9 cm)
Soldate 60; sprayed glaze; slip trailing; electric fired; alcohol reduction, stretched with sodium silicate
Photo by artist

RICK BERMAN
Raku Bottle, 2008
$8^1/_2$ x 7 x 7 inches
(21.6 x 17.8 x 17.8 cm)
Wheel thrown Standard 239; dipped
glaze; overglaze; gas fired
Photo by Erik Haagensen

To produce charcoal, hardwood is heated in a kiln in the absence of oxygen; the charred results are shaped in either natural lumps or briquettes. (Briquettes are formed by combining the smaller pieces and dust left over from the manufacture of the lump charcoal, with wheat starch or glucose as a binder.) Briquettes burn longer than lumps, but lump charcoal definitely burns hotter. The so-called charcoal briquettes found in supermarkets and hardware stores aren't wood. They're made from a coal base, contain petroleum-based bonding agents and fillers, and don't burn as hot as either of the natural wood products. The nature of their bonding agents alone should steer you away from using them.

For our purposes, natural lump hardwood charcoal is the preferred fuel for a coal-fired kiln. With the proliferation of natural food supermarkets, it isn't as difficult to find as it used to be. For other sources, look in the yellow pages under "charcoal" or try a wholesale restaurant supplier. For more about firing with charcoal, see pages 86–87 and 135–136.

DORIS BOSCHUNG-JOHNER
Medusa, 2007
$8^1/_4$ x $4^3/_4$ x $4^3/_4$ inches (21 x 12 x 12 cm)
Hand built stoneware; poured glaze;
wood fired; controlled cooling
Photo by Josef Kollar

To Buy or Build

Do you need to build your own kiln? Absolutely not. In general, commercially manufactured kilns are fine, and given the number on the market—from simple to complex in design—you can't help but find one to meet your needs.

For many years, the commercial standard was an ordinary wire frame, lined with ceramic fiber and set on top of a loosely assembled, soft brick base, but although these kilns are lightweight, easy to fire, and still the most popular, they've given way to more sophisticated designs that incorporate winch-operated or counterweighted cranes, clamshell chambers, heavy-duty welded frames, and other features. A wide range of sizes and configurations is also available, and the necessary combustion equipment (burner, hose, and regulator—and sometimes even an empty propane tank) is sometimes included in the package. Below left shows an Olympic raku kiln, photo 12 shows a Bracker portable raku kiln, and photo 13 shows a Zen raku kiln.

12

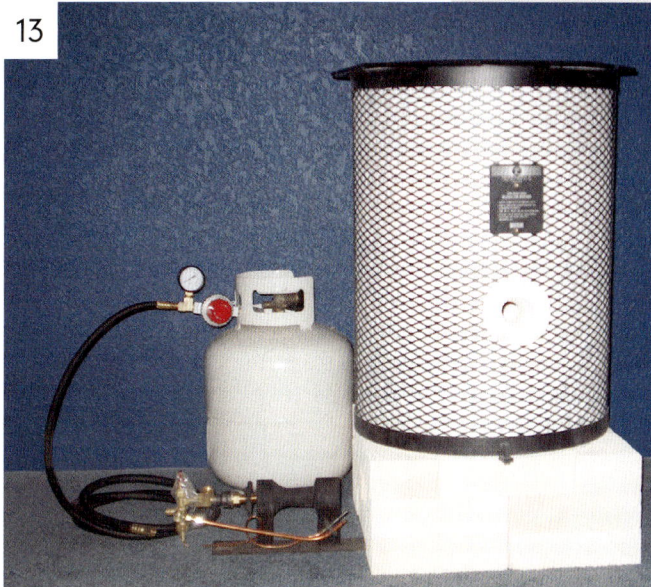

13

Kilns are available from large, well-known suppliers and manufacturers, as well as from one-person shops that custom design and build kilns according to your needs and specifications. In fact, kiln builders often allow and even welcome your help as they construct your kiln. Take advantage of this opportunity: it gives you greater insight into kiln design and some hands-on experience with construction methods.

If you do choose to buy a kiln rather than build one, research carefully first. Compare construction methods, materials, prices, quality, and features. Ask about customer support and technical advice. If you'd like to try your hand at building a kiln instead, move on to the next chapter.

RICHARD HIRSCH
Altar Bowl with Ladle #3, 2007
24 x 31 x 14 inches
(61 x 78.7 x 35.6 cm)
Relief sculpted, hand built and wheel thrown clay; sprayed and sponged glaze; carved, faceted; gas fired; selective smoking for reduction
Photo by Geoff Tesh

building
Your Own Kiln

Although building a 50-cubic-foot (1.4 cu. m), downdraft, sprung arch, high-fire kiln can be daunting, making a small raku kiln is truly easy—and please understand that I'm not a do-it-all-yourself kind of guy. It can also save you a lot of money. The real reason to embark on a project of this kind, though, is the invaluable knowledge you'll gain from the experience. Constructing a kiln helps you understand how it works, how to control its firing, and how to make repairs and alterations. Ultimately, the exercise will help you gain an understanding of the entire raku process.

STEVEN BRANFMAN
Vessel, 2002
15 x 11 inches (38.1 x 27.9 cm)
Brushed and splattered multi layered stoneware and commercial
low fire glaze; combed and impressed surface texture

First Steps

Common to most kiln-building projects are a few steps you'll need to take in advance, including checking out your local building codes, choosing the type and size of kiln you'd like to build, purchasing the appropriate burner for it if you plan to use natural gas or propane as fuel, selecting a site that's both safe and practical, and creating a foundation.

Considering Building Codes

We potters often carry on with our quiet and benign activity as if we were immune to local town ordinances and building codes. However circuitous some of these requirements and regulations may seem, they're designed with safety in mind. They aren't always easy to deal with, but you should approach them with only the highest regard for your safety, the protection of your surroundings and neighbors, and the legal issues that govern.

Obviously, natural gas lines or a 500-gallon (1893 L) propane tank must be professionally installed; you must have a building permit in hand before you start, and the finished job requires an inspection and approval. But problems arise and frustration takes hold when in order to get official permission to operate a small raku kiln, you try to explain to the powers that be just what a raku kiln and post-firing reduction are. These powers rarely have any firsthand experience with kilns and are sometimes less than receptive to being educated.

What should you do? Your situation (is the fire chief your next door neighbor?); location (do you live in a rural area without another house in sight?); and various other circumstances dictate the proper course of action. The best advice I can give you is this: First, consult with potters in your area who may have hand-built kilns, and find out how they handled codes and inspections. Second, when you describe your proposed kiln to an inspector, try to equate it with something that he or she has some experience with—a gas grill, smoker, or fire pit, for example.

Choosing a Kiln Style and Size

Once you've decided to build your own kiln, ask yourself some basic questions: What is the size of my work? Do I want to work with a top-loading kiln, a front-loading kiln, a kiln on wheels, or a *car kiln* (a kiln set on a wheeled, rail-mounted cart)? Will I be firing multiple loads or one load at a time from a cold kiln? Will I be firing alone, or will I have helpers? And will the kiln be a permanent structure, or will I have to dismantle it after every use?

The answers to these questions—and the rest of this chapter—will help you determine the style and size of kiln to build. Raku kilns vary widely in size and complexity of design. Yours might have an elaborate, welded-steel frame and a hinged door, be built on rails, or include an overhead lift-off device. Most kilns, however, don't require these complex design elements and are

NESRIN DURING
Untitled
Hand-built Westerwald Clay; wood fired;
smoking for reduction
Photo by Stefan During

1

MICHAEL HOUGH
Reds, 1990
24 x 38 x 3 inches
(61 x 96.5 x 7.6 cm) Carved,
textured and hollowed clay;
underglaze, overglaze; raku fired;
reduction in trash can of newspaper
Photo by artist

simple enough to be within reach of mortal kiln-builders. In fact, raku kiln construction techniques are relaxed, and design specifications are flexible.

Popular designs for the novice kiln builder include loosely stacked, soft-brick kilns; fiber-lined drums; fiber-lined wire-mesh frames; and sectional electric kilns that can be converted to gas firing when their useful first lives have ended. Each has its strengths and weaknesses, depending on your particular situation, but the basic designs and construction processes are all covered in this chapter. The last thing I want to do is make doing raku more complicated than it has to be; the few complex processes described are optional—and more relevant to the advanced raku potter who's ready to participate in some customizing and fine-tuning.

Top-Loading and Front-Loading Kilns

For several reasons, I prefer top-loading kilns to front-loaders. First, there's nothing more frustrating than discovering that your pot is 1 inch (2.5 cm) taller than your kiln. The advantage of a top-loader is you can vary its height easily. If the kiln is brick, you just lay on another course of bricks to make it taller. If it's a trash-can or wire-frame fiber kiln, you build the base up to raise the kiln to the height you need.

Second, when you remove the lid from a top-loader, all the pieces in the kiln are visible, which greatly facilitates the unloading process. In a front-loader, if you want to remove a particular pot and it happens to be in the rear of the kiln … well, you see what I mean. In addition, a top-loader doesn't require any special

design or construction skills. Unlike the vertical, hinged lids of front-loaders, the lids of top-loaders double as their doors, so no hinges or metal frames are necessary.

Any kiln gives off a terrific blast of heat when you open its door or lid, but when you unload a top-loader, you can shield yourself from that heat by looking into the kiln from a slight angle while you reach in with your tongs. The wall of the kiln itself acts as a heat barrier. There's no getting away from the heat when you unload a front-loader or remove the chamber of a *top-hat kiln* (a kiln the chamber of which lifts directly up off the base); you have to stand directly in front of the kiln, with the blast of heat coming right at you. The one advantage that a front-loader does have over a top-loader is that you can stack pots in it more tightly by using more than one kiln shelf.

Kilns on Wheels

Most raku kilns aren't considered permanent; they tend to be small and are easily dismantled when necessary. Because they're small, you can build them on wheeled steel platforms, as Michael Hough did with his (see photo 1). Rolling a mobile kiln of this sort out of its storage shed and into position for firing is easy. Some folks push the envelope, of course! Photo 2 shows the entire raku facility at the Northern Clay Center in Minneapolis, Minnesota, assembled on a cart with a steel roof, complete with front-loading kiln and ample space for the storage of gloves, containers, and other raku paraphernalia. Even though my kilns are easy to move, for planning purposes, I think of them as permanent, thereby eliminating one variable from the construction equation.

Choosing an Appropriate Burner

Unless you plan to build a wood- or coal-fired kiln, you'll need to consider the relationship between your kiln design and the burner it requires. Once you've determined how large a kiln you want to make, you must purchase a compatible burner that's suited both to the interior volume of the kiln and to the materials from which it's made. The kiln's burner port and flue must be sized appropriately as well (see page 70).

Assuming that you've decided to base the desired size of your kiln on the size of the work you plan to fire in it and on the size of the kiln shelf you want to place in it (see page 71), calculating the interior kiln volume is easy. Just use either of these formulas:

Cylindrical kiln:
π (or 3.14) x radius^2 x height = volume
Rectangular kiln:
length x width x height = volume

All dimensions must be in the same measurements. If your dimensions are in inches, divide the result by 1,728 to convert to cubic feet.

Now consider the materials with which you will build your kiln. The chart, right, provides the approximate (key word!) heat input that your burner must provide, depending on which building materials you used for your kiln. Since it's always better to err on the high side, my figures are generous.

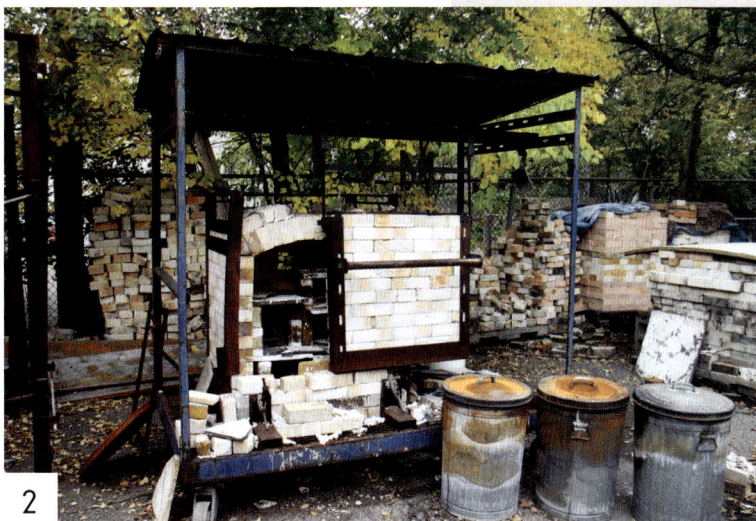

2

Recommended Refractory Materials	Heat Input per Hour per Cubic Foot (in Btu's)
1-inch 8-pound-density refractory fiber blanket*	30,000
2-inch 8-pound-density refractory fiber blanket	15,000
2½-inch 2300°F insulating fire-brick	32,000
4½-inch 2300°F insulating fire-brick	18,000

*Densities for refractory blanket are usually given in pounds per cubic foot.

Let's walk through an example, using a cylindrical kiln lined with 1-inch 8-pound-density fiber. Our kiln interior is 20 inches (50.8 cm) in diameter and 33 inches (83.8 cm) tall. First, we'll calculate the interior volume, using the formula π (or 3.14) x (radius^2) x height = volume.

If you're tempted to build an electric kiln, let me encourage you not to. Doing so just isn't practical. You have to deal with too many important aspects of construction, such as calculating the correct resistance for the coils, fashioning the coils, shaping bricks to accept them, and choosing the appropriate types of wiring and switches. These factors require special skills that are often beyond those of the average potter. When you take into account the effort, time, cost, and the likely overall quality of the result, purchasing an electric kiln for raku makes more sense than trying to build one.

The advantage of a top-loader is you can vary its height easily. If the kiln is brick, you just lay on another course of bricks to make it taller.

NESRIN DURING
Untitled
Hand-built Westerwald Clay; wood fired;
smoking for reduction
Photo by Stefan During

$3.14 \times (10)^2 \times 33 = 10{,}362$ cubic inches (169803 cu. cm)

$10{,}362 \div 1{,}728 = 6$ cubic feet (.17 cu. m)

Now, referring to the chart, note that the fiber you plan to use requires 30,000 Btu's per cubic foot. Your 6-cubic-foot (.17 cu. m) kiln therefore requires a burner with a heat output of 180,000 Btu's.

Here's another example: this time we'll consider a rectangular $2\frac{1}{2}$-inch-thick (6.4 cm) insulating firebrick kiln, with an 18 x 18 x 27-inch (45.7 x 45.7 x 68.6 cm) interior. Your calculations would look like this:

Interior kiln volume = $18 \times 18 \times 27 = 8{,}748$ cubic inches (.14 cu. m)

$8{,}748 \div 1{,}728 = 5.1$ cubic feet (.14 cu. m)

$5.1 \times 32{,}000 = 163{,}200$ Btu's

Once you've selected an appropriate burner system based on these calculations, you need to adapt the burner port and flue in your kiln to it. The burner port should be about 2 inches (5.1 cm) larger in diameter than the diameter of your burner. For example, if the burner is 3 inches (7.6 cm) in diameter, the burner port should be at least 5 x 5 inches (12.7 x 12.7 cm) or 5 inches (12.7 cm) in diameter. The flue should be about $1\frac{1}{2}$ times (150 percent of) the area of the burner port. Larger openings are always preferable to smaller ones. Unless you're building a true downdraft kiln, you don't have to worry about a stack or chimney; your kiln won't need one.

Creating the Foundation

Regardless of the type of kiln you build, the nature of its site (whether the terrain is flat, sloping, rocky, or soft, for example) is important. You must be able to create a level surface for the base (or foundation) of a brick or fiber-lined kiln. The prevailing wind direction is important, too; the wind has a direct bearing on your management and control of the air-to-fuel ratio during combustion. If possible, plan to position your kiln so that the wind blows toward and into the burner port or firebox. Remember to place the kiln well away from low-hanging tree branches and any vegetation that might be affected by the flame or heat (see page 24).

All kilns require a solid foundation. A patch of reasonably level ground serves quite well, but the most durable and permanent foundation is a concrete slab. Having a slab poured professionally is expensive but worth it; constructing the forms and pouring the concrete yourself are ambitious undertakings. Here's some advice: whether you pour the slab yourself or not, make sure it's large enough to accommodate at least twice as many kilns as you think you're likely to need. A large slab not only provides a smooth, level base upon which to erect your kiln but will also accommodate your bottled gas supply and can even serve as a surface for all your post-firing work. Creating a large slab first is much less time-consuming and expensive than tackling the job piecemeal.

Building a Top-Loading Soft-Brick Kiln

Tops on the hit parade of easy-to-build kilns is the top-loading soft-brick rectangle. It's simple in design, expandable, adaptable to various styles of firing, and very serviceable.

Building the Base

The best bases (or stands) for most kilns, whether built on concrete slabs or bare earth, are made with concrete builder's blocks. These are manufactured in many different sizes and shapes, so it's possible to configure a base to exacting specifications. I use standard 8 x 8 x 16-inch (20.3 x 20.3 x 40.6 cm) blocks, which are heavy enough to provide a firm base and large enough to raise the kiln to a comfortable height. Keep in mind that the *actual* dimensions of these blocks are each ³⁄₈ inch (1 cm) less than their *nominal* measurements; the smaller dimensions make up for the thickness of the mortar joints when mortar is used. The fact that these block dimensions are compatible with those of bricks makes it easy to construct a neat installation.

When purchasing your blocks, note the difference between *corner* (or *end*) blocks and *line* (or *stretcher*) blocks. Corner blocks have flat tops and squared edges, unlike line blocks, which are designed to have the concave areas between their butted ends filled with concrete for strength. Since you won't be bonding your blocks together with mortar or concrete, corner blocks are preferable, as they lend a neater, more finished look to the base.

Before building the base, your first task is to decide how wide and deep to make the kiln's firing chamber. In the instructions provided here, the interior dimensions are based on the size of the kiln shelf you plan to use, as well as on the dimensions of your brick. Because you're going to use standard *insulating firebrick* (also called IFB or soft brick; see the next section) that measures 4¹⁄₂ x 9 inches (11.4 x 22.9 cm), the kiln is designed in multiples of 4¹⁄₂ inches (11.4 cm). The plans call for an 18-inch square (45.7 cm sq.) interior dimension so that you can use a readily available 16-inch-square (40.6 cm sq.) kiln shelf.

Now lay out the design for the kiln base on paper, making sure that the base is larger than the footprint of the kiln so that you'll have space around the kiln for preheating and cooling pots and for other objects you want to keep nearby. Next, if you're building on grass, remove the sod. The square flat end of a garden rake will facilitate smoothing the ground. Set the concrete blocks on the ground one at a time, leveling them in all directions as you go and tamping them down firmly by standing on them; they shouldn't rock back and forth (see photo 3). A bucket of sand comes in handy when you need to level the soil under a block. Set the blocks tightly against each other to ensure a smooth surface, and position them so that any holes in them face the outside; this will provide a solid surface on top and will also provide a vent for the hot air that builds up under the kiln.

3

4

Selecting and Working with Bricks

Basic to the craft of kiln building are refractory bricks—both *firebrick* (hard brick) and IFB. Both are manufactured in many different shapes and sizes and in a variety of temperature ratings. Under no circumstances should you use hard brick to build your kiln, except for the floor and around the burner port. Hard brick has little or no insulating value and requires an enormous heat input to reach temperature. For raku kiln building, when hard brick is called for, the lowest rated (and least expensive) variety is more than adequate.

IFB is most commonly available in three temperature ratings: 2000°F, 2300°F, and 2600°F (1093°C, 1260°C and 1427°C). You might think that the 2600°F (1427°C) bricks offer better insulating qualities, are more durable, and have a longer life, but in fact, they have a lower insulating value and are no more durable. Because raku temperatures don't even approach their upper temperature limits, the 2300°F (1260°C) bricks last just as long. Certainly, 2000°F (1093°C) IFBs are serviceable, but since the cost is virtually identical to the 2300°F (1260°C) bricks, there's no reason to use them.

Depending on the dimensions of your kiln and how brick features in its design, you'll have to do some cutting. Don't let the "softness" of IFB bricks fool you. While they're relatively easy to cut, they dull even the best saws, knives, files, and drill bits, so use inexpensive tools. A drywall saw—which is stiff and short and has large, coarse teeth—works well. Most of the soft-brick cutting you do involves cutting the bricks in half. Since the bricks are twice as long as they are wide, use an-

other brick as a cutting guide (see photo 4). Remember to protect your eyes from airborne particles!

Cutting hard bricks is a little more difficult. If you have access to an industrial-strength wet saw, take advantage of it. Most of us, however, have to use a hammer and a cold chisel, mason's chisel, or brick set. Put on eye protection and draw a cutting line on the brick. Score the marked line all the way around the brick by tapping the chisel with a hammer. One final blow with the hammer should fracture the brick on the line (see photo 5).

5

Constructing the Floor and Walls

Next comes a layer of soft insulating brick on top of the base (see photo 6). On top of that is the layer of hard brick that will serve as the floor of your kiln (see photo 7). I use hard brick for this layer because it's durable enough to withstand all kinds of abuse, including placing work on it, standing on it—and knocking into it, as potters are apt to do. To accommodate your burner, add a concrete block centered along one side of the base, and top it with two layers of hard brick. (Only one layer is shown in photo 7; I added the second as I built the walls.) Now position the first two courses of IFB for the kiln walls, making sure to incorporate an opening for the burner port (see photo 8).

Different schools of thought exist regarding the best-functioning kiln shelves. Clay shelves (made of cordierite, mullite, and sillimanite) are the standards for use in electric kilns. They're durable and, if treated with care, will last for hundreds of firings when used in electric kilns as intended.

Silicon carbide shelves are the standards for use in fuel-fired kilns. These are heavier and more durable than clay shelves and will also last many years when used as intended. They're also more expensive.

Either type works well in a raku kiln, but save your money. Due to the thermal shock that raku kilns are subjected to, even the most durable shelves will soon crack, so buy the least expensive ones, treat them as carefully as possible, and replace them when they're no longer serviceable.

Before laying more courses of brick for the walls, place three 6- to 9-inch-long (15.2 to 22.9 cm) *soaps* on the floor of the kiln to support your kiln shelf, positioning one of them—the *target brick*—in front of the burner port (see photo 9). Soaps are 2-inch-square (5.1 sq. cm.) hard bricks cut to various lengths for use as shelf posts; using full hard bricks instead greatly increases the amount of mass that must be heated, which lengthens the firing and increases fuel consumption. The target brick splits the flame and directs it toward both sides of the chamber for even heat distribution. To isolate your pots from direct contact with the flame, the kiln shelf should sit 6 to 9 inches (15.2 to 22.9 cm) above the kiln floor—high enough so that its top is above the burner and allows all of the flame to go underneath it. A major cause of cracking of pots during firing is direct contact with the flame. A firebox that's too small adversely affects combustion.

Next, add another course of IFB to the walls, placing a *lintel*—the brick over the top of the burner-port opening—as you do (see photo 10). For durability and strength, use hard brick for the lintel.

Then position the kiln shelf on the soaps (see photo 11). Continue laying the IFB, course after course, staggering the joints for strength until the kiln is the height you want. If the ratio between the width and height is too great, the heat in the bottom and top of the kiln will be uneven. As a general rule, keep the interior height to within $1\frac{1}{2}$ times the interior width.

12

13

Leave one removable brick in every few courses, alternating locations between opposing sides of the kiln (photo 12). When you pull these bricks out, the openings serve as peepholes and allow you to monitor the firing from different angles and heights.

To help the kiln contract to its original size after firing, you may want to tie it together with a series of corner braces and cable or pipe clamps. (This step is optional: in practice, a kiln this small won't expand much and can be pushed back together easily if it does.) First, use a saber saw or hacksaw to cut short sections of steel angle iron, available at most hardware stores (see photo 13).

Next, bind the steel to the corners of the kiln with the cable or clamps (see photo 14). I prefer stainless steel hose clamps (also available at hardware stores) because they're strong and last forever. I just gang them together to form a band as long as I like and tighten it down firmly around the kiln. If you use cable instead, you must use a turn-buckle to tighten it.

14

15

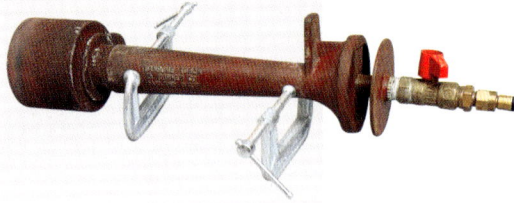

16

Making the Burner Support

A firm, stable support to hold the burner in place is crucial. If you'd like to liberate the Rube Goldberg in you, feel free to clamp all kinds of braces and stands around the burner, but you can fashion a good support easily from a soft brick. Using the burner as a template, carve and file out a groove in the brick for the burner to rest in (see photo 15). C-clamps also work as braces (see photo 16). Commercial burner stands and supports are available. The excellent support shown on Tom Clarke's kiln at Dakota Potters Supply adjusts both forward and backward (see photo 17).

18

Making the Lid

Any extra kiln shelves you may have lying around your studio can work well as kiln lids. They're durable, strong, and reasonably good at insulating. By using two shelves, you can create a space between them that acts as an adjustable flue opening (see photo 18).

An alternative is a refractory fiber lid, made from wire mesh and fiber; it's easy to construct, lightweight, easy to remove, and reasonably durable. (For instructions on working with fiber, see pages 77–81.) Commercial landscaping and garden-supply stores carry an interesting product that I've found useful here—it's a wire-mesh circle designed for placement over new plantings to protect them as they grow. These mesh circles come in different diameters and make perfect kiln lids when they're covered with refractory fiber. Discarded metal refrigerator shelves and barbecue grills covered with fiber also work well as lids (see photo 19). Alternatively, use an old electric kiln lid; simply cut a hole through it for the flue (see page 82).

17

You can also construct a strong, relatively lightweight lid with good insulating properties by tying individual IFBs together with threaded rods and angle iron. If you plan to have help with your firings, build this brick lid as a single unit with handles that two people can grab for lifting. If you anticipate firing on your own, build the lid in two halves to facilitate its removal by one person. To make a brick lid, you need predrilled, heavy-duty angle iron and an assortment of ⅜- or ½-inch (1 or 1.3 cm) threaded rods, nuts, washers, and lock washers—all available from hardware stores.

Start by referring to photo 20. Then drill holes through the bricks so you can pass the threaded rods through them. Rather than measuring the hole placement on each brick individually, fashion a cardboard template to use as a guide. Lay out the bricks on a flat surface, and cut the angle irons a little longer than necessary to provide short lengths at each end that you and a helper can use as handles.

Because the bricks are compressed from only two sides, two smaller flue holes, rather than one large one, better preserve the integrity of the lid. Cut these holes out with either a saw or a hole-cutting attachment. Pass the rods through the angle irons and the holes in the bricks, and bolt them down tightly against the irons, tightening the nuts evenly so you don't end up with a tight row of bricks next to a loose row. The bricks naturally expand and contract during use, so make a habit of regularly checking the nuts for tightness.

Building a Refractory Fiber Kiln

Fiber kilns—the ones most closely associated with raku—are simple in concept and construction, as well as being lightweight and truly portable. A well-built one will serve you well and has the potential to last a long time. My own small fiber kiln has been fired more than 1,000 times and is still going strong (see photo 21).

19

Metal trash cans or large metal drums are often used as the shells, but you can fashion your own frame from hardware cloth, chicken wire, or wire mesh. Expanded metal mesh—used, among other things, for fabricating safety guards on machinery and as space dividers in trucks—works very well. Available at metal scrap yards and steel suppliers, it's much stronger than regular mesh and provides a rigid but slightly heavier frame for your kiln. It's sold in 4 x 8-foot (1.2 x 2.4 m) sheets as well as in various thicknesses and diamond sizes. You can decide which gauge is appropriate for your kiln. Whatever mesh material you use, avoid any that's so flexible it won't hold a cylindrical shape well. I prefer hardware cloth or expanded metal because they're both rigid and easy to fabricate.

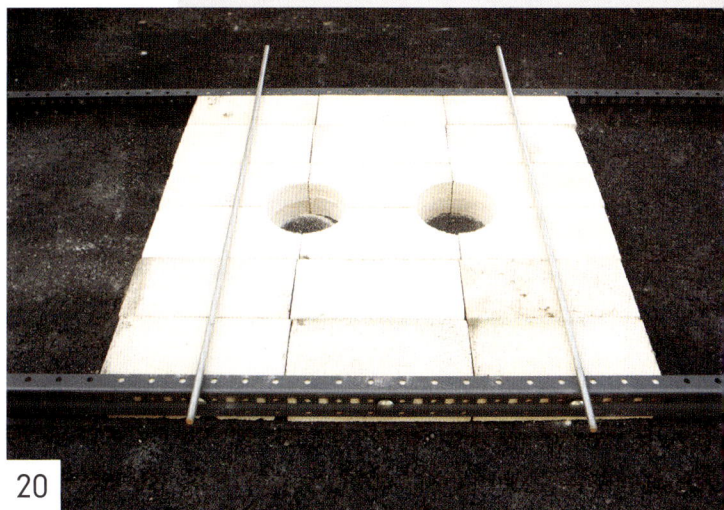
20

21

22

The *refractory ceramic fiber* (or RCF) blanket with which these kilns are made is an alumina/silica combination spun into a fiber-like material. Available in many forms, RCF has brought kiln building within reach of people who might otherwise have been too intimidated by the need for steel frames or complicated brickwork. Photo 22 shows (clockwise from left): pieces of 1-inch (2.5 cm) fiberboard, 2-inch (5.1 cm) fiberboard, 1/2-inch (1.3 cm) rigid fiberboard, 1/4-inch (.6 cm) refractory board, and fiber blanket.

Regardless of how hot the weather is, wear a respirator, a long-sleeved shirt, gloves, and long pants when working with RCF—it's an extreme skin and lung irritant. At the very least, the airborne fibers will make you itchy and uncomfortable, while prolonged inhalation can result in a lung disease similar to asbestosis.

Blankets made from a relatively new magnesium-silicate fiber offer significant advantages over RCF. The higher compression recovery rate of this material makes it a better insulator than RCF, the insulating properties of which are compromised when it's compressed. When the magnesium-silicate fiber is compressed, its high rate of "bounce back" allows it to expand back to a state close to its original loft. Even more important, it dissolves in lung fluid and is excreted from the body, thereby eliminating the serious health hazard associated with ceramic fiber. The down side of this material is that it's a bit more unwieldy to work with and is serviceable only at low temperatures very close to the upper limits of raku; some potters have experienced material failure.

23

Forming the Mesh Frame and Roof

Before beginning construction, determine how tall and wide you want to make the firing chamber. Its interior diameter should be as wide as the kiln shelf you plan to use, plus about 1 inch (2.5 cm) to allow for air flow. Common round or multi-sided shelf diameters are approximately 17, 23, and 26 inches (43.2, 58.4, and 66 cm). A fiber kiln wide enough to accommodate a 26-inch-diameter (66 cm) shelf would be too large to maneuver easily, so I recommend either of the other two sizes. The kiln shown in photo 35 is 20 inches (50.8 cm) in diameter, and is made to fit a 17- or 18-inch-diameter (43.2 or 45.7 cm) shelf. Though most fiber raku kilns are round, they don't have to be. Be creative, and let your ingenuity take over. Harold Takayesu assembled discarded metal appliance shelving to make a very nice kiln (see photo 23)!

Cut your frame material to size and bend it into a cylinder (see photo 24). If you have the skills and equipment, or a friend with both, you may want to weld together the ends of material that's thick (expanded metal, for example). A local welding shop can do this for you inexpensively, or better yet, try coaxing the industrial arts or shop teacher at the local high school into helping you out. You can never be too resourceful!

24

25

26

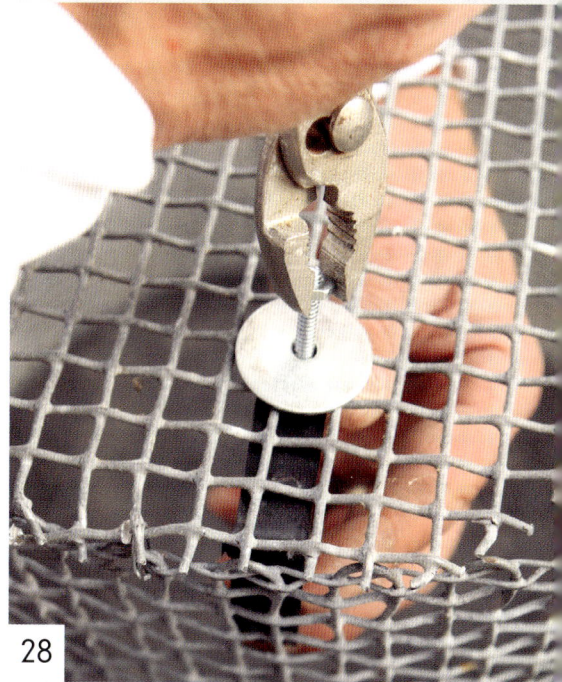
27

28

29

If welding isn't an option, sew the edges of the cylinder together with wire, or use small bolts, washers, and nuts (see photo 25). Next, while access to the interior of the frame is still easy, attach two sash handles to the exterior, about midway up the chamber, using bolts, washers, lock washers, and nuts to fasten them in place (see photo 26).

Cut a piece of the frame material for the roof (or top) of the kiln, and cut out an opening in its center for the flue. Then attach the roof to the frame with heavy wire (see photo 27) or with small angle braces spaced 6 inches (15.2 cm) or so apart (see photo 28). Be careful to keep the chamber as cylindrical as possible.

Depending on the height of the chamber, decide on the number of peepholes you'd like, and cut them out (see photo 29). Three at different heights and spots are usually adequate.

30

31

A minor disadvantage of ceramic fiber is its fragility. Because it isn't resistant to abrasion either, you may want to brush, roll, or spray a *rigidizer* onto its interior surface after fastening it to the frame. Available from ceramic fiber dealers, rigidizer is a liquid solution that hardens the fiber surface, minimizes abrasions, and prolongs the life of the blanket.

I've spoken with several potters who've had good success with this substance, but I find its surface too thin to be useful: extreme temperature changes, lifting of the chamber, and the rough treatment to which kilns are often subjected can all cause cracking. I suggest using rigidizer only if you find after several firings that the surface of the blanket is giving you problems. If you don't use rigidizer, be careful to not allow your pots to come in contact with the blanket; any glaze melt that sticks to it will tear it away from the frame.

Lining the Frame and Roof

Using the roof of the chamber as a template, mark a section of the fiber blanket (see photo 30). Then use a mat knife or shears to cut it out, and place it against the interior of the chamber roof.

Although fiber blanket is a strong material, it tears easily, and it can't be sewn. To fasten the blanket to the roof frame, use a simple, neat, and effective system (patterned after industrial systems) that includes buttons or strips cut from rigid insulating board, with lightweight 17- or 18-gauge wires inserted through them (see photo 31). The best alloys to use for the wires are Kanthal or Nichrome.

Press the wire ends through the fiber and frame (see photo 32), twisting them together tightly on the exterior. Porcelain buttons work just as well; I've never used them, but I've fired kilns made with them. You may also substitute strips of insulating board about 2 inches (5.1 cm) wide and installed vertically; these add a measure of rigidity to the structure.

32

34

Measure the interior circumference and height of the chamber, and cut a piece of fiber blanket to fit, beveling the end cuts so the ends will butt together to create a tight, smooth connection without overlapping (see photo 33). Wrap the blanket around the inside of the cylinder (see photo 34), and attach it by using the same method you used to attach the blanket to the roof frame. The number of buttons you use and the spaces between them aren't critical, although too many buttons are better than too few. Apply enough buttons to prevent the blanket from draping or sagging. Try setting them 8 to 10 inches (20.3 to 25.4 cm) apart; they're easy enough to remove and reposition if you have to. Trim the fiber close to the flue and peephole openings, and secure it with buttons and wire. There's no need to cover the exposed edges of the frame with fiber.

Building the Base

You may be wondering where the burner fits into this kiln. Many fiber kilns of similar design do include a burner port cut into the chamber, which allows you to place the kiln on a flat brick base. I prefer to keep the fiber chamber intact and to create a base by recycling an old, burned-out section from an electric

33

35

36

Line the can with refractory fiber the same way you line a mesh frame: attach the fiber with fiberboard or porcelain buttons, and insert their wire ends through holes drilled in the wall. As an alternative to buttons, use a wide paint-brush to apply a thin coat of sodium silicate to the can's interior, and press the blanket in place over it. A brick (either IFB or hard brick) burner port, without a lintel, forms the base of the kiln shown.

kiln with an opening cut in it for the burner (see photo 35). The base is portable and already bound together for strength. (See page 82 for instructions on cutting out the burner port.)

To build a brick base with a burner port in it instead, follow the instructions for the soft-brick kiln (see photo 10 on page 74), but be sure to include the lintel. To round off the rectangular, partially built walls so you can set the cylindrical kiln on top of them, insert additional bricks in each inside corner. By keeping the wire-frame chamber intact and using this brick base, you can increase the height of the kiln just by adding one or more courses to the brick walls.

Fiber-Lined Trash Can Kilns

You can also make a kiln shell from a trash can (see photo 36). Cut an open-ing in the bottom for the flue (the bot-tom of the can becomes the top of the kiln) and one in the wall to serve as a peephole. You can attach sash handles if you like, but using four ladder-hanging brackets for the same purpose keeps your hands a little farther from the kiln when you lift it. They can also support a kiln shelf that will give you room to preheat pots for the next firing.

Fiber-Lined Car Kilns

A fiber-lined car kiln consists of three elements: a firing chamber, rails, and the combined floor and back wall. All three are separate from one another, so the kiln can be stored indoors if necessary.

An arched, expanded-metal frame lined with fiber forms the firing chamber. Expanded metal, cut to fit, also forms the front wall of the kiln. Welded to the bottom edge of the chamber frame are four grooved steel wheels. Two lengths of angle iron tied together with two flat metal braces form the rails. The ends of these rails slide under the stationary kiln floor and back wall, which are built from loosely stacked IFB. Two burner ports are cut into the back wall. The chamber rolls on the rails, encloses the brick floor, and butts up against the back wall. The car kiln shown in photo 37 was designed and built by Nathaniel Dubbs, glass and ceramics studio man-ager at the GoggleWorks Center for the Arts, in Reading, Pennsylvania.

Sodium silicate is most of-ten used as a clay defloc-culant, especially in cast-ing slips. A deflocculant causes the fine particles of clay to be dispersed and makes the slip more fluid. Because of its sticky nature and refractory quality, sodium silicate works well as a glue.

37

Recycling an Electric Kiln

My raku kiln of choice is one made from a recycled electric kiln (see photo 38). It's well built, lightweight, can be assembled in a variety of widths, and is stackable for increased height. If many potters—or a supplier who does kiln repair—live in your area, chances are you'll find burned-out, ready-for-the-junkyard kiln orphans just waiting for you to take them away. Although you may be able to get these for free, don't be surprised if you have to pay. Approach your regular supply house in a friendly way, too; you may be able to coax someone there into letting you take an old kiln off his or her hands.

Don't be greedy and expect the electric parts to be intact; somebody's likely to have salvaged those already. All you need are the brick sections wrapped in their fine steel jackets. If you can't find a lid and bottom, don't worry; they're easy enough to fashion yourself.

Once you have the old kiln in hand, the first step is to make some accommodation for the burner. One way to do this is to place the kiln on top of three or four courses of bricks, with a burner port incorporated into them, as described in the section for constructing a soft-brick kiln (see pages 71–77). It's just as easy, however, to make a complete unit without the need for a separate brick base by cutting a burner port into the side of the old kiln. You can use tin snips to cut an opening in the steel jacket, and then cut a hole in the brick with a keyhole drywall saw, although an easier and much neater method is to use a drill and hole-cutting attachment.

First, cut a hole through the steel jacket only, approximately 3 inches (7.6 cm) larger in diameter than the diameter of your burner. The center drill bit of the hole cutter penetrates the brick, leaving a small hole. Next, cut out the burner port in the brick. Its diameter should be smaller than that of the hole in the jacket and approximately 2 inches (5.1 cm) larger than that of the burner. Place the center drill bit of the hole cutter into the hole left by the previous cut, and drill halfway through the brick (see photo 39). Because the brick is so thick, you'll have to drill the rest of the hole from the other side. The larger hole in the jacket will keep the burner flame from contacting it, thereby increasing the life of the metal.

Rather than cutting a burner port into the chamber, you may want to buy one of the clever conversion units available from several commercial manufacturers. These kits consist of completely assembled one-, two-, or four-burner combustion systems and kiln-base units. Cutting into the kiln floor to accommodate the burners (a template comes with the kit) gives you a neat, updraft gas kiln.

Once the burner port is in place, set the chamber on the floor—or on the bottom of the original electric kiln if you were able to obtain it. Position a kiln shelf on posts that raise it above the height of the burner port so that the flame is kept under the shelf and away from direct contact with your ware (see page 74). Remember to place the target brick with one of its corners directly in the path of the flame.

Typically, the standard peepholes in electric kilns are too small to be useful for much of anything. Enlarge them

38

39

40

with a hole cutter or tin snips. Soft bricks cut to size serve as peephole plugs.

If you plan to use the lid that came with the kiln, you must cut a flue hole in its center that's 1½ times the diameter of the burner port. If you can't find a hole-cutter large enough for this task, cut two smaller holes, or use a drywall saw to cut out a larger circle. No, the bricks won't collapse, but periodically, do check the tightness of the band that holds the lid together. As a finishing touch to the flue hole, seal the surface of the brick with a thin coating of refractory cement. Complete the lid by attaching two aluminum or steel sash handles—or a second sash handle opposite to the one that may already be on the lid. Notice the sash handles attached to each section of the kiln in photo 38. These make it possible to lift off individual sections of the chamber when you're ready to remove the hot ware (see page 106).

A recycled electric kiln may also be used on its side. Potter Edge Barnes cut the burner port into what was the bottom of his kiln and let the hinged lid function as a door (see photo 40). Be creative. Use your imagination!

Constructing a Wood-Fired Kiln

Wood is the most basic source of fire and heat. Wood is true to pottery tradition. Wood is romantic. And there's no question that the effects of wood firing are hard to duplicate, whether in high fire or raku. So what are its drawbacks? The firing creates a lot of smoke, so you must locate your kiln in an area where smoke can be tolerated.

Building and firing a wood kiln is hard work, too. Aside from having to gather and cut the wood and the continuous stoking required to keep the kiln going, the major drawback is the inability to be spontaneous. More often than not, I decide to do a raku firing almost on the spur of the moment or—if I really plan ahead—the night before. Resigning myself to a full day of chopping, hauling, and stoking definitely cools my fire.

Because my goal is to keep the projects in this book within reach of every potter, I won't go to extremes in this section by walking you through building a form for the construction of a formal arched firebox. Instead, I'll describe two kinds of simple wood-fired kilns: the first one I ever built (see photo 41) and a soft-brick version built on a concrete block base.

41

My first raku-kiln building and firing experience was with a wood-fired kiln. Crazy, you say? Absolutely. Doomed to failure? No question about it. Certain to discourage me from ever doing raku again? For sure. To complicate matters further, I'd never built a kiln of any kind. And the final test of my inflated sense of confidence? I'd never actually observed, let alone participated in, any kind of raku firing from start to finish.

I went to work on the kiln with only a vague idea of the process, a sketch of a kiln given to me by a fellow graduate student, and all the bricks and materials I needed supplied by the prep school where I was teaching. Watching me was a herd of high school students and art teachers who thought I was a pottery god. That first wood-fired kiln was a resounding success, but only because I was lucky.

A few weeks later, with the help and participation of some fellow graduate students, I built an identical kiln at a different site. No matter how much wood we stoked, we just couldn't get the kiln to reach temperature. At the time, I had no idea what was wrong. Only after many more firings of all kinds did it become clear that our failure was a simple case of poor combustion resulting from a lack of sufficient air sources. If only I'd had a book like this one!

42

Building a Brick-Lined Earth Kiln

Unless money is no object, building a wood kiln similar to my first one—or any kiln for that matter—is an exercise in resourcefulness. I used firebrick and IFB, as well as iron bars or grating for the wood to rest on, and materials such as old kiln shelves, lintel bricks, sheet metal, or spanning tile for roofing the firebox. Try your local scrap metal source or junkyard. Even if you have to pay, you should be able to escape with minor financial damage.

The structure and dimensions of a wood kiln's firing chamber are much the same as the other kilns described in this chapter. The differences are related to the use of wood instead of gas as a fuel. A firebox replaces a conventional burner port, and essential provisions are made to ensure a sufficient primary air source and efficient combustion.

I sited my first wood kiln on a small hillside. In a way, the kiln was an adaptation of a traditional Asian *climbing kiln*, in which the heat rises upward from the firebox to the firing chamber. I dug the firebox and ash pit at the bottom of the incline, providing ample combustion space and a place for the ashes to collect. At the top of the hill was the firing chamber. The earth surrounding the kiln added useful insulating properties.

To build a similar kiln on sloping ground, first dig a 36-inch-long (91.4 cm) firebox/ash pit. Make it approximately 30 inches (76.2 cm) below ground level and 25 inches (63.5 cm) wide at its opening, and gradually decrease its depth and width to 9 inches (22.9 cm) below ground level and 18 inches (45.7 cm) wide at its terminal end (the eventual level of the firing chamber floor). Line the walls with firebrick. The firing chamber floor can be made with either firebrick set directly on the ground or with concrete blocks set with their tops at ground level. The only advantage that blocks afford is a more solid structure.

To support the wood during firing, set three or four iron bars across the pit, 4 to 8 inches (10.2 to 20.3 cm) apart (see photo 41 on page 83). Leave a 9- to 10-inch (22.9 to 25.4 cm) clearance between the bars and the roof of the firebox. Keeping the wood suspended on this grating promotes combustion by allowing air to flow clearly around it. Build up the height of the firebox to approximately 8 inches (20.3 cm) above ground level.

Set the kiln shelf in place on standard 9-inch (22.9 cm) soaps, and build the firing chamber up to the height you want. This kiln has a 23-inch-diameter (58.4 cm) shelf and is about 27 inches (68.6 cm) tall. As you build up the chamber, be sure to integrate the firebox and firebox roof with the kiln chamber in a neat, tight fashion. I used kiln shelves to make the firebox roof and the lid. For added insulating value, top off the firebox with earth (see photo 42). Leave a large flue opening for a draft and efficient combustion.

A

As a cost-saving measure, many potters use common red bricks, as I did, to build their wood-fired kilns. Theoretically, these bricks should be adequate for the temperatures reached in raku firing, but I've found that even in the relatively low temperatures of raku, they can fail and become a physical hazard as they crack apart and explode.

Building a Soft-Brick Wood-Firing Kiln

Nesrin During, an experienced wood firer from Holland, designed a beautifully simple kiln design (see photo 43). She built her kiln with about 50 loosely stacked soft bricks set directly on the ground. An iron grate or appliance shelf supported by a few strategically placed bricks holds the wood. Bricks also hold the shelf in place at its corners. To further support the shelf, During placed a metal bar across the front bricks and under the front edge of the shelf. As you can see, her kiln is a very informal affair in which the firebox and firing chamber are one and the same. She fires with locally gathered waste wood and rebuilds the kiln to the size she wants for each firing session (see photo 44).

A more permanent, durable wood-fired kiln is easy to build. Take a look at the one shown in photo 45. The interior of its firing chamber is 18 inches square (45.7 cm sq.), and the firebox interior is 9 x 12½ x 36 inches (22.9 x 31.8 x 91.4 cm). The exterior of the entire kiln is 63 inches (160 cm) long.

Start by laying 17 standard concrete blocks: eight to form the base under the firing chamber and nine to form the longer, narrower base under the firebox. On top of the base, set a layer of standard 9-inch (22.9 cm) IFB, installed so that it's wider and longer than the kiln on top of it will be. Then set a layer of hard brick on top to create the floor of the firebox and firing chamber.

Using IFB again, lay the first three courses of bricks for the rectangular firebox and square firing chamber. Across the tops of the bricks that form the firebox/ash pit, set 10-inch-long (25.4 cm) kiln posts to hold the wood. You may substitute iron bars or a grate if you wish. To accommodate the kiln posts, position the next course of bricks slightly farther outward (see photo 46).

After setting two more courses of IFB, top the firebox with bricks, spanning tile, or two kiln shelves. (Note that one of the two shelves has been removed in photo 45 right.) Position another kiln shelf inside the firing chamber so that it's level with the top of the firebox, and continue to build up the chamber to the height you want. Remember to incorporate peepholes! Use a lid of your choice. This kiln can function either as a top-loader or, with slight modifications, as a front-loader.

43

44

45

46

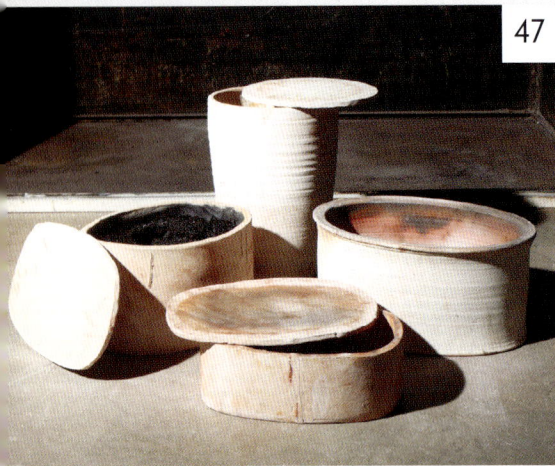

47

Building a Coal- or Charcoal-Fired Saggar Kiln

Coal or charcoal—probably the fuel of the first raku potters, though we can't know for sure—is rarely used today, but the fact is a coal-fired raku kiln is easy to build, easy to fire, and requires no electricity, gas tanks, hoses, or burners.

To use coal or charcoal as a fuel, the ware must be completely surrounded by—but isolated from—the fuel. A *saggar* (a clay container used to hold the ware whenever direct contact with the atmosphere, or in this case the fuel, must be avoided) serves this purpose (see photo 47 and figure 1). Potters today usually load their saggars with organic material and fire them in high-fire kilns for certain kinds of reduction effects, but the successful use of saggars in raku has been documented and is definitely worth experimenting with. (See pages 135–136 for information on the creative use of saggars.)

Although saggars can be thrown, the best are usually slab-built from highly grogged clay that's resistant to thermal shock; their structure is generally more thermal resistant than that of thrown forms. No matter how the saggars are formed, many potters wrap them with wire to hold them together in case they crack. If you don't want to go to the trouble of building a saggar and lid, just use a standard red clay flowerpot and accompanying dish,

available at any garden shop or home center. These are inexpensive, come in a variety of sizes, and work really well, but expect them to last for only a few firings at best. Clay recipes formulated for making saggars are provided on pages 161–162.

A lid is only necessary when you want to fill a saggar with combustible material in order to saturate the atmosphere within and create intense reduction effects. If you do use a lid, make sure it's easily removable so that you can view the pots during the firing cycle and retrieve them when they're ready. A peephole in the lid can serve the same purpose.

A coal (or charcoal) kiln is little more than a chamber that encloses the saggar and fuel, built from IFB, castable mix, or even fiber-lined mesh. The shape of the chamber isn't critical; it can simply consist of a fiber-lined wire cylinder, similar to the fiber-lined kiln described on pages 77–81 but open at both ends. The interior of the fiber-blanket is also lined with mesh, which protects it from abrasion by the burning and settling coal.

Begin construction with a hard-brick floor laid directly on the ground or on a concrete-block base. Then build up your walls in any configuration you like, allowing 4 to 6 inches (10.2 to 15.2 cm) of space between the interior wall of the chamber and the saggar so there's plenty of room for the fuel to collect and burn (see photo 48). A 4- to 6-inch (10.2 to 15.2 cm) space between the top of the saggar and the top of the chamber aids in combustion.

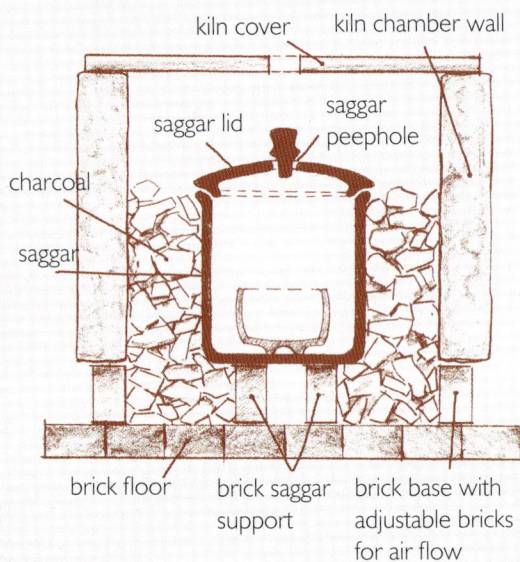

kiln cover — kiln chamber wall

saggar lid

saggar peephole

charcoal

saggar

brick floor — brick saggar support — brick base with adjustable bricks for air flow

FIGURE 1

48

Accessories and Repairs

Kiln building has made some impressive and useful advances in recent years. Technology in the areas of electronics, element design, computerized firing controls, timing devices, venting, and more have made their way to the pottery community, many as by-products of industrial demands. As tempting as getting the latest high-tech accessories may be, none of them are critical or even necessary for the raku potter whose needs are modest. The advancements that *are* useful and sometimes essential, however, are ceramic mortars, patching compounds, and coatings. All these materials can help you ensure durability, make repairs, and increase firing efficiency, thereby lowering both fuel consumption and costs.

Mortars and patching compounds are great for repairing loose or missing sections of brick and for coating the brick surfaces around burner ports and flue openings to increase their durability. Ceramic coatings have become almost common. These commercially prepared materials are formulated for different applications. For example, some are sprayed over bricks to increase their insulating value, and others are sprayed directly onto electric kiln elements to make them less susceptible to failure. If your pottery supplier carries refractories, they carry materials of this type, too, and can advise you as to their use.

49

No matter what your kiln is made of, place three or four bricks on the floor to support the saggar and to direct the air flow (see photo 49). Once the fuel is loaded and the firing has begun, these bricks are untouchable, so you'll need to experiment over the course of a few firings to find out where best to position them. Make the chamber as tight as possible to assist in heat retention, but also make sure that two or more of the first-course bricks are moveable so you can adjust the air flow during the firing. To raise the temperature more rapidly, a blower—or vacuum cleaner that doubles as a blower—can provide additional air. Place a lid of any kind, with a flue cut into it, on top of the chamber to increase the draft and thus the temperature.

ROBERT COMPTON
Vase, 2006
12 x 5 inches (30.5 x 12.7 cm)
Wheel thrown; dipped glaze;
gas fired; smoking for reduction
Photo by artist

50

Protecting Your Kiln from the Elements

Unless you store your kiln indoors, you need to protect it from the elements, particularly rain and snow, if you want it to outlive currently popular rock music. Occasional rain won't hurt a brick kiln, but continuous exposure is harmful. Also, if a kiln is wet when you fire it, it takes longer to reach temperature and therefore uses more fuel. Even a fiber kiln can withstand a little moisture, but rain is more harmful to it than to a brick kiln. The water, along with its impact, quickly compromises the integrity of the fiber. If you're ambitious and your firing site allows for it, build a roof over your kiln—it's the best possible solution. An 8- to 10-foot-tall (2.4 to 3.0 m) freestanding wood structure topped with corrugated metal roofing is perfectly adequate to allow the heat of the kiln to dissipate. (If you can't find metal roofing at your local building supply store, try a farm supply or feed store.) Make the structure large enough to accommodate unencumbered movement around the kiln.

The simplest way to protect your kiln, of course, is to cover it after it has cooled down. You may be able to find a grill or smoker cover to fit your kiln at your local hardware store, home center, or discount store. Air conditioner and patio furniture covers also work well (see photo 50). Inexpensive waterproof tarps can help, but they're unwieldy and difficult to secure.

Custom-fit a cover for your kiln instead—one that fits around the burners and bricks, as well (see photo 51). Even complex shapes can be fashioned by stapling or sewing sections of tarp together and sealing the seams with duct tape or the seam sealer made for tents. The disadvantage of using a cover rather than building a roof is that you must wait until the kiln is cool before you can cover it, which usually means coming back later that night. More often than not, I forget to do this—until it starts to rain.

51

Creative Problem-Solving

Ultimately, your goal should be to custom design and fine-tune an entire firing style—one that incorporates your kiln, kiln site, reduction containers and method, and the physical requirements for the firing. After some years of raku firing, Ronda Liskey did just that. Her ingenious raku facility features two identical firing pads, each including a burner where both firing and post-firing take place (see photo 52).

A fiber-lined, expanded-metal firing chamber and a 22-gauge metal reduction container swing from one brick pad to the other with the aid of a counterweight and long arm, thus eliminating the need to lift pots out of the kiln. When a firing cycle is completed, Liskey lifts the firing chamber, covers the ware with reduction materials, and lowers the reduction container over the ware. As this load smokes, the firing phase begins on the second pad, and the cycle is repeated. When a smoking phase is completed and the pots have been removed, Liskey loads a fresh batch of glazed pots onto that pad and lowers the firing chamber over it. Other good examples of creative problem-

solving are the mobile raku kilns and the indoor raku facility presented on pages 25 and 68.

My best overall advice? Stay simple and within your construction capabilities. Don't worry too much about the tiniest details. Be creative, be resourceful, and ask for help from others who may have skills you don't (welding, for example). And if you can't afford to pay them, offer to barter with your work. You'd be surprised how often I've done this.

For the potter on a budget, a raku kiln can't be beat; you can build one successfully from many kinds of found materials, including used bricks and other refractories. Very experienced kiln builders can sometimes even assemble crude, primitive-looking structures that seem to defy logic but do work. If you're new to kiln building, however, take pride in your work, and build your kiln using sound, tried-and-true design principles and construction methods. After you're more experienced and confident, you can get a bit more carefree and know you'll be able to solve problems if your device doesn't quite work.

LOU SMEDTS
Hagi Travel Chawan, 2008
$4^5/_{16}$ x $3^1/_8$ x $5^1/_2$ inches (11 x 8 x 14 cm)
Thrown and altered Ceradel Clay; dipped glaze; faceting; raku fired in wood kiln; reduction no smoking air cooled; cone 03
Photo by Gerda Gewyw

52

the firing

Process

"When all this has been done, prayers are offered to God with the whole heart, ever thanking Him for all that He gives us. Fire is taken, having an eye however to the state of the moon, for this is of the greatest importance, and I have heard from those who are old in the art and of some experience that, if the firing happens to take place at the waning of the moon, the fire lacks brightness in the same manner as the moon its splendour. In doing this, therefore, pay attention to it, especially when it is in the rainy signs, which would be very perilous and must be allowed to pass over, remembering always to do all things in the name of Christ Jesus."

Cipriano Piccolpasso,
The Three Books of the Potter's Art, 1556

STEVEN BRANFMAN
Vessel, 2005
17 x 9 inches (43.2 x 22.9 cm)
Poured raku and stoneware glaze

LEO VAN DER HEYDEN
Bird Jar, 2007
$5\frac{1}{2}$ x $6\frac{5}{16}$ inches (14 x 16 cm)
Relief sculpted and wheel thrown Westerwald Clay; brushed and sprayed glaze; slip
trailing; gas fired; quick cooling, smoking for reduction
Photo by artist

Your feelings about firing your ware are no doubt more earthbound than those of Cipriano Piccolpasso, the renowned Renaissance potter, and you'll probably feel more in control, too. Nonetheless, if there's a heart and soul of the raku technique, it's the firing process he describes. Our pots, no matter how beautiful they seem to us, are lifeless until they emerge from the kiln. Firing is the process during which all of our preparations—technical, mental, and aesthetic—come together; it's the rope that binds them. Yet even in raku firing, which is simple and relatively straightforward, many variables can work either against us or to our advantage.

Safety First

In my work and teaching, I stress spontaneity, but please don't confuse spontaneity with carelessness. Raku firing isn't a random or haphazard activity. It isn't a chance encounter between fire and clay, and it's definitely not something to be frivolous about. I've already covered some vitally important safety

issues (see pages 22–28), but here we'll focus on staying in control of your firing and getting successful results. To avoid predicaments that might ruin what would otherwise be a successful day at the kiln, you must plan and choreograph your raku firing carefully. There's nothing more frustrating than being faced with a problem that you could easily have anticipated and planned for.

You've located your kiln in an appropriate place, you've glazed a batch of pots, and you're almost ready to embark on your first firing. But there's more to do before you begin. First, take a look at the basic preparation checklist at the right; then read the rest of this section.

Make it a habit to inspect all your tools and equipment prior to every firing. Examine your tongs, checking the pivot bolts or rivets for looseness or weakness. Check the hinges and handles on your kiln, and check its lid for tightness and strength. Scrutinize your gloves for rips, tears, and holes.

Before every raku firing, take the time to go through the preparation checklist that follows.

▮ If your kiln is fueled by propane, wood, or coal, make sure you have an adequate supply of fuel for your planned firings (see page 93).

▮ Situate any gas tanks at a safe distance from the kiln and post-firing area.

▮ If your kiln includes burners, assemble them, and test them for leaks and hose integrity (see pages 93–94).

▮ Gather the reduction containers you'll need (see pages 94–96), and place them where they're easily accessible but won't obstruct movement around the kiln. Place your reduction material at a safe distance from the kiln but within easy reach for quick access during post-firing.

▮ If you'll need assistance during any part of the firing (lifting the lid off the kiln, applying reduction materials, and/or turning off the fuel supply), make sure your helpers know exactly what their jobs and responsibilities are.

▮ Make sure you have access to a continuous water source. You'll need water to wash your pots and, of course, for any fire-related emergencies that might arise.

▮ Secure the kiln and firing site from onlookers.

▮ Provide safe, clear avenues for completely unencumbered movement around the kiln.

▮ If you'll be firing multiple loads, have the next batch of pots preheating and situated for easy loading into the kiln (see pages 112–114).

1

Shelves and kiln furniture that are no longer in good enough shape for conventional firing—ones that are slightly warped, pitted, or chipped—are often just fine for raku firing, but you should scrape and coat them with kiln wash prior to each firing session. Glaze drips on shelves are inevitable, especially early in your raku career, but shelves caked and encrusted with glaze have uneven surfaces, can transfer glaze to the bottoms of stacked pots, and are prone to premature cracking due to uneven heating. I use an ice chopper to scrape all drips and most of the previous coat of kiln wash off mine (see photo 1). For a good kiln-wash recipe, see page 169.

Even if you're a one-person operation, planning your moves in advance and setting the stage by placing your tools and equipment in assigned, safe locations are critical (see photo 2). If you have assistants, make sure each one has a designated role, knows what it is and when to perform it, and is wearing the appropriate clothing. Leather work gloves, for example, are adequate for handling the covers of reduction containers and reduction materials, but reaching into the kiln, removing the lid, and other close-up, hot-faced jobs require gloves made of Kevlar fiber.

As you go through this planning process, remember that potential dangers abound. When you're working with other people, it's all too easy during the frenzy of removing pots from the kiln, reaching for tools, and applying reduction materials to swing around with a pot in your tongs while you aim for your reduction barrel, only to have your once-clear path obstructed by someone's leg. Ouch! If you're new to raku, take the time to make some trial runs. Reach into a cold kiln and pull out some bisqued pots that are typical of the ones you'll be firing. Take note of how much space you need around you as you do this, and situate your reduction material and containers, equipment, and any helping hands accordingly.

Also keep in mind that although firing against the backdrop of a dark sky is dramatic and exciting, it requires special caution. The reduced visibility increases the chances of accidents. Even if your site is well lit, shadows from the lights will make seeing difficult. Keep the number of participants to a minimum, maintain careful control over each person's activity, and stay acutely aware of all the activity going on.

Clear the firing area of all combustible materials, such as leaves or any stray reduction material left over from a previous firing and any low-hanging branches or other intrusive landscape features. Flying sparks or a dropped pot could result in an impromptu open-pit barbecue.

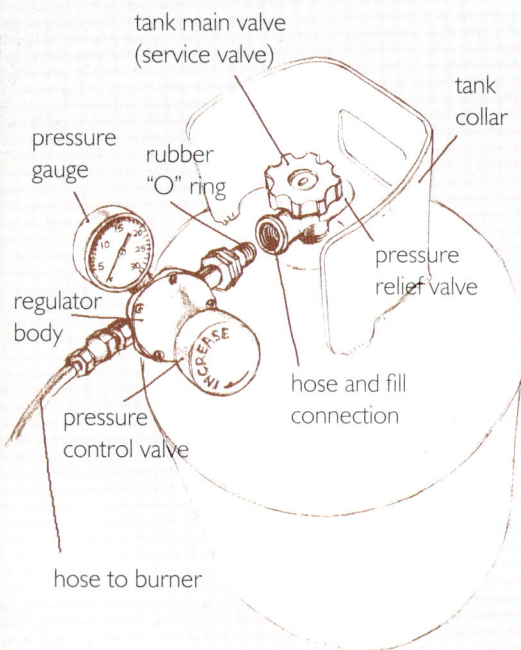

FIGURE I

- tank main valve (service valve)
- tank collar
- pressure gauge
- rubber "O" ring
- pressure relief valve
- regulator body
- hose and fill connection
- pressure control valve
- hose to burner

2

If you unload your kiln by removing the lid altogether, make sure a cement block or brick pad is in place to receive the hot lid so it won't contact grass or other materials that might ignite.

Raku Firing in an Electric Kiln

Firing raku in an electric kiln is much the same as firing it in a fuel-burning kiln, with one important exception. Accidental contact between your tongs and the electric elements in the kiln will result in an electric shock that can cause injury. I've seen elaborate setups to prevent this, including muffles or saggars in the kiln chamber to separate the potter physically from the coils. These not only make unnecessary work but also decrease the interior dimensions of the kiln. If your kiln shuts off automatically when you lift the lid, you're in no danger. If it doesn't, be sure to switch off the kiln before you reach into it. Remember to switch the kiln back on after you remove your ware.

Raku Firing in a Fuel-Burning Kiln

Before firing your ware, you must prepare your fuel (unless you have a natural gas system), assemble your burner, situate your reduction containers and materials, and stack your ware in the kiln. Planning and preparation are vital elements of success. As the firing process unfolds, the importance of paying attention to details becomes even clearer.

Preparing the Fuel

Having an adequate fuel supply on hand is an absolute must. If you're using propane, make sure you start your firings with full tanks. For any of the LPG-fueled kilns described in the last chapter,

a 20-pound (9.1 kg) tank should give you three or four firings, depending on how quickly you fire. Fifty pounds (22.7 kg) of charcoal should be enough for one firing in the charcoal kiln (see page 100), but keep 100 pounds (45.4 kg) or even more on hand for longer or multiple firings. Planning for a wood firing is difficult the first time around; the required amount of fuel will depend on the type of wood you have on hand, the sizes of the pieces, and your rate of stoking. I recommend a half cord (64 cu. ft. or 1.8 cu. m).

Assembling and Testing the Combustion System

A natural gas system and its associated fittings require professional installation. When you contract this work, ask the installer to connect the burner assembly via a *quick-release mechanism*, which allows you to disconnect the burner easily in order to store it indoors. Whether your LPG burner system came with your kiln or you purchased a separate burner system, follow the manufacturer's instructions for attaching any necessary fittings. When you purchase your burner, hoses, and fittings, if you're given the option of having them assembled for you, take advantage of it. An assembly that's been pressure-tested and is ready to use is well worth any extra cost. All you have to do is screw the system onto your tank and attach the burner if it hasn't been attached already.

If you store away your burner and equipment after each firing session, you must reassemble them before each new session. Using figure 1 (on the facing page) as a guide, thread the male brass fitting on the regulator onto the female receptacle on the tank (see photo 3).

Popular myth has it that when electric kiln elements are hot, the danger of electric shock is eliminated. Nothing could be further from the truth. Kiln elements are no different from unsheathed electric wires; whenever they're carrying current, they're just as dangerous, and you must avoid contact with them. While it's true that the layer of oxidation that forms on the surface of an element over a period of use does afford a minimal degree of insulation, it's not enough to protect you from shock.

3

4

If the fitting has a rubber O-ring, you can hand-tighten it; if it doesn't, use a wrench. Remember that propane tank fittings tighten *counterclockwise*!

For storage, cleaning, and to change the orifice, you can remove the burner from the valve assembly (see figure 2 on page 59). Simply hold the valve and unscrew the burner from the orifice stub. To remount the burner before firing, screw it back onto the stub. Place the burner on its stand, with the hose stretched out and arranged neatly on the ground. Don't uncoil any more hose than necessary. Keeping extra hose out of the way helps maintain a safe firing environment (photo 4).

With the burner valve closed, open the *main* (or *service*) valve on the tank, and check all connections for leaks by brushing them with a soapy water solution. Tighten any connection where bubbles form.

Preparing Reduction Materials and Containers

Well in advance of firing, you must choose and arrange reduction materials and containers for the post-firing reduction phase of raku. Any material that's carbon-based is suitable as a reduction material (see photo 5). Medium to coarse sawdust, wood shavings, and wood chips are the most popular and are my first choices. They ignite easily and are dense enough to release a sufficient amount of carbon.

Cabinet and furniture manufacturers as well as sawmills are great sources for free sawdust and other wood scraps. Lumberyards and home centers are, too, but avoid pressure-treated stock, plywood, waferboard, and other composite goods; sawdust from them can emit fumes and gases from the binders, glues, and chemicals used in their manufacture. Leaves, hay, straw, pine needles, shredded paper, and cloth are also popular materials.

5

6

8

Galvanized buckets and garbage cans with matching lids are the most common reduction containers and are ideal for most applications (see photo 6). They meet all three basic requirements: they're available in various sizes to accommodate your ware, they're fire and heat resistant, and their lids fit snugly to create airtight chambers. If you store them in a dry place, they last a long time, too. Galvanized cans, tubs, and basins in 5-, 10-, 20-, and 30-gallon (18.9, 37.9, 75.7, and 113.6 L) sizes are available at hardware stores and home centers. Farm supply stores carry long galvanized troughs, and some hardware stores can special-order them.

Cookie, popcorn, and other gift-item tins also make great reduction containers. Other useful containers, including larger ones, can often be found by checking the "barrels" or "cans" listings in the yellow pages. Manufacturers and distributors frequently sell seconds and used goods at reasonable prices. Resourceful potters sometimes make use of discarded refrigerators and freezers (after removing the plastic interiors), as well as all kinds of steel drums and barrels. Use your imagination. Even an old grill can serve as the perfect container for your pot (see photo 7).

7

The sizes of your containers are just as important as having an adequate number on hand. As a rule of thumb, use the smallest container that fits a pot. I should be embarrassed to admit it, but several times, I've found myself with a pot hot from the kiln, only to find that I've filled all my reduction barrels or that the piece I'm holding is too large for the nearest container. Make sure you have enough containers and that they're the right sizes.

If your work is taller than your tallest available container, dig a shallow hole in the ground, place the piece in it for post-firing reduction, and cover the piece with the container (see photo 8). This technique also works well with containers that don't have lids, though kiln

Just as the participants were about to unload a kiln during a workshop presentation I once gave, I realized that we were short on reduction containers. I quickly grabbed some cardboard boxes, soaked them with water, and lined their bottoms with wet newspaper (see photo 9). The flaps at their tops, covered by pieces of wood, formed the lids. The water sealed the pores of the cardboard, and the boxes turned out to be perfectly airtight. They even lasted through three or four post-firing cycles.

9

shelves, sections of sheet metal, or even wooden boards soaked with water work well as lids. In order to create a good seal, wrap the rim of the container with a gasket made of wet newspaper (photo 10).

Building a custom reduction container sometimes makes sense. To accommodate my tallest pieces, I fashioned a double-height container out of two 20-gallon (75.7 L) trash cans and a modified lid (see photo 11). Using metal shears, I cut out and discarded all but the rim and about 2 inches (5.1 cm) of one trash-can lid and then made cuts along its circumference. I bent the cut metal sections down to create tabs (see photo 12), then placed the piece on top of one trash can and riveted the tabs to its interior walls. The open end of the other can fits perfectly into this modified rim.

Any containers are fair game as long as you can adapt them to your particular

needs and requirements, but be careful to remove any nonmetal parts before using them. And don't forget to add your reduction material to them before you begin your firing. A $\frac{1}{2}$- to 1-inch (1.3 to 2.5 cm) layer is usually sufficient, depending on the size of your ware.

Arrange your containers in a way that will allow you to move freely as you remove pots from the kiln and that will help you avoid back stress created by having to reach too far as you place the pots in the containers (see photo 13). A concrete-block platform that you can stand on when unloading a tall top-loader can be useful. A car kiln like Robert Compton's (see photo 14) or a kiln

chamber that lifts off exposes the entire load of ware at a height that's usually comfortable and easy to access.

Stacking the Ware

You've been stacking and firing kilns for years, so you think you can skip this section and rely on your own expertise. Back up! The goal when stacking a conventional kiln is to load the ware as efficiently as possible—in other words, the more pots the better. In raku, however, your primary goals are to isolate your ware as much as possible from the flames of the burner (unless you choose to ignore this for creative purposes), to avoid blocking efficient draft in the kiln, and to make removal of your pots as easy as possible. Ideally, you should be able to remove the pots one at a time, in any order you like; no pot should block access to any other.

Flames are ever-present in fuel-fired kilns. Direct contact with them early in the firing is a major cause of breakage. If you've designed your burner port properly so that it's under the kiln shelf (see page 74), the flames will travel upward and hug the wall of the kiln. As long as your pots are stacked away from the wall, you shouldn't have any flame-related breakage problems.

Arrange the ware in a way that facilitates its removal without blocking the draft during firing. Wide forms such as bowls and plates that are stacked directly under the flue act as dampers; they'll block the path of the draft, may slow the kiln, and may prevent it from reaching the desired temperature. Even if they don't inhibit the draft, glazed pieces stacked near the flue—say within 3 inches (7.6 cm) of the top of the kiln—may not reach matu-

rity because that part of the chamber tends to be cooler than the rest of the kiln. Place unglazed ware or ware with lower-maturing glazes there instead. Alternatively, you can load your ware with a plan for sequential removal in mind. If you like, you can stack plates and other flat pieces on their edges, which usually makes them easy to grab with tongs, but ware loaded in this manner may be prone to warping, and glazes will likely drip in ways that you may not have planned for. Take these considerations into account before you stack.

Can pieces of ware touch one another in a raku firing? Since you're too embarrassed to ask a question with such an unmistakably clear and unequivocal answer, I've asked it for you. The answer: sure they can! Your decision rests on your aesthetic expectations and how much work you feel compelled to load into the kiln at one time. Just as in a bisque firing, unglazed surfaces can contact other unglazed surfaces with no ill effects. In group and workshop situations, where there always seems to be more work than could ever be fired, I load the ware foot to rim, with pieces all over each other (see photo 15).

Allowing glazed surfaces to touch each other can create interesting surface effects, but until you're more experienced, you may want to avoid this. Molten glaze behaves like melted candy; glazed pots in contact with one another will stick together. As you pull one pot from the kiln, a thin thread of hot glaze connected to

Some potters preheat their kilns before stacking the first loads in them. Although a kiln can be reloaded and fired multiple times during the same raku firing session, preheating the kiln for the first load is unnecessary, has no positive effects, and can lead to breakage.

14

15

16

another pot may form and stretch out as it stays attached to both. Be careful! This thread will harden quickly and may cut or burn you if you touch it.

Kiln furniture is certainly useful for stacking in some kilns. Shelves in front-loading and car kilns offer more stacking efficiency, while still giving you full and reasonably easy access to all of your work. You may also use shelves in kilns with chambers that lift off to expose the ware. Just make sure when you raise and lower a kiln of this type that it clears the edges of the shelves—a task that requires some skill. A solution to this is a kiln guided by cables or tracks like this one from Ceramic Services that keep it from moving side to side (see photo 16).

In top-loading kilns, shelves are obstacles and nuisances. Having to remove a kiln shelf to expose the ware stacked beneath it is difficult, and reaching for a

pot under a half-shelf is awkward. Typically, the only furniture I use in my top-loaders are bricks or kiln posts to raise the work closer to the top of the kiln or to allow pieces to clear each other and fit more efficiently. However, I have placed a small shelf or shelf shard on top of a piece—even directly on the unglazed rim of a pot—and stacked a pot on top of it, but only when removing the shelf or shard with tongs to expose the pot underneath is quick and easy.

Bricks, posts, and shelf shards are useful in another important way. A major cause of breakage is heating work too fast and unevenly. Raising a pot off the shelf by placing it on one of these objects slows down the heating of the pot, especially its bottom.

Facilitating easy removal of the ware from an electric kiln is important, but other factors also come into play. If your electric kiln is a top-loader, stack your ware on a kiln shelf so that the tallest piece is within 2 to 3 inches (5.1 to 7.6 cm) of the top of the kiln. This eliminates the need to reach deep into the kiln, to open its lid very wide, or to get too close to the kiln itself when you're ready to remove the ware. In a front-loader, stack the ware as close to the front of the kiln as possible for the same reasons. In any electric kiln, arrange your pieces 1 to 2 inches (2.5 to 5.1 cm) away from the kiln wall (see photo 17). This space helps you avoid touching the brick or elements with your tongs and helps keep glaze drips off the kiln walls.

17

The Firing Cycle

Depending on the type of fuel your kiln uses, management of the firing cycle differs slightly, but all fuels require careful supervision for safety. Electricity requires the least tending; in fact, up to the point of maturity, it requires no tending at all. Gas requires careful (but minimal) attention, while wood and coal demand continuous tending. While this section focuses primarily on gas systems, the other types—electric, wood-fired, and coal-fired kilns—are mentioned wherever appropriate.

Igniting the Fuel

Remember, LPG is heavier than air and takes time to dissipate, so check to see that the valve at the burner is closed. Open the main valve at the tank all the way, and leave it in the open position for the duration of your firing. Treat this valve as an on-off switch, *not* as a tool for controlling the gas flow or pressure.

To ignite the burner, use a welder's sparker (see photo 18), a self-igniting propane torch (see photo 19), some rolled-up newspaper lit with a match (see photo 20), or a butane lighter with

a long tip (the ones designed for lighting barbecues). These tools keep your hands a safe distance from the burner tip. I confess I've never been entirely comfortable using a sparker; I don't like putting my hand that close to the flame, and every time the burner lights, no matter how well prepared or safe I am, I always jump.

Open the burner's primary air control (the burner should be in place), uncover the flue, have your igniter in hand, turn on the gas at the burner until you can barely hear it flow, and light the burner by placing the igniter close to or in front of the burner head. If the gas flow is too weak, the burner won't light. If it doesn't light within about three seconds, shut off the gas, wait a minute or so to give the gas that's entered the kiln time to dissipate, then turn it on and try again. If you don't allow the built-up gas to escape, the next time you attempt ignition, a loud pop—or worse, a small explosion—could result. Though natural gas dissipates much more quickly, take similar precautions with it.

18

19

20

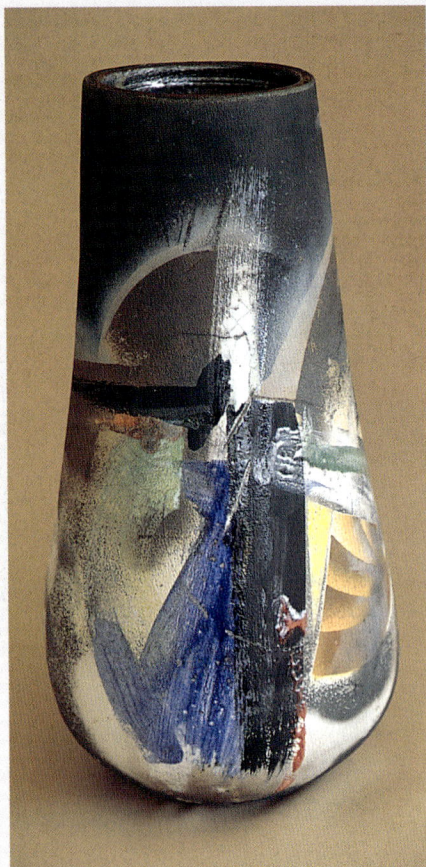

Igniting wood and coal is a bit trickier. You can't turn up the power with a convenient valve; the "valve" is your own manipulation of the fuel. Place a layer of newspaper, wood shavings, excelsior, twigs, or any other kindling in the firebox. On top of this, place some of your larger pieces of wood, 4 to 5 inches (10.2 to 12.7 cm) or even larger in diameter. Light the kindling with a rolled-up sheet of newspaper, and allow the kindling to ignite the larger pieces of wood (see photo 21). To preheat the chamber and ware, add more large pieces of wood on top of the grate. As the firing progresses, gradually decrease the size of the wood you add. At the height of the firing, use pieces 1 inch (2.5 cm) in diameter or smaller.

Light charcoal (or coal) on grates in the same way. In a coal-fired saggar kiln, arrange the kindling in the bottom of the chamber, cover it with a layer of charcoal, and light the kindling. When the coals begin to turn ashen, pour in more charcoal right to the top of the saggar. Continue adding charcoal as the firing progresses.

Controlling Combustion and Temperature Rise

You must understand and be comfortable with your firing system. Three different parts of a gas-fired system affect the gas flow, and although they all appear to do the same thing, their functions are very different and shouldn't be confused.

The main (or service) valve turns the gas on or off. It should always be either in a fully open position or a closed one—never between the two. In a propane system, the main is a valve on the tank. A natural gas system usually has two mains.

21

One is a valve located on the gas line before the meter; it's used to shut off the gas when the meter needs to be replaced. The other main is located near the point at which the gas enters the building. In an outdoor kiln area, it's located on the plumbing where your burners connect.

A regulator controls the gas pressure. Natural gas systems have a fixed regulator (the pressure is preset and can't be changed) positioned between the meter and the second main valve. Propane systems have one or two regulators, depending on the size of the tank and the pressure you're firing at; one or both are positioned after the main. Most raku propane systems have a single adjustable regulator. If, however, your system is a low-pressure one with a large tank—250 gallons (946 L) or more—it's likely to include a step-down regulator that leads to a second regulator. Adjust the regulator (or regulators) to the pressure recommended by your burner supplier and then leave it (or them) alone.

JIM ROMBERG
Untitled
19 x 9 inches (48.3 x 22.9 cm)
Wheel thrown Soldate 30; brushed and sprayed glaze; oxide wash, stains; gas fired
Photo by artist

Finally, all systems have a valve that controls the burner; this same valve directly governs the heat in your kiln, and it's the one you manipulate. Don't confuse the controls in the system and use one to do something for which it wasn't intended. Use the valve on the burner—*not* the valve on the tank—to control the gas flow.

The temperature in your kiln depends on a combination of factors: the gas flow (or the wood you stoke); the primary and secondary air; and the flue and wind. Probably the most difficult concept to master is the effect that air has on temperature rise.

Think of air in respect to your kiln as the fine-tuning control on a radio. As you move the control on a radio, the sound gets clearer until it reaches optimum quality. If you continue to move the control, the quality deteriorates. In your kiln, insufficient air produces a yellow flame, resulting in a reduction atmosphere. As you "tune in" by increasing the primary, secondary, and/or flue air, the flame gets bluer, hotter, and more efficient. Continue to "tune," however, and too much air creates a flame that's blue, but not hot. To lower the temperature in the kiln, turn down the gas, and then adjust your air for an efficient blue flame (see photo 22).

Another potentially confusing concept related to air and temperature rise is the adjustment of the damper or flue. The flue controls the power of the draft in the kiln—that is, how strong the air-pull or sucking action is. Assuming that you begin with a flue that's the right size, in general the more open the flue is, the more draft; the more draft, the more air;

the more air (up to a certain point), the bluer and hotter the flame. When the flue is open and you can feel the radiant heat from it, understand that while some heat is escaping, it should. The single most common error that novices make is not allowing sufficient air into the kiln. Resist the apparently logical tendency to think that closing the flue causes the temperature to rise by retaining the heat. It won't work! Often, the best way to raise the temperature is to open the flue.

The warmth of the kiln also affects the draft. At the start of the first firing of the day, the kiln is cold and the draft is weak. You'll see flames in the kiln, and achieving a blue oxidizing flame at the burner tip may seem impossible. As the kiln heats up, however, the draft and your ability to control the kiln improve. In extreme situations, a poor draft causes flames to shoot out of the burner port. To avoid a fire hazard, build a brick enclosure or wall to enclose the flames temporarily (see photo 23). Remove the enclosure when the draft improves.

Here are a couple of reminders: Don't block the flue with your ware, and be careful not to stack the kiln too tightly. Both can negatively affect the draft. Occasionally, when the draft is poor, you may have to resort to more unusual methods to increase the air intake, such as propping open the lid of a top-loading kiln with bricks or leaving the door of a front-loader ajar. Be careful: the heat that comes from the space between the lid or door and the kiln itself is dangerous.

Wind—obviously a great source of air—provides a free power-burner system. Orient your kiln so that any wind blows into the burner port. Wind blowing from

If you're just starting out, be conservative: fire slowly until you've gained enough experience to be able to recognize an appropriate temperature rise.

the opposite side of the kiln or down into the flue can prevent an efficient draft, which in turn can result in a cooling effect. Wind can also blow the flame back out of the burner port, which poses a fire hazard. To prevent this, build a brick shield to protect the flue (see photo 24).

Other weather conditions can also affect firing. Firing an unprotected kiln in the rain is usually nothing more than uncomfortable. I'm often asked if I fire in cold weather or when there's snow on the ground. I certainly do! But low temperatures cause your ware to cool faster and inhibit preheating subsequent loads—conditions that vary in importance from one potter to another. Extreme cold will cause premature freeze-ups and pressure loss in propane tanks (see page 61). The smaller your tank, the more likely you'll encounter these problems. Snow presents a different problem. While the heat generated by the kiln keeps you warm, it also melts the snow around the area and can create a real mess, depending on the surface the kiln is sitting on. Mud and slippery grass create a potentially dangerous situation, especially with all the movement that takes place around the kiln during the unloading phase. A concrete slab or similar hard surface is less affected by wetness, but you must guarantee yourself sure footing.

The Firing Schedule

Knowing how to manage the firing and recognizing when the ware is ready to remove from the kiln are the most intimidating and mystifying aspects of the entire raku process. Take a deep breath, relax, and …

One of the core attractions of raku is the rapid firing. Cycles can be as short as 15 or 20 minutes; I've even witnessed ones only 10 minutes long. However, lightning-speed firings don't improve your work, and if fast firing is your goal, you'll need to experiment in order to avoid breakage, most of which occurs during the heating stage when the ware is moving from cold to hot, not during the cooling stage. My firings take one to three hours, depending on the size of the work. Your own will depend on the clay body you've used, your preheating success, and the initial temperature advance once the ware has been placed in the chamber. If you're just starting out, be conservative: fire slowly until you've gained enough experience to be able to recognize an appropriate temperature rise.

Electric kilns are either controlled manually, by means of switches, or through a computer control. There's nothing complicated about turning on an electric kiln, and there's no firing schedule to follow with it. Just turn the kiln on high— and go have a snack. Come back later in this chapter, when I talk about recognizing glaze melt, maturity, soaking, underfiring, and over-firing. Depending on the size of your kiln and the condition of its coils, the firing takes two to three hours.

A reasonable, yet conservative initial firing schedule for a gas system follows. Start by lighting the burner and adjusting the flame so that it's clearly audible. (A reminder: control the gas with the burner valve, not the regulator or main valve!) The sound of the burner is an accurate indicator of the intensity and power of its operation. Too soft a flame, and you run the risk of it blowing out. To lessen the chance of extinguishing the flame by adjusting it too low, begin with the burner head positioned just inside the kiln (see photo 25). Open the primary air control completely, and uncover the flue. Remember that until your kiln is thoroughly hot, draft is minimal and the flame may be yellow. At this stage, there's little you can do to eliminate flames in the chamber; they're normal and nothing to worry about.

As the kiln heats up, the draft improves and, if you've done everything correctly, you should have no trouble achieving a blue oxidizing flame. After 15 minutes or so, pull the burner outward until it's 1 or 2 inches (2.5 or 5.1 cm) away from the kiln and turn up the gas until you notice a difference in the quality of the flame and loudness of the burner. Every 15 minutes, until the glazed surfaces and the bare clay begin to take on a dark, gray quality, increase the gas flow just enough to notice a difference in the sound the burner makes.

Once the gray quality is visible on your ware, it's safe to turn the burner up more quickly. If you're not sure you've reached this stage and prefer to be cautious, then by all means continue slowly. As the temperature continues to advance, the appearance of the glazed surfaces begins to change. You'll observe this change long before there's any melting of the glaze or a uniform orange color in the kiln.

Determining Glaze Maturity

The climax of the firing is the stage at which the glazes reach maturity. Being able to recognize this stage requires patience and comes with experience. In conventional firings, melting cones indicate the progress—and ultimately the maturity—of the glaze, as well as the end of the firing. In raku firing, cones aren't commonly used; rapid firing, changing atmospheres, and the firing of multiple loads make their use awkward, clumsy, and sometimes inaccurate. Instead, raku potters determine when a firing should end by relying on direct observation of the ware's surface—and on their intuition.

During the firing, the glaze evolves from a dry state through various degrees of melting. Within the temperature range of raku, the color and brightness inside the kiln enable you to see these stages on the surfaces of your wares. Look into the kiln through the peepholes and down into the flue. Try viewing the work from different angles, and spy across its surface rather than looking straight down at it. (Be careful; blasts of heat come from every kiln opening.) As the kiln approaches firing temperature, the interior of the chamber begins to change from colorless to a bright glowing orange. The first visible change in the glaze takes place at this stage (and sometimes even before), just as the dry glaze begins to melt. Its surface takes on a living appearance, similar to flowing lava, moving and changing almost second by second. I refer to this stage as the "ugly stage" because … well, the glaze looks truly ugly. It's just slightly shiny, and its surface looks as if it's about to separate from the pot and leave bare areas behind.

Cones can unfortunately become elements that separate you from closer contact and dialogue with your ware. I welcome variations in approaches, though, so I don't completely disregard the potential value of cones in raku firing. For example, they can aid in the firing of a load of unglazed or matte-glazed ware from a cold kiln, where you know the preferred cone. Regardless, in order to use cones, you must know which ones your glazes mature at, and this information isn't often a part of raku-glaze descriptions.

25

26

DOMI GRUSZECKA
Vessel, 2006
14⁹/₁₆ inches (37 cm) tall
Hand built Witgert MS Clay; brushed
glaze; overglaze; gas fired, quick
cooling, smoking for reduction
Photo by artist

This next phase of the firing cycle is when adjusting the firing becomes more finely tuned and critical; it includes firing the glazes on each of your pots to maturity, possible reduction effects, and the process of soaking. As the temperature increases, the glaze surface begins to smooth out, and the glossiness intensifies. During this process, if you observe carefully, you can see small, pimple-like eruptions and pinhole craters on a very shiny surface.

As a novice learning how to recognize proper maturity, you're aiming for a smooth, defect-free, shimmering, gloss-like surface (see photo 26). This final stage of melting has been likened to the reflection of water on ice in the sunlight—an accurate as well as poetic description. Resign yourself to the fact that recognizing this stage takes practice; there's no substitute. Depending on your rate of firing, the time between the first visible signs of meltage and subsequent maturity can be anywhere from 15 minutes to an hour. Then, depending on the glaze, the ultimate maturing point may lie within a very narrow temperature range or a very wide one. Only experience will tell.

Over- and Under-Firing

If only kilns fired perfectly evenly and all glazes matured at the same time! This doesn't usually happen. The bottom of a kiln often fires hotter than the top, and one side of the kiln may be hotter than the other. If you don't have much experience with raku, you may over- or under-fire some glazes in an effort to melt others. You'll know you're over-firing if you see vigorous boiling on the glaze surface. The visible eruptions will be similar to the ones you saw as the glaze first reached temperature, but these pimples won't smooth out.

Although you can't repair an over-fired pot, if you recognize the problem early on, you can sometimes nip it in the bud by soaking. During this process, gases and atmosphere flow throughout the kiln, and the heat in the chamber balances itself. Unless you've over-fired the glaze completely, some of it is still immature. When it's soaked, it will melt and flow over the over-fired glaze, filling the pits and smoothing the surface. Soaking also allows glazes that haven't yet reached temperature to catch up with the rest of the load—and it can be a creative approach as well; it allows glazes to mature, flow, drip, and establish depth. The time to start soaking is late in the firing (but not too late!), when you notice sections of the chamber firing unevenly. Cover up the flue ever so slightly, and cut back on the air just a bit. Be careful not to overdo it: cutting back on these air sources too much may cause the temperature to drop or create a reduction atmosphere that you don't want. (See page 57 for more on reduction firing.)

Is there an optimum length of time for a firing? As far as its effect on glaze quality is concerned, the firing time in raku isn't as consequential as it is for a high-fire cycle. There are some advantages—as in the case with soaking—to be gained from a longer firing cycle, but your aesthetics and common sense regarding safety issues should govern the length of a firing.

Removing the Ware

The next phases are removal of the ware from the kiln and the ensuing post-firing reduction. We'll talk about these two phases separately, but they're inextricably linked.

You usually remove the glowing ware from a kiln with tongs, which keep you at a safe distance while allowing you to reach into the kiln and maneuver as necessary to grab it. Purchase tongs that are appropriate for your pots; these tools are available from pottery suppliers in different shapes and sizes (see photo 27). Fireplace supply shops are good sources, too, but tongs for fireplaces tend to be heavier and shorter. Beware of inexpensive, low-grade tongs designed more for display than use. Yours should be sturdily made of a strong material, such as iron or aluminum, and have substantial pins or bolts at their joints. I've never

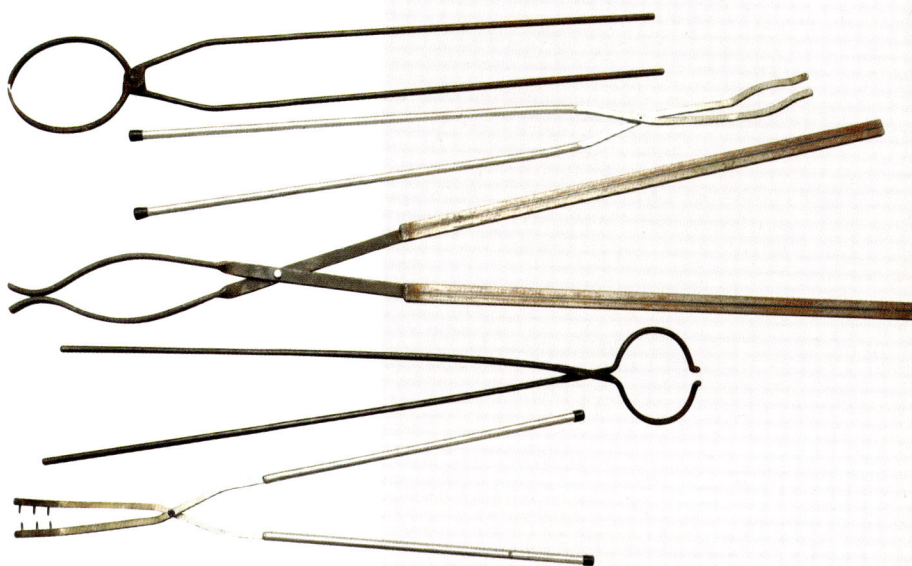

27

had a set of tongs fall apart during use, but I can imagine the disappointment I would feel if they did.

You may need custom-made tongs for your work. Bob Compton makes a four-point design (with two points on each side) rather than the traditional single-jaw one, for example, which makes the secure handling of large and awkward forms easier. I've made my own tongs and have had some made for me by a class at a local industrial school. The teacher was more than amiable; he enjoyed having a new and interesting project to assign his students. Be resourceful!

Tongs may or may not leave a mark on your pot at the point of contact. In traditional raku firing, the tongs are cooled in water before they enter the kiln; their cooled surfaces immediately harden the glaze and prevent any impressions from being left in it. In your own firing, the first pots you remove from the kiln may show tong marks, but as the ware remaining in the kiln cools, tong marks are less likely. The marks shouldn't necessarily be viewed as defects anyway but as integral effects of the raku technique.

28

A

Approaching a pot from its sides is easier than approaching from directly above it, so one feature of my recycled electric kiln that I like and often take advantage of is the relative ease with which you can lift off a section or two when the firing is complete. I do this when I want to lift out a tall pot, whether I'll be using tongs or my gloved hands. To adapt your recycled kiln, simply attach at least two large sash handles to each of its sections (see photo 38 on page 82.)

Grasping pots firmly but carefully while keeping them under control takes practice, as does becoming aware of and sensitive to your own strength as you squeeze the tongs. If the shape of your pot permits, grabbing it with one tong jaw on the inside and one on the outside is usually easier than wrapping both jaws of the tongs around the outside (see photo 28). Avoid grasping very thin rims and necks, but if there's no other way to lift the piece, keep it as upright as possible, allowing its weight to hang freely so you don't place unnecessary stress on the neck itself (see photo 29). Be careful! Depending on the shape of the pot, the extent of its glazed surface, and how you grab it, it may slip out of your tongs.

Another way to remove your pots is to lift them with your gloved hands. While you might think not having to master the use of tongs will make your life easier, using gloves does have disadvantages. Ones thick enough to provide adequate protection from heat (you have to stand closer to the kiln than you would if you were using tongs) reduce dexterity; ones thin enough to permit dexterity won't protect you adequately from burns.

In addition, a crowded firing chamber makes grabbing a piece without disturbing the others tricky. And gloves leave marks on glazed surfaces.

Use your gloved hands rather than tongs *only* to remove pieces so large that you can't physically lift them with tongs or when absolutely no other way to proceed exists. And when you use gloves, take some added precautions. Make sure your gloves are long, put on your protective mask, and use a second pair of gloves as potholders to ensure protection from the

29

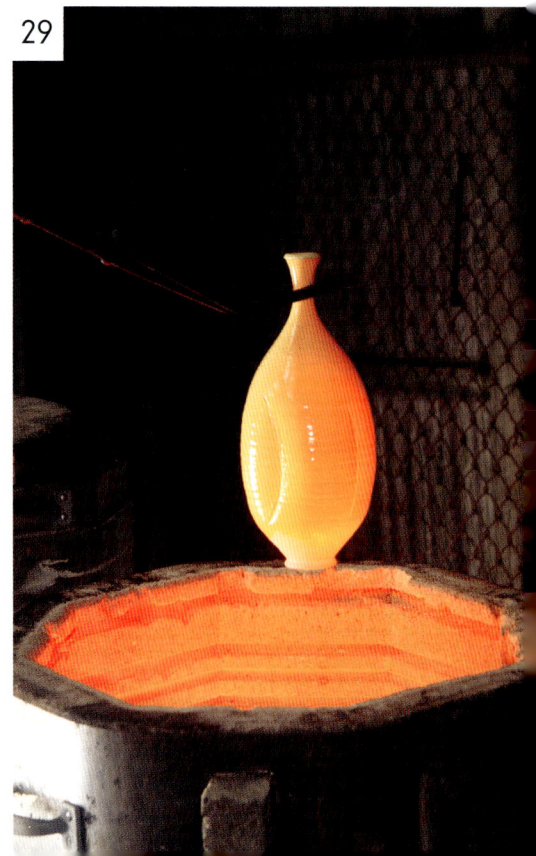

hot ware. Go through a dry run beforehand, too, to make sure you're strong enough to lift the piece and place it in your reduction container (see photo 30). Practice runs are a great way to get over the potentially intimidating process of removing hot ware; they can help you gain confidence and dispel some of your fears. But there's nothing like doing the real thing for the first time.

A team of two can lift out a large and/or heavy piece by gripping its opposite sides. This does require exacting teamwork and communication—unless, of course, you want to end up with two or more pieces for the price of one!

Despite helpers, custom-made tongs, and other specialized tools and procedures, you may still encounter work that for one reason or another, you can't remove from the kiln—work that's too heavy or fragile, for example. The solution in this case is to do your post-firing work on the kiln base or in the kiln itself. (A kiln designed expressly for this purpose, with two chambers and two pads, appears in photo 52 on page 89). For instructions on reducing in place, see page 124.

Pieces too small to be lifted with tongs also present removal problems. The only effective way to remove beads or other small objects—and avoid raku-induced nervous breakdown—is to fire them on a bead tree, in a clay container large enough to grab with tongs, or on a small kiln shelf (see photo 31). When the firing is ready, remove the tree, container, or shelf, and use it to transfer the individual pieces to your reduction container.

Be creative, respond to particular circumstances, and use your intuition. If your work is small and the flue in the lid of your kiln is large enough, you may not have to remove the lid at all. Just reach in through the flue to remove your pots (see photo 32).

Standard Post-Firing Reduction

Post-firing reduction is the heart of Western-style raku. Just as it's important to learn how to fire your glazes to smooth and glossy maturity before attempting more advanced approaches, so is mastering the basic, vanilla-flavored reduction technique. If you take every step correctly (glaze application, firing to maturity, and so on), standard post-firing reduction produces the effects shown in photo 33: crackled glazes (by the author); matte black clay (by Karen Mahoney), and metallic lusters (by Debbie Winnick).

The post-firing phase begins with turning down the gas at the burner, switching off the elements in an electric kiln, or ceasing the stoking of a wood- or charcoal-fired kiln. (Expect flames in the chamber from still-burning wood.) If you've fired several pots, leaving the burner on as you remove them keeps the pots still inside the kiln a bit hotter. If you've fired only one pot or are removing the final piece from a load, turn the gas off.

Open the kiln or, in the case of a fuel-burning top-loader, remove the lid. Make sure you've prepared a safe, fire-resistant spot for a removable lid; don't set it down on grass or against a fence or tree. If your kiln is electric, grab the handle with tongs (the radiant heat of the kiln is too severe for gloved hands), and raise the lid on its hinge (see photo 34). Practice this beforehand with a cold kiln, being careful not to get the tongs caught between the handle and the top course of bricks or electrical boxes when you close the kiln.

Reducing the Fired Pieces

Preparation and speed are essential for success during this stage; I can't emphasize them enough! Reach into the kiln, lift out your pieces, and place them in your containers as fast as you can (see photo 35). Unless you're unloading pieces in quick succession, close the kiln in between removals. Set each pot down gently in its container, positioning it so it doesn't tip over, hit the container

wall, and possibly break. Release your grip carefully, so you don't nick the rim of a piece as you pull the tongs away. Add more reduction material if necessary— the equivalent of a small handful of sawdust—dropping it in from close range. Don't throw it in from a distance; lightweight materials such as sawdust or leaves tend to blow all over the place, and hot air rising from the container may also prevent the material from entering.

To ensure efficient smoking for glaze and clay-body development, cover the container within 15 seconds of the point at which the material ignites. Intense reduction effects are a result of how efficiently and quickly you position your ware, ignite the material, and cover the container; they're *not* a result of the amount of reduction material you use. Be sure to allow the material to ignite

36

before covering the container (see photo 36). If it smolders instead, little or no reduction effect will take place.

On page 95, I suggested placing very tall pieces in shallow holes in the ground and inverting containers over them. Shoveling sand or dirt around the edges of an inverted container creates an excellent airtight seal that prevents oxygen from entering. Inverting the lid of a container over a flat piece set on the ground also works well (see photo 37).

Throughout the post-firing process, never forget that combustion and fire are dangerous and sometimes unpredictable. If the lid to your container is lightweight or doesn't fit snugly, air may be sucked in and cause a sudden burst of flames that could blow the cover off. Likewise, if you uncover a container in which a pot is smoking, either to insert another piece or to add reduction material, stand well back with your face protected. The mixture of air and heat in the container can cause a sudden, powerful flare-up.

37

Here's a true story to emphasize the importance of planning ahead and trying to anticipate any problems. Early in my raku experience, I was preparing to fire in a populated area and was concerned that onlookers might be frightened if they saw the post-firing process. I chose a firing area hidden behind a row of small retail shops, I located the kiln far enough from the buildings and any other flammable sources to be safe, and I planned every other aspect of the firing in advance—or so I thought. All went well, including the post-firing reduction, which produced very little smoke. The process was over, and I was finally calm.

A few minutes later, though, I heard fire engines roaring down the block! One of the shops—an ice-cream parlor, no less—had been filled with just enough smoky odor to alarm the employees. The one thing I hadn't considered was their ventilation system; it was located on the roof of the building and had very effectively sucked in the minimal amount of smoke my post-firing produced. By the time the fire trucks arrived, the smoking had stopped, of course; the ventilation system had done its job, and the shop was clear. Soon thereafter, we moved our raku kilns to a friend's house in the country.

MICHAEL SHEBA
Raku Wallpiece "Transcendence"
$6^{11}/_{16}$ x $42^{1}/_{8}$ x $3^{1}/_{8}$ inches (17 x 107 x 8 cm)
Slip cast raku clay; sprayed terra sigillata; carved, sgraffito, burnished; raku fired in propane kiln; controlled cooling, smoking for reduction, selective smoking for reduction; cone 06
Photo by artist

While you should definitely be cautious, don't be afraid of the flames coming from the container. As long as you're wearing gloves and appropriate clothing, the flames won't hurt you. The initial burst of smoke during the post-firing reduction phase lasts only about 30 seconds to one minute and may be no more noticeable than the smoke from a barbecue. The more airtight the seal, the better the reduction and the less smoke that escapes. If you're doing raku in your yard and would rather not attract too much attention, less smoke can be critical.

Some types of work may require reducing a piece in place. If you're using a fiber kiln the entire chamber of which lifts off to expose the pots, remove it, place your reduction materials in a container, and invert the container over the pot or pots right where they're stacked. (Make sure your container is large enough to fit over them.) Then seal up the burner port and

any other places where air might enter the container. This post-firing reduction technique is effective if you provide a good seal between the rim of the container and the base of the kiln. A strip of insulating fiber used as a gasket usually works well.

If you're firing a top- or front-loading brick kiln, shut off the burner, close up the peepholes and burner port, and drop or shovel your reduction materials into the kiln, as Doug Johnson does with his kiln in photo 38. Immediately close the kiln and seal the flue to make the chamber as airtight as possible. When the chamber is cool, open the kiln and sweep away the charred reduction material (see photo 39). Be careful with any material that may still be smoldering. I've had mixed results with this technique, mostly because in a brick kiln, creating a chamber airtight enough for effective smoking is difficult.

Cooling the Pieces

In workshop situations, I keep the work in the containers until the next batch of pots is ready to come out and I need the containers again. This takes anywhere from 15 minutes to an hour, which is sufficient time both for reducing and for cooling most of the work. I keep my own pots covered for at least two hours and sometimes longer. Slow cooling lessens the likelihood of cracking and is especially important for work 16 inches (40.6 cm) or more in height.

A common misconception about raku—specifically about the post-firing phase—is that pots must be quick-cooled in water. Quick-cooling is unnecessary and raises the risk of cracking, so I practice patience. If you insist on speed-cooling, here are some tips to help you prevent cracking problems:

• Unless your pot has a thin neck, dunk it as quickly as possible so that one side doesn't cool off while the other is still hot; avoid setting up a "shocking" situation!

• With a narrow-necked form, allow the water to enter carefully and slowly until the piece fills up rather than submerging the opening all at once. If it's filled too quickly, the boiling water inside and the subsequent pressure buildup causes the water to spit out the narrow top like a geyser, which can shatter the piece—a scary as well as dangerous event.

• The buoyancy of a hollow form makes it difficult to submerge, so as the piece is filling, pour water on the outside to cool it as evenly as possible. Be careful not to break the neck.

38

JIM ROMBERG
Ode to a Canyon, 2004
21 x 18 x 8 inches (53.3 x 45.7 x 20.3 cm)
Slab built Soldate 30; brushed, sprayed and sponged glaze; gas fired;
selective smoking for reduction
Photo by artist

39

Can you fire multiple loads in an electric kiln? Conceivably—if you preheat your ware in a separate kiln, if your clay body is particularly resistant to heat shock, and if you don't care about the potential negative effects on the kiln itself—but you should really assign multiple loads to fuel-burning kilns. Electric kilns cool down much more slowly than other types because their electric elements take so long to stop radiating heat. Their slow cooling and the lack of instantaneous temperature control generally make them unsuitable for this job. In addition, the prolonged exposure to cool air required in order to cool and reload the kiln (as opposed to the quick opening and closing of fuel-burning kilns) shortens the life of the hot brick face, metal hardware (such as handles and hinges), and elements.

• One final cautionary note: hot pots quickly heat up the water buckets they're placed in, so be careful when reaching in to retrieve your ware.

Controlled cooling (different from quick cooling) of the ware prior to post-firing reduction is a technique that's sometimes used to produce particular glaze effects. See page 126 for more information.

Successive Firings

Firing successive loads of raku, a practice that Western potters have embraced, allows you to fire more pots during a session than a single kiln can handle at one time, but it's not a necessary part of the raku process. My own work is too large to preheat safely for multiple firings. Then again, I do have six kilns that I can fire simultaneously, which obviates the need to fire multiple loads in a single kiln (see photo 40).

Preheating the Ware

To fire multiple loads of raku successfully, you must preheat the next batch of pots before loading them into the hot kiln. Remember that most breakage occurs when ware is going from cold to hot, so be patient here. The more porous and shock-resistant your clay body, the more successful you'll be. Yes, I've seen

40

41

cold pots fired in a preheated kiln without any breakage, but treat this event as a miraculous gift from the kiln god. Lest she think you greedy, make it a habit to preheat your ware.

Glaze is also subject to heat shock of a sort. If you heat it too quickly when it's still wet, either during preheating or in the kiln, it can curl and flake off the ware (see photo 41). Make sure it's dry before commencing this phase.

Preheating is usually accomplished by placing the pots on the top of or around the kiln so the radiant heat warms them (see photo 42). Rotate them frequently

42

GEOFFREY PAGEN
Magmatic, 2007
23 x 20 x 2 inches (58.4 x 50.8 x 5.1 cm)
Hand built personal clay; brushed glaze; sgraffito, glaze trailing; gas fired; smoking for reduction, cone 05
Photo by Stephen Cridland

STEVE MATTISON
Sky Series, 2008
$25^{9}/_{16} \times 23^{5}/_{8}$ inches (65 x 60 cm)
Press molded Westerwald Stoneware;
brushed glaze; colored and laminated
clays; gas fired; selective smoking for
reduction; 1000°C
Photo by artist

weak fiber lid, the pots won't rest on it steadily. Some potters go to great lengths to ensure complete preheating, including setting up additional kilns dedicated solely to that task, but preheating rigs can be as simple as topless brick enclosures, metal basins, or sections of 55-gallon (208.2 L) drums warmed by small burners at very low settings. You can even use a gas grill effectively.

Reloading the Kiln

Once you have a load of pots ready to remove from the kiln and you've preheated your next load of pots, you're ready for the transition stage—unloading, post-firing, and reloading. Before you remove the present load, move your preheated pots away from the kiln. Be careful: successfully preheated pots are too hot to touch without gloves. Move the pots to a noncombustible surface where they won't get in your way. Then unload the kiln and complete the post-firing reduction phase with the fired ware.

By the time you're finished, your preheated ware has cooled considerably. If your kiln is a top-loader, arrange this ware around its rim to preheat it again before placing it in the kiln. If you're us-

so they don't get hotter on one side than the other and crack. And don't allow them to block the flue; they may interfere with the draft. Don't worry if you notice a piece turning black as it sits atop the kiln; the carbon that you're seeing fires off once you place the ware in the kiln.

Arranging pots on or around the kiln can be a nuisance and, depending on your kiln, may not even be effective or practical. Ware placed on the lid can block your view into the kiln and can impede your movement if positioned around the base. If your kiln has an arched top or a

MARCIA SELSOR
Great White Heron, 2008
$2\frac{1}{2}$ x $19\frac{1}{2}$ x 1 inches
(54.6 x 49.5 x 2.5 cm)
Slab built Raku Smooth Alligator Clay
MC117; brushed and sprayed glaze;
gas fired; straw smoked face down
for reduction
Photo by artist

ing a lift-off kiln, place the ware around the perimeter of its base. Reheating the ware this way may seem overly cautious; feel free to experiment and find out what works best for you.

In about a minute, or when you think the ware is sufficiently hot, place a cold IFB or kiln shelf shard on the kiln shelf, and using tongs or your gloved hands, immediately place a pot on it. The cold brick or shard minimizes heat shock on the foot of the pot and on the pot as a whole but only if you position the pot on it before it has a chance to heat up. Cover or close the kiln, close the damper, insert all the peephole plugs, and leave the burner off for a few minutes to allow the pieces to preheat some more in the still warm chamber.

If any pieces break during the early stages of heating, open the kiln and remove the broken shards, especially any that might have landed inside or on an unharmed work.

Then uncover the flue and light the burner. (If you light the burner with the flue closed, there will be no draft, and the flame will back up on you.) Start to raise the kiln temperature slowly, using the same guidelines as before (see pages 102–103), but keep in mind that the temperatures can rise faster in a warm kiln than they can in a cold one. If any pieces break during the early stages of heating, open the kiln and remove the broken shards, especially any that might have landed inside or on an unharmed work.

Techniques
CHAPTER 8

Once you become familiar with the basic raku technique, I hope you'll experiment with more complicated variations, some of which are described in this chapter. Don't hesitate to try a technique you come across in an article or book, even if you feel you don't have enough information to get started. You'll often be pleasantly surprised by the results.

STEVEN BRANFMAN
Vessel, 2007
26 x 12 inches (66 x 30.5 cm)
Brushed multi layered commercial low fire glaze;
pressed surface texture

Firing Variations

Although the essential characteristics of raku—fast firing, removal of the mature ware, and fast cooling—are almost universally practiced, additions and innovations by Western potters have been and continue to be many and significant. Manipulating the firing itself leads the list.

Reduction Firing

The atmosphere in which you fire your work has a significant effect on color, texture, and overall appearance, but even though raku firing takes place in atmospheres ranging from clean oxidation to smoky reduction, raku potters often overlook intentional manipulation and careful control of the atmosphere as a creative tool.

A reminder before we start: An oxidation atmosphere is the result of a highly efficient fuel-to-air mixture and is desirable when the goal is a speedy temperature advance or clean, bright colors. A reduction atmosphere is one in which there's insufficient oxygen for complete combustion, and as a result, the fuel must look to other sources, the most readily available of which are the clay and glaze. The chemical reactions that take place during reduction alter glaze effects. Reds, purples, blues, and other variations are possible.

You should start reduction during a firing when your glazes are on the brink of reaching maturity. Begin by partly closing off the primary air to your burner and partly covering the flue. Experiment with their control; you may find that you can control the atmosphere with the flue adjustment alone.

Make these adjustments slowly, and observe the changes taking place in the kiln. The interior of the chamber should become intensely orange in color and take on a cloudy, swirling appearance. Flames begin to emanate from the flue and peepholes, and you should detect a distinctive odor (see photo 1).

To have any appreciable aesthetic effects in raku, reduction must take place for at least 30 minutes. Exploring the various effects obtainable through different degrees of reduction, different glazes, and the post-firing phase requires some experimentation.

HARVEY SADOW
Chesapeake Veneer Series #21, 1982
12 x 11 x 11 inches (30.5 x 27.9 x 27.9 cm)
Wheel thrown Laguna Rod's Bod; brushed, sprayed and dipped glaze; carved, sandblasted, chiseled; raku fired in gas kiln; controlled cooling, smoking for reduction, multi fired
Photo by artist

The first time I heard the term "reduction" was when my college pottery teacher asked me to check on the progress of the reduction in a kiln. As a first-year student, I'd never been asked before, so I was full of pride. I happily drove the mile to the kiln shed, only to realize once I got there that I didn't have the foggiest idea of what I was supposed to be looking for. A shrinking kiln? Did kilns reduce in size during the firing? Luckily, some advanced students were at the kiln site, so I was able to fake my way through. But you can be sure that I went back to the library that night and looked up every reference to reduction firing I could find.

Multi-Firing

Firing your ware two, three, four, or more times produces colors and textures unobtainable in any other way. You may fire pieces with or without additional glaze applications between firings. You can fire successively—that is, remove ware from the kiln, manipulate it through a post-firing phase or reglaze it, and immediately refire it—or cool and fire it the next day. Physically altering the surfaces between firings by sandblasting, grinding, or filing them is also possible, as is varying the temperature of each firing. For example, you can fire at progressively lower temperatures so that the glaze melt of the previous firing isn't unduly affected. The finished surfaces can display extraordinary depth and fascinating textures.

Because raku ware is fragile, to avoid breakage, you must take extreme care when you fire the same piece multiple times. For successive firings, make sure you preheat the piece and allow your kiln to cool before firing the piece again. Avoid complacency if you're firing a cold pot from a cold kiln: fire slowly and patiently.

Salt and Soda Firing

Salt (and *soda*) *firing* is a form of *vapor glazing*—a process during which vapor within the kiln creates a glaze on the ware. Developed in Germany as early as the fourteenth century, salt firing was widespread by the mid-1500s. Salt-glazed crocks, jugs, mugs, and other wares appeared in the United States by the 1730s, were common by the mid-eighteenth century, and were still in wide production well into the early twentieth century.

A true salt glazing requires that a clay body be mature when you introduce the salt (in one of various forms) into the

Because successful raku firing depends on a clay body that is porous and highly refractory throughout the firing, clay maturity is rarely reached, so actual salt glazing seldom takes place. However, salts do react with glazes, engobes, and clay regardless of the maturity of the clay body.

kiln. As the salt volatilizes, sodium oxide combines with the silica and alumina in the clay to form a glaze. Because successful raku firing depends on a clay body that is porous and highly refractory throughout the firing, clay maturity is rarely reached, so actual salt glazing seldom takes place. Salts do, however, react with glazes, engobes, and clay regardless of the maturity of the clay body. Any firing in which you introduce salt, whether the end result is a glaze or some other effect caused by the salting process, is naturally attractive to many raku potters precisely because it works at low temperatures. You can carry out successful salt firing at any temperature above 1472°F (800°C)—the melting point of the salt.

A word of caution: Salt in a firing creates two dangerous by-products: hydrochloric acid and chlorine gas. In order to avoid exposure to these, potters now use salt substitutes, most notably soda (sodium oxide) in the form of sodium carbonate, commonly known as *soda ash*. In the descriptions that follow, my use of the word "salt" refers to both salt and soda.

Raku salt firing can affect your ware in many different ways. Salt introduced into the kiln creates an intense reduction atmosphere immediately, which—as with any reduction atmosphere—causes glazes that contain copper to turn red. The depth of the red depends on the glaze and the degree of reduction. Salting tends to bring out subtle shades of blue as well. It can cause the surface of highly mature glazes to pit and take on delicate textures. And a salt vapor atmosphere tends to impart a silvery sheen to unglazed surfaces—one that acts as a resist to the effects of carbon during post-firing reduction.

Instead of soda ash, you may use noniodized table salt, rock salt, kosher salt, sea salt, or canning salt. Each has its own characteristics; the most important is the degree of coarseness. Coarse salts, such as rock salt, tend to pop and explode, sending dangerous projectiles out of the burner port, peepholes, and flue, so be careful. Table salt is fine grained and therefore volatilizes efficiently. Sea salt contains trace minerals that can add interesting effects.

Because clay maturity is a moot point in raku, potters typically begin salting just as their glazes are approaching maturity. The traditional method of adding salt to a firing is to shovel or scoop loose, dry salt through the opening above the burner port. A more controlled method is to fashion salt packets made of twisted newspaper or paper cups. For my 7-cubic-foot (198.2 cu. dm) kiln, I divide 2 cups (473 ml) of salt evenly among several packets. At the low temperatures of raku, I find that diluting the salt slightly by dipping a packet in water just before I insert it through the burner port aids the volatilization process (see photos 2 and 3). If you prefer, you may insert the packets through the flue or peepholes. After introducing the salt, I close the flue about halfway to allow for complete saturation of the atmosphere. Over the next 45 minutes to an hour, I repeat the process, keeping the flue closed halfway and opening it only to introduce more salt through it.

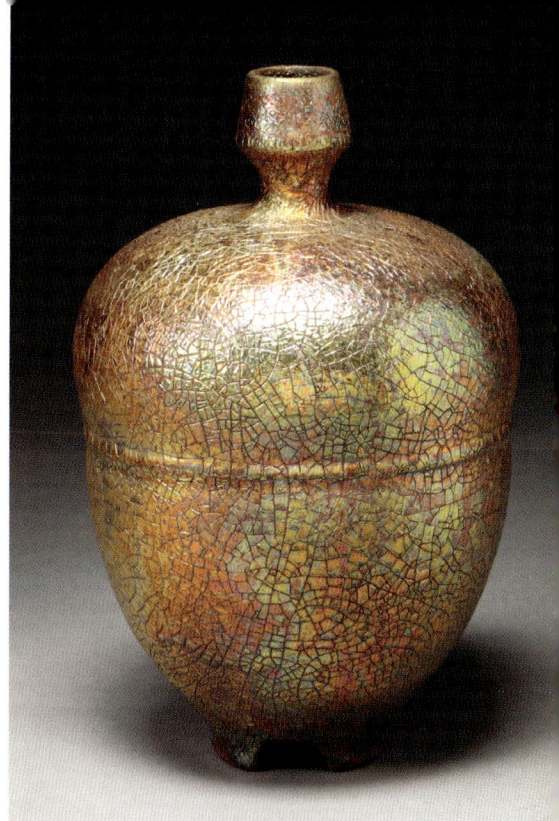

JAMES C. WATKINS
Bottle Form, 2007
15 x 8 inches (38.1 x 20.3 cm)
Wheel thrown personal clay;
brushed glaze; fuming; gas fired
Photo by Jon Thompson

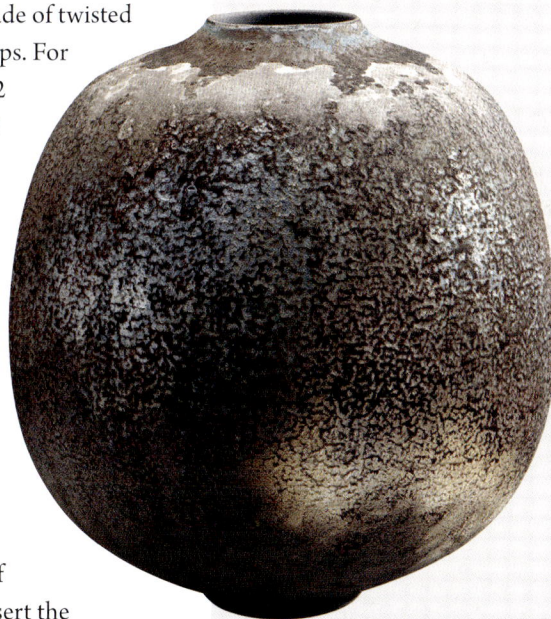

HARVEY SADOW
Tanja—Sacred Sites Australia, 1991
12 x 11 x 11 inches
(30.5 x 27.9 x 27.9 cm)
Wheel thrown Australian
Stoneware; brushed, sprayed,
and dipped glaze; sandblasted and
chiseled; gas fired; smoking for
reduction, controlled cooling
Photo by artist

119

KATHI TIGHE
Raku Bowl, 2006
10 x 10 x 3 inches
(25.4 x 25.4 x 7.6 cm)
Thrown and altered Deco
Porcelain with molochite and
kyanite; sprayed glaze; gas
fired; smoking for reduction;
cone 05
Photo by Monica Ripley

Other methods of introducing salt into the firing include soaking your pot in a saltwater solution before loading it in the kiln, wrapping salt-soaked rags around it, spraying it with a saltwater solution, sliding dry salt down an angle iron into the flue (see photo 4), and placing salt in your saggar if you're saggar firing (see page 135). If you're firing with wood, you can soak the wood in saltwater and allow it to dry out prior to firing. Variations on low-temperature salt and soda firing abound and are limited only by your imagination. Try a 50/50 mix of borax and salt (or soda). Borax, which acts as a low-temperature flux, aids in the development of a salt glaze even when the clay isn't mature. Some potters combine salt with oxides for different effects.

4

RAMON CAMARILLO II
Wailana, 2003
19 x 18½ x 18½ inches
(48.3 x 47 x 47 cm)
Wheel thrown Soldate 60; poured
glaze; raku fired; smoking for reduction;
fumed, then transferred
to reduction can with paper
Photo by Donelle Sawyer Camarillo

Fuming

Fuming—the application of vaporized metallic salts to the surface of the ware—is yet another technique the roots of which aren't in raku but that has been adapted to the American raku process. Related to salt firing and vapor glazing, fuming adds lustrous gold, silver, and mother-of-pearl effects to glazed surfaces. In addition to the metallic and soluble salts mentioned on page 119, cobalt nitrate, cupric chloride, chromium nitrate, silver chloride, and zinc oxide all work well.

You may apply the salts as washes or as components of glazes, but I'd like to describe two other fuming methods—ones that produce different, though not necessarily better, effects: fuming as a part of the firing process and (see page 126) as a post-firing process. No matter which method you choose, protect yourself from fumes by working only outdoors, and make sure you stand upwind. Wear a respirator and protect your eyes as well.

As a firing process, introduce the metallic salts into the kiln during the last stages of firing. Prepare a liquid solution by diluting a few crystals of the salt—approximately 5 grams (.2 ounces)—in 1 cup (236.6 ml) of hot water. Then, during the last stages of the firing, use a garden sprayer with a metal spray wand (you don't want to melt a plastic wand and tip) to spray the solution into the kiln through the flue or peepholes (see photo 5). Alternatively, slide the dry crystals down an angle iron and into the flue.

Creating a Copper Matte Effect

A *copper matte* surface is characterized by a rough to velvety texture and by multi-colored iridescence. Typical recipes are comprised of frit (10 percent) and copper carbonate (90 percent). The minimal fluxing action offered by the frit causes the glaze to fuse just enough to bond to the surface, which creates the rough texture. Potters occasionally add other oxides for enhanced color variations. For the most consistent results, mix the glaze to the consistency of milk and apply a very thin layer before firing. Spraying it on with an airbrush and compressor is the best application method, but in a pinch, a garden sprayer works. Copper matte recipes are provided on pages 169–170.

Recognizing the proper firing temperature is tricky because copper matte doesn't fuse and melt to a glossy state that's easy to discern. Furthermore, the maturity range of copper matte glazes is limited. For these reasons, using a handheld digital pyrometer here is worthwhile.

Using your regular schedule, fire to 1850°F (1010°C). Shut down the burner, and let the kiln cool to 1250°F (677°C). Relight the burner and fire in a reduction atmosphere to 1600°F (871°C). Move your pot to your reduction container, allow the combustible material to ignite, and cover the container as quickly as possible. Use a minimal amount of reduction material (a thin layer of sawdust or newspaper), and make sure the container lid fits well to ensure an airtight seal. After a 6- to 8-minute period of smoking (you'll have to experiment), open the container and observe the color that's developed on the pot's surface. A friend of mine aptly calls this stage "blooming." As the color blooms, freeze the effect by using a spray bottle to spray the surface with water.

A slight variation involves firing to 1800°F (982°C) and cooling to 1000°F (538°C). Fire back to 1400°F (760°C) in a reduction atmosphere. Carry out the same post-firing application I've just described, but lengthen the smoking period to 8 to 12 minutes. Uncover, observe, and cool with water as before. In both approaches, slow cooling in the reduction container is essential; the piece must still be hot when you uncover it. To ensure this, fashion an insulated reduction container (see page 127).

5

EDUARDO LAZO
Vapor Glazed Funerary Vessel, 2008
12 x 12 x 12 inches (30.5 x 30.5 x 30.5 cm)
Wheel thrown Soldate 60; stannous chloride and bismuth subnitrate fuming over base glaze; electric fired; no reduction air cooling
Photo by David Lazo

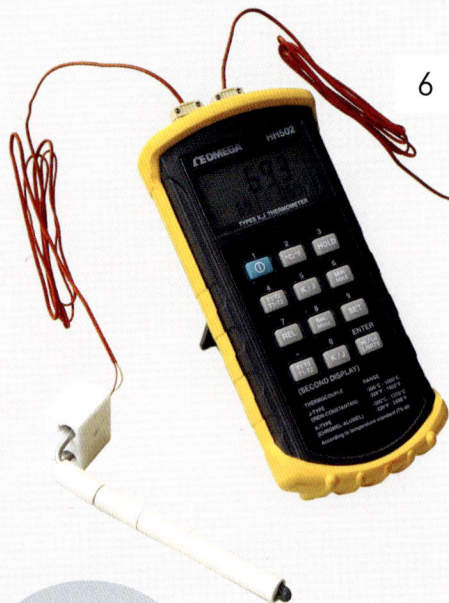

On occasion, determining the maturity of your wares by means of visual observation isn't practical or possible. A digital pyrometer, with a thermocouple inserted into the kiln and wired to the pyrometer, gives accurate temperature readouts. Both mountable and handheld units are available, and some handheld versions include dual thermocouples, allowing you to monitor two kilns at the same time (see photo 6). Stay away from inexpensive models, as their accuracy is questionable.

A less technical approach involves applying the glaze prior to bisque firing. The raku firing is carried out to red heat, with a 15- to 30-minute period of atmospheric reduction, and followed by the post-firing reduction phase. Some potters have found that multi-firing, with an additional glaze application before each firing, creates rich effects.

You can produce another variation of the copper matte effect by rubbing a thin iron-oxide wash or dry iron oxide onto the surface of the piece before firing. The iron acts as a resist to the carbon, resulting in an earthy surface reminiscent of reduction-fired stoneware clay or the familiar yellow blush often associated with copper matte. To achieve these results, partially reoxidize the piece after a 2- to 3-minute period of smoking by uncovering the container, adding more reduction material, and leaving the lid off.

Many different approaches to firing copper matte glazes are possible. Experiment and be patient, and you'll find the method that works best for you.

The Halo Technique

Paul Soldner developed this unique decorative effect during his early experiments with raku and the smoking phase. "Ghosting" as he calls it, or "halo," as it's now commonly known, is an example of carbon resist in which the very slight fluxing action of a material prevents post-firing carbon from being absorbed by the clay. In the case of the halo effect, the result is an easily distinguishable, although sometimes faint, white outline around the design.

PAUL SOLDNER
Untitled, 1990
15 inches (38.1 cm) tall
Hand built and wheel thrown stoneware;
brushed glaze; terra sigillata;
gas fired; ghosting
Photo by Armstrong's Gallery

Soldner's method starts with the application of a thick white slip to the bisque ware. Over the dry slip, he paints his designs with a thin, watercolor consistency 50/50 copper-iron wash and then fires the ware to approximately cone 010. Heavy post-firing smoking, followed by a brief but bright period of reoxidation (similar to the copper matte method), creates the halo effect. This post-firing technique is subtle and full of nuance, and you must manipulate the process to achieve the desired results. (See page 170 for a halo slip recipe.)

Alternating between smoking and oxidation during the post-firing phase can yield unusual results.

A variation is to substitute a commercial underglaze for the copper-iron wash. Adding a few grams of gerstley borate or borax to each 3-ounce (88.7 ml) bottle of underglaze causes just enough fluxing around the edges of the painted or slip-trailed design to resist the carbon smoking. Achieving the proper maturing temperature and degree of reduction takes some experimentation. Since the melting is so slight and difficult to observe, one way to determine the correct firing temperature is to include the piece in a load of your regularly glazed pots and use a pyrometer to monitor the temperature. Remove the piece when the rest of the load is mature, and assess the results. If the surface is too glossy, lower the temperature by the equivalent of one cone. If you'd like more melting, raise the temperature by one cone.

Post-Firing Variations

The main objectives of a typical post-firing reduction are matte black unglazed surfaces, metallic luster effects, or heavily crazed areas. I say "typical" not to malign those effects; there's much about them to keep a potter busy technically and creatively. Once you're able to achieve these effects, however, you may want to move on to more complex approaches: developing different glaze and surface effects, more sophisticated imagery, and the use of various reduction materials in order to control and shape the final results more carefully. Success in all these areas begins with your choice of glaze, slip, oxide, or other materials;

their correct application and utilization; and sufficient maturity in the kiln.

Manipulating and Controlling the Smoking Phase

If you're interested in the different kinds of results possible through manipulation of the smoking phase, from intense luster and black effects to white and grey surfaces, you must first understand the properties and characteristics of smoke and carbon and how to regulate them.

Depending on its surface treatment (slip, glaze, underglaze, oxide, or stain), fired ware reacts to the smoking of post-firing reduction in different ways; each treatment has its own degree of resistance to or acceptance of the carbon. The post-firing atmosphere that surrounds your piece is a critical element as well. Your container should have an airtight seal and should be large enough to hold your piece but small enough to leave the least possible amount of space around it. A container of the correct size gives you more control: you need less reduction material, and the less you use, the fewer uncontrolled moments of oxidation you'll face and the faster the atmospheric reactions will occur.

Alternating between smoking and oxidation during the post-firing phase can yield unusual results. Opening the reduction container for very short periods allows oxidation to take place. Lift the lid off carefully, and if flames aren't present,

PATTY WOUTERS
Circles and Lines, 2006
$9^{13}/_{16}$ x $19^{11}/_{16}$ x $235^{13}/_{16}$ inches
(25 x 50 x 600 cm)
Wheel thrown Limoges Porcelain and Southern Ice Porcelain; poured glaze; burnished, terra sigillata; bisque fired in electric kiln, saggar fired in gas kiln; controlled cooling, selective smoking for reduction
Photo by artist

fan the interior to produce them; the flames are what have the most impact. Allow them to lick up onto the pot for 5 to 10 seconds, then apply more material and quickly replace the lid.

Localized reduction, executed outdoors, is another way to vary the degree of oxidation and reduction. Hold the piece over a bed of material, and manipulate the material to cover only a portion of it (see photo 7).

Using Specific Reduction Materials

Wood is the most popular reduction material. In my experience, the kind of wood matters less than its form—fine sawdust, chips, or shavings, for example—but some potters swear by certain species. Experimenting with different kinds may prove fruitful.

Three major factors to consider when selecting a material are particle size (as in the case of sawdust); density (as in different thicknesses of cloth); and dryness. Dry material ignites quickly, burns hot, and results in the strongest reduction effects. Using damp material is an interesting approach; the water content causes a slower post-firing reaction and can produce softer-looking surfaces and glaze effects.

Reduction material that contacts the ware almost always leaves traces of some kind. If the glaze hasn't hardened sufficiently before it comes in contact with the material, physical impressions are left on the glazed surface. Glaze thickness is an important factor here; the thicker the glaze, the longer it takes to harden and the longer it's receptive to impressions. Coarse materials, such as wood shavings and especially straw, hay, seaweed, and the like, leave very obvious marks. These needn't be random; you can arrange your material in intentional patterns. The fact that different materials resist the smoke to different degrees also makes it possible to create intentional patterns on your piece.

On unglazed surfaces, the material can leave intense black, mottled effects or other telltale signs of contact. The *Leaf Vase* on the next page shows a piece created by placing the unglazed surface on a sprig of leaves. Smoke that penetrated where the leaves were thin left black areas; where the leaves were thick, the areas that were protected by them are white. Pine needles or woods with heavy resin contents leave surfaces with a slight sheen, almost as if you'd rubbed them with oil.

7

RAMON CAMARILLO II
Waipi'o Stream, 2006
9½ x 12 x 12 inches (24.1 x 30.5 x 30.5 cm)
Wheel thrown Soldate 60; poured and dipped glaze; raku fired; immediately transferred to reduction can with paper
Photo by Donelle Sawyer Camarillo

8

KAREN MAHONEY
Leaf Vase, 2008
10 x 5 x 5 inches
(25.4 x 12.7 x 12.7 cm)
Wheel thrown earthenware;
unglazed; light burnishing, carbon
resist; fired
in metal trash can;
smoking for reduction
Photo by Steven Branfman

To avoid the effects produced by contact with the reduction material, first place a layer of material in your container. On top of it, place a brick, and on top of the brick, place a sheet of newspaper. Arrange some more reduction around the edges of the newspaper—not in the area on top of the brick. When you place your piece, hot from the kiln, onto the covered brick, it will ignite the newspaper, which in turn will ignite the material—but only the unglazed foot of your piece will be in contact with the newspaper.

An oil-impregnated rag or a bed of oil-soaked material also offers interesting reduction effects (see photo 8). The oil causes intense local reduction that often results in strong metallic effects and a fine network of small crazing and crackles. Avoid using fresh, clean motor oil; it's too rich, and the oily residue that it almost always leaves on the ware is difficult to wash off. Used 20- or 30-weight motor oil works well and is available free from many service stations. Do exercise caution: oil ignites immediately and creates a lot of smoke.

The fact that different materials resist the smoke to different degrees also makes it possible to create intentional patterns on your piece.

9

Just as a piece that's fired too quickly will crack, so will a piece that's cooled too quickly. Being able to identify the point at which a piece cracks is a critical step toward correcting the problem in the future. If melted glaze has flowed into the crack, then you can be sure the piece cracked during the firing cycle. If the crack runs cleanly and sharply through the glazed surface, it probably developed during the cooling phase, after the glaze had hardened.

Fuming and Other Post-Firing Techniques

Placing salt, powdered oxides, and soluble salts in your reduction containers along with more conventional reduction materials is a technique that falls somewhere between fuming and vapor glazing on the one hand and saggar firing on the other. Upon ignition, these materials volatilize and effect changes in your glazes and surfaces.

Fuming as a post-firing method differs slightly from fuming in the atmosphere of the kiln. Put on your respirator, remove your piece from the kiln, place it on a noncombustible platform, and spray a solution of silver nitrate, stannous chloride, ferric chloride, or other metallic salt onto it (see photo 9). You may want to control the final outcome by using localized post-firing reduction and water-cooling techniques (see pages 111 and 124) as well.

Another way to fume begins with placing a hard firebrick in the kiln with your glazed or unglazed ware and firing the piece to maturity. After allowing the piece to cool to approximately 800°F (427°C), move it to your reduction container—or even better, to a sand pit—and position the brick next to it. Place the fuming salts on the brick, and immediately cover both the piece and the brick. The hot brick instantaneously volatilizes the salts and glazes the piece. After 5 minutes, open the lid to release the fumes, add some reduction material, replace the lid, and allow the piece to smoke. (For a selection of fuming recipes, see page 170.)

Using a propane torch as a post-firing tool is another way to alter a glazed surface. Either prior to or after the post-firing phase, use the torch as a paintbrush to manipulate the color. Hold the flame close to the surface, and as the color shifts, use a water spray to fix the effect. To avoid cracking the piece, if you do this after the post-firing phase, make sure it is still hot.

Controlling the Cooling

Controlled cooling of your ware prior to the reduction phase—either in the kiln after shutting off the gas or outside the kiln—influences both its appearance and the successful finish on it by hardening the glaze and making both glazed and unglazed areas less susceptible to the effects of post-firing carbon reaction and penetration. A single piece can show both reduction and oxidation effects. Experiment by allowing your piece to cool for a period of time before placing it in the reduction container. Reducing your piece in the open (see page 124) is a form of controlled cooling.

The aggressive application of water to your piece shows immediate and permanent results. To lessen or eliminate the metallic lusters while accentuating color and brilliance on some of my pieces, I remove my ware from the kiln with tongs, and while an assistant sprays it with water, I move it to control the direction of the spray (see photo 10).

10

When the glaze has cooled sufficiently, usually in 15 to 20 seconds, I place the piece in my reduction container to complete the process. Sometimes I dip either the whole piece or only a portion of it in water momentarily to affect the ensuing smoking (see photo 11). Spraying with water is also an excellent way to develop and intensify crackle effects; it cools the glaze just enough to increase contraction of the surface. Subsequent smoking exposes the effects nicely.

If your pots are plagued by cracking during the cooling phase, make an insulated container for cooling them. Place three bricks inside a large, lidded container, and set a smaller lidded container on the bricks. The air space between the two containers slows down the cooling inside the smaller one. For even slower cooling, fill the void between the containers with refractory fiber or unfaced fiberglass insulation.

Possible variations on post-firing reduction methods are many, limited only by your vision and your ability to identify the materials and conditions that may affect your ware in some way. The more experience you gain with documented techniques, the more knowledge you'll be able to apply to your own. As in any form of experimentation, limit the variables and stick to one change in one technique at a time so that you can track an effect, whether desirable or not, back to its cause.

11

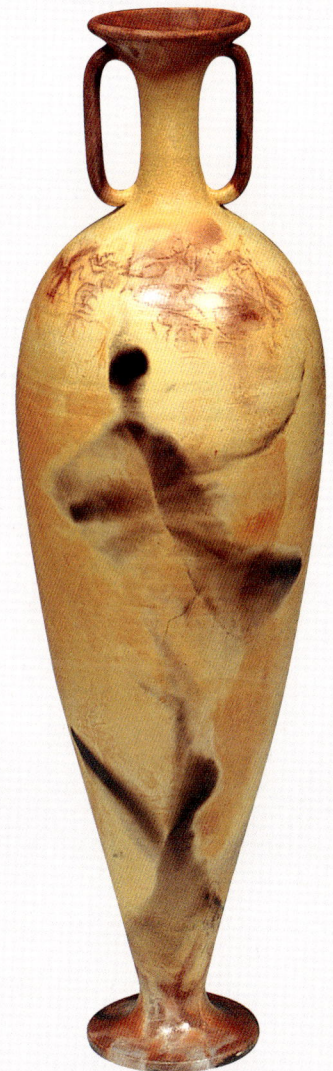

RAMON CAMARILLO II
Running Man, 2006
25 x 7 x 7 inches (63.5 x 17.8 x 17.8 cm)
Wheel thrown Soldate 60; brushed glaze; combustible material, foil wrap; raku fired
Photo by Greg Staley

related techniques for
Raku

Due to experimentation and advances in ceramic techniques, pottery processes not originally a part of traditional raku have become inextricably linked to it. Some, such as *slip resist* and *horsehair*, are now almost synonymous with the contemporary practice of raku. Others, including pit firing, smoke and sawdust firing, and saggar firing, are more remotely associated with it.

STEVEN BRANFMAN
Vessel, 2006
13½ x 9 inches (34.3 x 24.1 cm)
Brushed raku glaze; inlaid colored glass

Slip Resist (or Naked Raku)

Perhaps the first person to identify and develop this approach was Jerry Caplan, who called his technique "raku reduction stenciling." While experimenting with rust peelings that he'd applied to the surfaces of his plates prior to firing, Caplan discovered that although the peelings didn't fuse to the clay during firing, their aftereffects did mask the effects of carbonization during smoking. The slip resist technique (or *naked raku*, as it's more commonly known) that is common today entails applying a slip designed for wet ware onto a bisque-fired pot—a slip specifically designed to flake or peel away after firing rather than fusing onto the surface. (For naked raku slip and glaze recipes, see page 170.)

While the slip is wet, carve or draw a pattern through it with a needle or fine-pointed tool (see photo 1). (An aside here: the slip often curls away from the surface on its own, forming "islands" as it dries; you may not want to carve it at all.) Carefully, so as to not disturb the patterns, place the ware in the kiln and fire it to approximately 1700°F to 1800°F (927°C to 982°C). Equally carefully, remove the ware and place it faceup in your reduction container with your material of choice. The areas that remain slip-covered resist the smoking effects of the carbon.

CHARLES RIGGS
LINDA RIGGS
Golden Horsehair, 2008
11½ x 6 x 6 inches
(29.2 x 15.2 x 15.2 cm)
Wheel thrown stoneware; brushed terra sigillata, bisque fired, brushed with ferric chloride, fumed in aluminum foil saggar with sugar and horsehair; quick air cooling; 1100°C
Photo by Riana Riggs

1

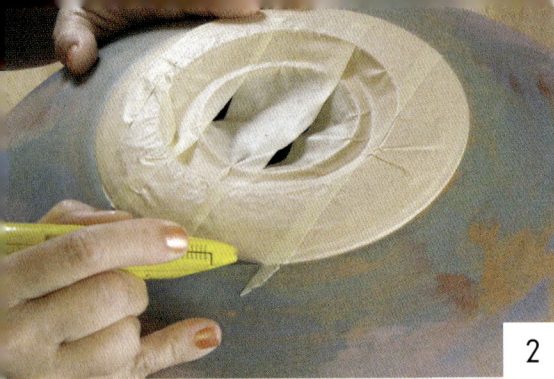

2

3

4

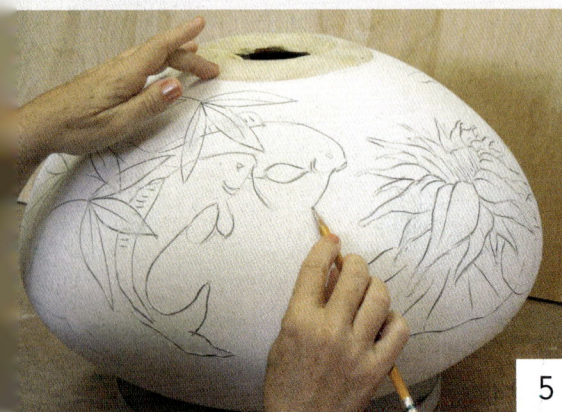

5

After about 10 minutes of cooling, take the ware from the container. Scrape and wash the surface to remove the slip. Don't worry about scratching the surface. This resist technique imparts a soft, quiet character to the piece, with white clay gradually giving way to grays and blacks, depending on the character of the original crawled-slip shapes or carved designs.

Many potters have added variations and nuances of their own to this technique. Burnishing the surface of the ware prior to bisque firing is now common practice; the polished surfaces accentuate the contrast between the smoked and non-smoked areas after post-firing. For even greater gloss and contrast, some potters apply a layer of terra sigilatta prior to burnishing. If color is an important aspect of your work, you may want to apply colored slips and commercial underglazes under the layer of resist slip.

Another way to vary the quality of the smoked pattern—a process known as *two-step naked raku*—is to incorporate a glaze on top of the resist slip, as

Kate Jacobson demonstrates in photos 2 through 10. After applying color (if desired) to the bisqued ware, if you'd like any areas of it to remain unaffected by the slip/glaze combination that you're about to create, use tape or liquid latex to mask them (see photo 2). Apply the slip resist on top of the color by dipping, pouring, or brushing (see photo 3). Its thickness and your application method depend on the fit between your clay body and the slip—and your own experiments with this technique. Next, apply a thin coating of clear glaze, again by pouring, brushing, or dipping (see photo 4). After the glaze has dried, create your designs (see photo 5) and carve them through the clear glaze/slip layer.

Fire the piece *only* until the glaze begins to melt and the surface looks uniformly rough—a bit like an orange peel (see photo 6). If you've mastered basic raku firing , you'll be able to recognize this stage of glaze melt. Uniform melting is important in this technique, so don't hesitate to rotate your pot during firing. Then carry out your post-firing phase according to your own style.

6

7

8

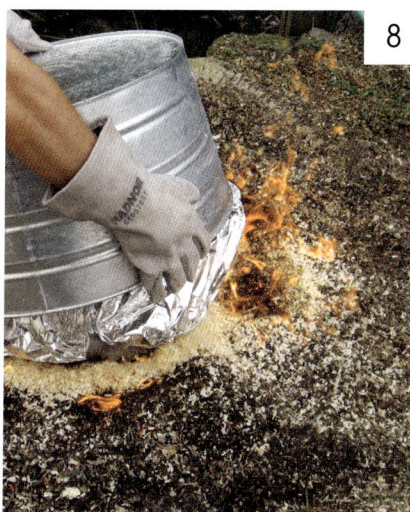

In this example, the piece was placed on a bed of reduction material, with additional material sprinkled over it (see photo 7). To protect the piece from any residue that might be in the reduction container, metal foil was placed over it before sealing it in (see photo 8).

After cooling the piece for about 10 minutes, spray it with water to release the glaze/slip layer (see photo 9). Scrape off any remaining slip with a knife or metal rib (see photo 10). The finished piece is shown below.

One tricky aspect of the naked raku technique is controlling the extent to which the slip adheres to the clay. Rough, textured, or porous clay surfaces tend to absorb the slip and make it difficult to remove. The thickness of the slip (typically ranging from milky to sludge-like) and the application method also affect the ease with which it comes off after firing. A firing temperature that's too high not only contributes to slip adherence but also causes the clear glaze to melt through the slip and onto the pot. Slip comes off tight, smooth, and burnished surfaces easily, but if the surface is too smooth, the slip may flake and peel away during the drying and firing. Follow the instructions that accompany the slip recipe, or experiment to find the correct approach. Make sure you scrape away any remaining slip before the pot cools to the touch.

9

10

KATE JACOBSON
WILL JACOBSON
Auntie's Garden, 2008
14 x 11 x 11 inches (35.6 x 27.9 x 27.9 cm)
Press molded, hand built and wheel thrown Laguna Clay, Amador; brushed and poured glaze; carved, paint/non-ceramic/non-fired, burnish porcelain slips; gas fired; smoking for reduction, sacrificial glaze, naked raku
Photo by artist

Resist Variations

Candy (or *sugar*) raku is another variation of the naked raku method. Adding sugar to the slip recipe causes carbonization to take place during the firing and alters the smoked crackle characteristics. (See page 170 for a recipe.) Mix only as much of the sugar/slip combination as you plan to use, and discard the rest, as it quickly turns rancid.

Another type of resist technique is something I call *shard resist*. Place your work in a bisque-fired plate, dish, or shallow bowl, and arrange a variety of shards (clay, brick, metal, etc.) around and on the work (see photo 11). After firing, remove the entire assembly intact from the kiln, and without disturbing the shards, place it in a reduction container. The shards offer a degree of resist to the smoking, resulting in variegated surfaces.

Horsehair Raku

In a quest to find new and exciting variations of established techniques, potters often make use of unusual materials. Such is the case with horsehair raku. In this post-firing process, strands of horsehair are applied to the surface of a hot pot; as they burn, they leave smoked trails. Horsehair is preferable to other types of hair because it's thicker. You may also use feathers. Although they're thin, they produce beautiful patterns if you apply them at the right stage of cooling. You may also sprinkle sawdust on the surface.

Begin by preparing a platform for the fired, still-hot pot with which you'll be working. Top the platform with refractory fiber, and locate it out of the wind. (The fiber pad keeps the pot hot and prevents marring of its bottom.) Next, fire your pot to approximately 1200°F to 1500°F (649°C to 816°C) or just until the kiln chamber begins to show color. Wearing gloves and using clean refractory fiber as potholders, move the pot from the kiln to the platform (see photo 12). Apply the horsehair (as Edge Barnes does in photo 13) by placing it carefully on the surface to "paint" lines, shapes, and patterns.

If the horsehair burns away without leaving a mark, the piece is too hot; wait a few seconds and try again. If carbonization appears in unwanted areas or is too

**CHARLES RIGGS
LINDA RIGGS**
Naked Raku Vase, 2008
8 x 5½ x 5½ inches (20.3 x 14 x 14 cm)
Wheel thrown stoneware; brushed terra sigillata, polished, bisque fired, cone 08; sgraffito, poured slip, brushed peel-off glaze; quick water and air cooling
Photo by Riana Riggs

13

14

dark, use a propane torch to reoxidize the surface. You can also use the torch to heat up any area that has cooled too much to carbonize the horsehair. When the piece is cool, wipe it with a clean cloth and polish it with any paste wax.

Pit Firing

Pit firing or *bonfire firing,* which was the first form of "kiln" firing, has its roots in ancient cultures, when ware was simply placed in an open fire. In its more refined state, it's a carefully controlled process. The pit, with its methodically stacked ware and fuel, can easily reach bisque temperatures and higher. Although pit firing is unrelated historically or technically to the raku technique, its open-air quality, exposure of the ware to combustibles, and resulting random patterns and textures have attracted raku potters to it. Contemporary variations include the use of slips, glazes, salts, and oxides on the pots and in the atmosphere.

In the example shown at right, Charlie Riggs dug a pit 12 inches (30.5 cm) deep and large enough to accommodate his bisqued pots, then filled the bottom with 6 inches (15.2 cm) of coarse sawdust. Next, he covered the sawdust with thin wood strips and added another layer of sawdust on top (see photo 14). After arranging his ware on top, he sprinkled copper sulfate, oxides, salt, steel wool, copper wire, and other materials on and around the pots for color and mottled effects (see photo 15).

15

EDGE BARNES
Horsehair Fired Vase, 2001
7 x 7½ inches (17.8 x 19 cm)
Wheel thrown personal clay; burnished; selective carbon markings with hair and feathers; polished paste wax finish
Photo by Nicki Pardo

16

Then Riggs stacked more strips of wood to a height of approximately 4 feet (121.9 cm), arranging them in a loose crisscross pattern. Using newspaper and kindling, he started the fire in several places (see photo 16). After it had burned down to ash and when everything was cool to the touch, he removed the ware. The finished pots are shown above.

17

Renowned potter Maria Martinez practiced a variation of pit firing by stacking her slip-decorated pots on raised iron grates. She placed wood under the grates and used sheet metal scraps to form a protective shell around the pots (see photo 17). To complete her "kiln," she stacked dried cow-dung chips (the primary fuel) around and over the pots (see photo 18). After firing, she smothered the ware with finely ground dung and sawdust, creating a carbon-filled reduction atmosphere not unlike that of the post-firing reduction atmosphere of raku.

18

Sawdust (or Smoke) Firing

Often confused with raku firing, this modern innovation is based on pit or primitive firing. The ware is completely surrounded by and filled with the fuel, and firing is carried out in a simple structure designed to contain the work and the heat. The sawdust burns without flames, creating a hot reducing atmosphere well below that needed to fuse even the simplest of glazes. A firing of this type may take anywhere from a few hours to a few days, depending on the size of the kiln, the ware, the wind conditions, and the type of sawdust used. After you've ignited the sawdust, you shouldn't disturb the firing or remove the ware until all smoldering and smoking has subsided.

To fashion a sawdust kiln from a metal trash can, drill or poke holes approximately 1 to 2 inches (2.5 to 5.1 cm) in diameter around its bottom and top circumferences and randomly all around its wall. The holes ensure enough air infiltration to keep the fuel burning. Then place a 5-inch (12.7 cm) layer of medium to coarse sawdust in the bottom. (Note: sawdust that's too fine may not burn.)

Place your largest and heaviest ware on this layer; then surround and fill the pots completely with sawdust. Continue to "stack" the ware by adding two or three alternating layers, first of sawdust and then of sawdust-surrounded and filled pots.

As the sawdust burns down, the pots settle onto one another, so be careful not to load the kiln with too much ware. To assist in stacking and to protect the ware, some potters place chicken wire or hardware cloth between the layers of pots or fashion a chicken-wire container for each pot. Top off the container with some crumpled newspaper, light it, and cover the barrel as soon as the sawdust ignites. It shouldn't produce visible flames; it should only smolder. You'll need to experiment in order to arrive at just the right amount of air flow through the holes in the can; use refractory fiber to plug any that seem unnecessary.

A sawdust kiln fashioned with common red brick or IFB, similar to the kiln described on pages 71–77, is easy to make. Load your pots as you build up the kiln, leaving some gaps between bricks and including removable bricks on each side of the kiln to allow for air flow (see photo 19). If flames develop during the firing, plug up some of the spaces. Top off the kiln with a trash-can lid, kiln shelves, or any other suitable material you have on hand.

Following a sawdust firing with a raku firing can offer interesting results. After sawdust firing, apply a clear raku glaze to the carbon-patterned pots. A moderate reducing atmosphere during the ensuing raku firing allows the subtle carbon shadows of the sawdust firing to remain intact under the glaze.

Saggar Firing

Saggar firing developed as a method of isolating ware from the potentially negative results of contact with either the fuel or the flames in a kiln. What has attracted raku potters to this type of firing is its capacity to produce intense atmospheric conditions.

Load your glazed or unglazed ware into a handmade saggar (see page 86) or a commercially available container such as a red clay flowerpot, and surround it with a variety of combustibles, oxides, salts, and/or other materials (see photo 20). Place the saggar in your raku kiln, and fire. The rest is up to you. When you think the kiln has reached sufficient temperatures, open it and the saggar, reach in, remove your pot, and commence with the post-firing phase. Alternatively, shut off the kiln, and allow the saggar and enclosed pots to cool inside it, omitting the post-firing phase.

19

20

Constructing a temporary saggar inside your kiln is another approach. Use bricks to build the saggar around your ware as you load it (see photo 21). Fill the saggar with combustibles (see photo 22), and top it with kiln shelves. You can stack additional ware on top (see photo 23). When using a saggar, expect the temperature inside it to be one to two cones below the temperature in the kiln chamber.

A creative variation on the saggar theme is wrapping your ware and combustible material in high-temperature foil, just as you'd wrap a piece of herbed fish for the grill. The foil encases both the pot and the atmosphere around it. After firing, let the piece cool before unwrapping it. Household aluminum foil isn't suitable; the temperatures reached in the kiln quickly turn it to ash. The thicker foil available from commercial restaurant suppliers and the high-temperature foil available from metal suppliers work well.

Are there other related techniques that may offer alternate paths for the raku potter? Can methods and procedures thought to be reserved for a singular pottery process be extended and incorporated into the raku technique? Of course! Imagination and bold experimentation are the keys to innovation and progress.

finishing your
Ware

CHAPTER 10

You've fired and cooled your piece after the post-firing— and it's beautiful. Is it finished? Not quite. You'll need to clean it, and you may want to alter its surface as well. And, of course, if it emerged from the kiln in two pieces, you'll want to repair it.

STEVEN BRANFMAN
Vessel, 2003
14¹/₂ x 10 inches (36.8 x 25.4 cm)
Brushed glaze; impressed texture

RONDA M. LISKEY
Paradise—It's All It's Cracked Up to Be!, 2000
4 x 15 inches (10.2 x 38.1 cm)
Wheel thrown and altered raku clay; brushed
glaze; overglaze luster; propane gas fired;
smoking for reduction
Photo by Raymond Kopen

Cleaning the Ware

The raku process, particularly the post-firing reduction phase, almost always leaves behind a layer of carbon, ash, and other kinds of "dirt." Sometimes, this contamination takes the form of a lustrous sheen on the glazed surface, one that's difficult to distinguish from the luster effects of copper and other metals. The former, which may appear as a shiny, silver coating, consists of a layer of carbon and soot and becomes evident as you wash it off. Your reduction material and the residue on the wall of your reduction container may produce other types of contamination. Whether or not you can see the muck and grime on your pot, assume it's there and proceed to the cleaning phase.

Unglazed work or areas of work are less affected than glazed areas; cleaning them is necessary, but doesn't have to be aggressive. Rinsing them with water and wiping them with a clean soft rag or towel are usually sufficient.

Glazed surfaces must be cleaned vigorously—but carefully; raku is fragile.

A stiff-bristled nailbrush (or for small pieces and crevices, a toothbrush) is the best tool to use. Green abrasive cleaning pads, steel wool, soap-impregnated steel scrubbing pads, and even fine sandpaper all work well. Unless your glaze is exceedingly soft and fragile, you needn't worry about scratching it.

A powdered or liquid abrasive cleanser is an absolute necessity. Look for one that doesn't advertise its gentleness; you want the hard abrasive quality! Test the cleansers on the market and choose the one that works best for you, or make your own by combining whiting (calcium carbonate), fine grog, and liquid dish soap or an industrial-strength liquid cleaner.

Wet the piece with hot water, apply liberal amounts of cleanser, and scrub well (see photo 1). As you remove the sheen, you'll expose the true colors of your work; they'll be especially noticeable on white and light-colored surfaces. Rinse thoroughly, making sure to remove any residue left by the cleanser on any unglazed surfaces.

1

A propane torch, used immediately after the post-firing, while the ware is still hot, is effective for cleaning off the carbonaceous material left over after smoking. Hold the flame 1 to 2 inches (2.5 to 5.1 cm) from the pot, and turn the pot as the carbon is oxidized away (see photo 2). You'll see the glaze brighten right before your eyes. Be careful to keep the flame moving so that you don't overheat any areas. If you'd like to use a torch after your pot has already cooled, heat the pot gradually to avoid cracking it, popping off a piece of glaze, or both.

Enhancing and Altering Surfaces

As a result of its functional and utilitarian origins, pottery has long been an art and craft form that's stayed faithful to the natural effects of the firing process on the materials. When contemporary potters make functional ware, this remains true. As pottery began to move from the production of strictly utilitarian ware toward nonfunctional decorative art, however, potters began to take creative liberties, including the use of non-ceramic materials and processes.

In this regard, today's potters push the creative envelope after firing and post-firing. Despite our intellectual acceptance of these practices, as soon as an artist plays around with paints, inks, glues, and other non-ceramic or refractory materials and processes, we question the integrity and honesty of the piece and challenge the artist's sincerity. We're still mired in clay! A piece needn't be 100 percent ceramic to qualify as pottery.

Clearly, non-ceramic applications have taken root and are no longer viewed as corrupt.

It's always tempting to accentuate crackle and crazed effects or the degree of blackness on unglazed surfaces. A historical precedent for this practice was set in Asia, where tea was used to enhance the crackle effects on celadon wares. You can do the same by applying ink, shoe polish, hobby paint, or acrylic-based paint specifically designed for use on ceramic surfaces. Coat the surface, allow the material to be absorbed for a minute or two, and then wash off the rest. You may have to do this several times to arrive at your desired result. Do I advocate this approach? Let your own conscience be your guide.

Even further removed from ceramic finishes are paints, stains, melted metals, and other art materials applied to the surfaces of your pots as supplementary—or even primary—decorative elements. Contemporary clay artists have blurred the line when it comes to design and decoration. Many are working in mixed media, combining disparate materials in creative ways to arrive at personal expressions.

2

RONDA M. LISKEY
Sunflower Jar, 2007
6½ x 14 inches (16.5 x 35.6 cm)
Wheel thrown raku clay; brushed glaze;
overglaze luster; propane gas fired;
smoking for reduction
Photo by Raymond Kopen

Waterproofing and Protecting Surfaces

You can't make raku ware and crackle glazes entirely waterproof. In an effort to seal the inner surfaces of ware intended for use as planters and vases, some potters apply sealers made for concrete, stone, and tile work—urethane; tung oil; grout sealer; and a variety of other coatings, including products now marketed specifically for this purpose. From my point of view, attempting to transform an object into something that it isn't is an effort in futility. I treat my work as decorative and advise my customers to put plastic or glass liners in their pots if they want to use them for flowers or plants. Regardless, never use raku ware to hold food or drink.

Paste wax works well to protect soft, unglazed, burnished surfaces that are easily marred by fingerprints and rough handling. Using a soft cloth or wax applicator, apply a coat, and buff it in to seal the surface. Apply a second coat, let it dry, and buff it vigorously with a cloth to a high gloss.

To protect lusters from the tendency to fade over time (see page 42), one approach is to coat the glazed surface with a plastic-based fixative spray (usually acrylic, sometimes urethane) or a brushed solution, and then keep the ware away from the elements. Expect a slight yellowing of the coating to develop over time. Here's a curious approach to glaze protection I picked up (although I haven't tried it, others have reported mixed results): Mix 3 teaspoons (15 ml) of medical-grade sodium silicate with 1.1 quarts (1 L) of water. Spray this solution onto your ware with a standard plastic spray bottle, and heat the pot in a 100°F (38°C) oven for 45 minutes.

DANIEL ACHERMANN
Untitled
13³/₈ x 8¹/₄ x 4¹¹/₁₆ inches
(34 x 21 x 12 cm)
Wheel thrown Potclays
T-Material 1161Y; dipped glaze;
oxide sprayed; gas fired; select
smoking for reduction
Photo by artist

JIM CONNELL
Red Carved Lidded Jar, 2001
15 x 15 x 15 inches (38.1 x 38.1 x 38.1 cm)
Thrown, carved, and altered Highwater
Raku; sprayed glaze; carved; electric fired;
smoking for reduction
Photo by artist

Mending Broken Ware

A pot emerges from the reduction container in two pieces, or a section of its rim has broken off. Suddenly the devious thought of gluing the pieces back together enters your mind. Quickly, you seek out counseling for your affliction. Well, go ahead and glue the thing back together! Legitimate precedents exist; historically, cracks in pottery were filled with melted gold and silver. Although I usually discard broken pots, I'll admit that I've successfully mended one or two. But how to make the repair is the question.

Professional restoration is one possibility (specialists now work in most large cities and even in many small ones), but it's expensive and is generally worthwhile only for very valuable items. Restoration classes and workshops are offered occasionally, but many specialists tend to be rather secretive about their methods.

Mending a broken piece involves two steps: gluing the pieces back together, and restoring the color and/or surface design. With so many glues on the mar-

ket, the choices can be bewildering. Stay away from instant, "five-minute-setting," or flexible glues; they're not strong enough or permanent. Instead, choose an industrial strength, heavy-duty paste epoxy that comes in two parts. The one I use sets slowly enough to allow me time to work, yet hardens quickly and, unlike many epoxies, can be filed and sanded when dry.

Mix the adhesive according to the manufacturer's instructions (see photo 3). Then apply it sparingly toward the inside edges of the pieces (make sure they're clean and dry) so that large gobs of it don't ooze out onto the exterior surface and mar your work (see photo 4). Press the pieces together, clean away as much excess epoxy as possible, and apply masking tape or gummed paper tape to hold the pieces in place while the epoxy hardens (see photo 5). Epoxy may also be used as a filler. Build it up in thin layers, allowing each layer to harden before applying the next. To color the repaired areas, apply acrylic paints or any paint or stain designed for unfired ceramic surfaces.

teaching
Raku

Some of the best raku teachers have only limited exhibition and production histories, while potters who've achieved great stature in the raku field can fail completely to light students' fires. Fame isn't what makes a good teacher. What does is a thorough understanding of all phases of raku and the ability to solve problems on the spot. Whether you want to teach raku as a technique in and of itself or use it as a vehicle for introducing students to pottery or crafts in general—whether in an elementary school classroom, high-school ceramics studio, adult education class, or raku workshop—you must be well-versed in raku and have the confidence and ability to share what you know.

STEVEN BRANFMAN
Vessel, 2007
14 x 8 inches (35.6 x 20.3 cm)
Dipped and rushed multi layered
commercial low fire glaze;
pressed surface texture

Teaching Raku in Schools

Is raku firing too dangerous for elementary or middle school students? Are young children capable of grasping the necessary concepts, participating in the physical aspects of raku, and being inspired? In our classes at The Potters Shop and School, we routinely did raku firings with five- and six-year-old students. Many schools today are introducing children from kindergarten to high school age to pottery through a hands-on experience with the raku technique.

Raku is an effective way to introduce students to pottery in general: the excitement, speed, and unusual nature of the process motivate them, eliciting their attentiveness and involvement. But raku in the classroom shouldn't take on an instant-gratification, circus-like atmosphere. To oversimplify or trivialize a craft technique of such historical and cultural significance does a disservice to it and to potters who engage in it respectfully and in earnest.

When raku is taught seriously, with a respect for its origins and history, it *is* appropriate for any school situation, and as a teaching tool, it offers advantages that other ceramic techniques don't. As students view the pots in the kiln and remove them red-hot from the chamber, the relationship between clay and fire is made very obvious. Glazes and fix how they mature—from sintering through smoothing out—are brought to life visually. And the short time span from completing the clay work to glazed and fired pots makes offering students a comprehension of a complete pottery process relatively easy. In these respects, raku becomes more than an individual pottery process; it becomes a gateway to pottery making as a whole.

Assuming that your school doesn't already offer a raku class, your first hurdle is justifying teaching one to the person whose permission you'll need to create flames and smoke. This can be done! When I started teaching in public high school, I raku fired in an electric kiln located in a cramped office/storeroom, lifted the hot pot with tongs, climbed out a window, and placed the pot in a barrel that the students had thrown sawdust in and would then cover. The barrel was in a concrete, recessed window well that measured only 5 x 15 feet (1.5 to 4.6 m). The space was also below ground level, so smoke would routinely escape into the classrooms above. Not the safest or most tranquil of raku environments—but the principal agreed that the class had educational value.

As a teacher, I've always had difficulty justifying the case for deliberately subjecting students to making common mistakes, all in the name of learning. That's not to say that students should be protected from making them. Failure—or lack of immediate success—can certainly be a strong impetus for learning. But one of the joys of teaching is helping your students avoid obvious pitfalls.

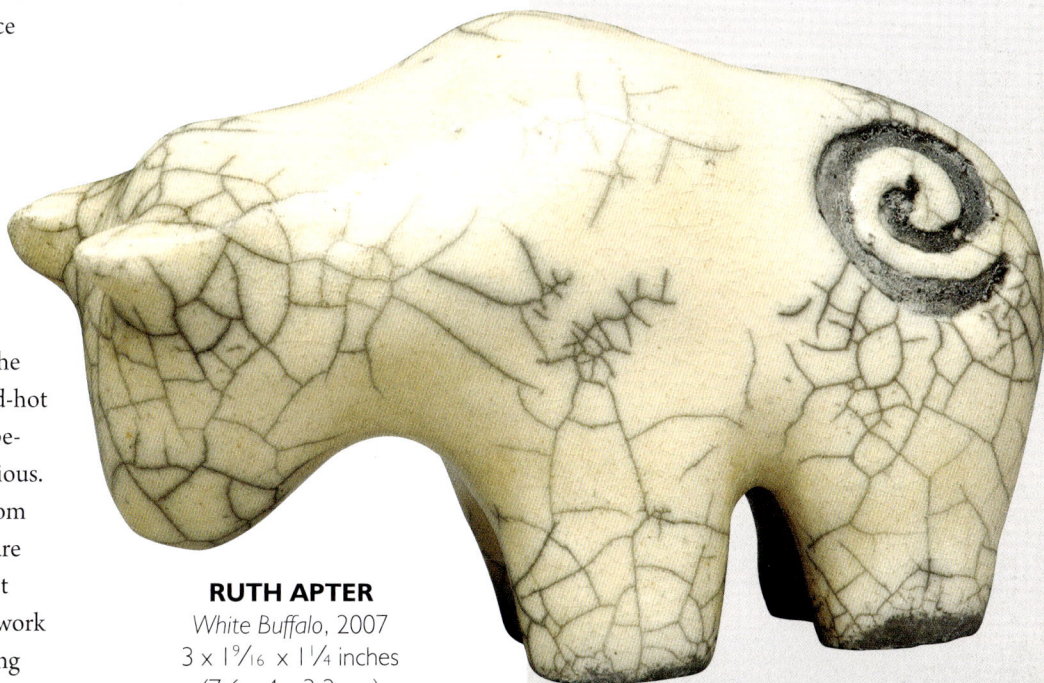

RUTH APTER
White Buffalo, 2007
3 x 1⁹⁄₁₆ x 1¹⁄₄ inches
(7.6 x 4 x 3.2 cm)
Press molded and hand built Laguna WSO; brushed glaze; stamped, underglaze brushwork; electric fired; smoking for reduction
Photo by Frank Ross

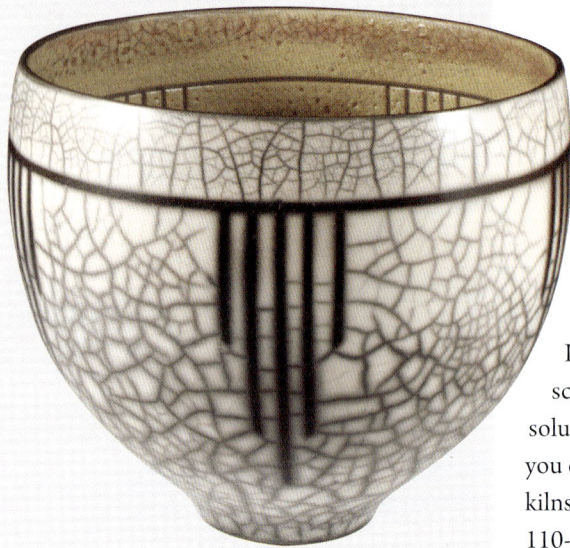

CATHERINE WEIR
Shadow Crackle Bowl, 2008
6 x 6½ inches (15.2 x 16.5 cm)
Wheel thrown Sheba raku;
brushed and poured glaze; tape
resist; raku fired in propane kiln;
controlled cooling, smoking
for reduction; cone 08
Photo by Christie Gruppe

The next hurdle, of course, is setting up a safe working environment. A raku kiln isn't a prerequisite (an electric kiln will do), but you may have to overcome some serious logistical concerns anyway. If a firing area similar to the one described on page 24 isn't available, one solution is to place the kiln on a cart that you can wheel outdoors. Small electric kilns that run off a standard household 110-volt, 15-amp circuit can be used anywhere electric outlets are available. Of course, using an electric kiln isn't as exciting or hands-on as using a gas kiln, but beggars can't be choosers. Take whatever your school supervisors give you and run with it.

The following paragraphs are descriptions of a few of the special aspects of teaching raku to youngsters that you should consider. You'll undoubtedly encounter others, too, depending on your own circumstances.

Explain the firing process first so that students know exactly what to expect, and choreograph the whole event in advance (see photo 1). Assign each student a particular task, and limit his or her movements to a small, well-defined area. Students who will lift pots out of the kiln *must* know where they'll need to take them.

Chances are you'll have more students than available tasks, so divide them into teams, and let each team participate in a firing while other teams wait for subsequent loads. As a general rule, the younger the children, the fewer should take part at one time. No more than two children (or people of any age for that matter) should remove pots from any single kiln load. If during a firing, you've assigned students to tasks such as glazing and washing, locate areas for those tasks at a safe distance from the firing area.

Assign each student a particular task, and limit his or her movements to a small, well-defined area. Students who will lift pots out of the kiln must know where they'll need to take them.

1

Safety is a primary concern, especially with younger students. Don't ask a child to lift a pot and carry it to a container that's on the other side of the kiln; place all reduction containers in closer, safe spots. As the leader and director of a firing, you won't be able to keep an eye on every child, so assign this monitoring to another adult—one to whom you've already explained the process.

Schedule enough time for the students to experience the entire process without their having to rush off to the next class. A well-designed conclusion to each session is important for the students' understanding and appreciation of the technique, process, and results (see photo 2). This may entail a special after-school time slot.

Once you've taken your students beyond the preliminaries, place the raku technique in the context of other pottery processes so they'll realize that raku isn't the only form pottery takes. Don't let raku—or any one approach—run your program. The appeal of raku's spontaneity, ease, and visual results often comes at the expense of an open attitude toward other firing methods. Stress to students that raku is just one of many pottery processes worth experiencing and exploring. Explain that the knowledge and experience of other pottery processes can make raku itself even more creative. Getting this across to your students may be difficult; they tend to become addicted to raku!

Giving Workshops and Demonstrations

In a workshop forum, you don't have the luxury of the classroom teacher who meets with students regularly and who therefore has an opportunity to understand their perceptions, intentions, and learning styles. You can't reiterate points, elaborate on particular details, or correct mistakes that attendees may make. You have only one chance to present yourself and your knowledge, and the information you provide is the information that people will remember and use when you're no longer present.

A well-planned, successful workshop or demonstration revolves around fulfilling the needs and expectations of the participants; it doesn't have to traverse the subject of raku from cover to cover. You're more likely to do a thorough job, please the participants, meet attainable goals for yourself, and be able to measure your success if you restrict your presentation to one or two limited areas, such as the firing process, glazing techniques, kiln building, or traditional raku. To help you plan well, find out if the participants will be experienced potters, whether

ANDREAS RUHRNSCHOPF
Windeye, 2008
78³⁄₄ x 23⁵⁄₈ inches (2 m x 60 cm)
Hand built Witgert 2sg; sprayed glaze; wood fired; quick cooling, selective smoking for reduction; 1100°C
Photo by artist

2

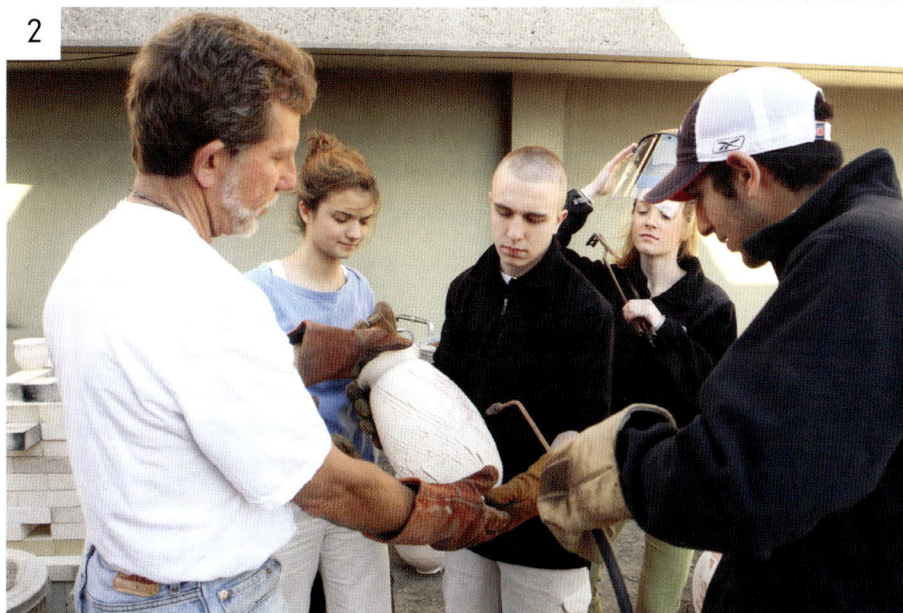

145

DORIS BOSCHUNG-JOHNER
people on the edge, 2008
17^{11}/$_{16}$ x 37^3/$_8$ x 6^{11}/$_{16}$ inches
(45 x 95 x 17 cm)
Pressed stoneware; brushed glaze;
wood fired; controlled cooling
Photo by Josef Kollar

they've done raku before, and what they expect to learn.

Make sure you communicate the workshop contents to participants in advance. Set some educational goals, but be prepared to shift your focus with the participants' leanings. Prepare all necessary materials and props; you should never find yourself running out of gas or reduction containers, lacking appropriate tools, or being unable to fix or replace a malfunctioning kiln.

Leading Group Firings

Firing your work is a process best confined to the privacy and control of your own kiln site and studio. Often, however, groups of potters cooperate by sharing a kiln or kilns and conducting their firings together. Group firings offer some advantages. They're sensible when access to a kiln isn't otherwise available; a group solves the problem of finding helpers for certain tasks; and the camaraderie, individual styles, and mutual interests of a group can result in new ideas and directions for your own work. But group firings also have the potential to be disorganized, confusing, frustrating, and dangerous.

The paragraphs that follow list some ways to keep your group firings successful.

Ideally, the group should be small. Discuss and agree on the goals and expectations of each member before you load any pots and light the burner. Make sure required tools, equipment, and materials are on hand and available for each participant to use.

Plan each kiln load in advance so you know the ware is compatible with the firing temperature and with the type of atmosphere that you'll create. Keep loads small to maximize the necessary control during the firing, removal, and post-firing phases. When the pots are ready for removal, each person must have adequate space and time to carry out his or her post-firing method. Finally, everyone should share responsibility for the fuel costs and upkeep of the grounds, kilns, and related equipment.

Remember that a raku firing is never a completely predictable event. Enjoy the gathering, but be prepared to deal with any tricky situations that might arise. Remember to take advantage of the opportunity to learn from other potters and share with them what you've learned yourself.

DANIEL ACHERMANN
TACHI Vase
11 x 13 x 13 inches (28 x 33 x 33 cm)
Wheel thrown Potclays T-Material 1161Y;
dipped glaze; wax decor painting; gas
fired; smoking for reduction
Photo by artist

Conclusion

I'd like to wrap up this book with a few "Knute Rockne: Pottery Coach" words of inspiration that I hope will help you to move along enthusiastically in your raku learning experience.

Don't let a lack of experience or instruction in any aspect of the raku process hold you back. More often than not, you'll discover that you know more than thought you did. Whether or not a particular process or technique works "correctly" by someone else's standards is less important than whether the result satisfies your expectations.

By applying your inner knowledge and searching out new connections freely and boldly, you can open up new worlds. Keep an open mind; allow—and even embrace—unexpected results, without encumbering yourself by adhering strictly to predetermined formulas. Throughout your entire creative involvement, maintain your own aesthetic standards and expectations. A dedication to veracity, not compliance with technical matters, is what forms the most basic boundary of creativity.

Within these pages, I've included as much information as I could on the raku process and its variations, but covering every technique, material, and subtlety would have been impossible. Too many deviations, modifications, and individual nuances exist in the world of raku; in fact, they're limited only by the boundaries of your own vision and your ability to make connections between that vision and existing techniques.

I urge you to seek out and share influences and experiences; refrain from working in an isolated, self-absorbed manner. Read books and journals; visit studios; and attend classes, workshops, symposia, and conferences. View exhibitions, ask questions, and engage in dialogue. Use everything you learn; apply it all to your work. And complete the cycle by giving something back: provide assistance, teach what you've learned, and offer your own contributions to future students of the craft.

In raku, there are no conclusions—only beginnings and thresholds of departure from "accepted" ways—so blaze your own trail of excitement and expression.

WALLY ASSELBERGHS
Enceinte, 2005
13 x 13 x 13 inches (33 x 33 x 33 cm)
Coil built Westerwald Clay; splashed glaze; burnished; gas fired; smoking for reduction
Photo by Lucille Feremans

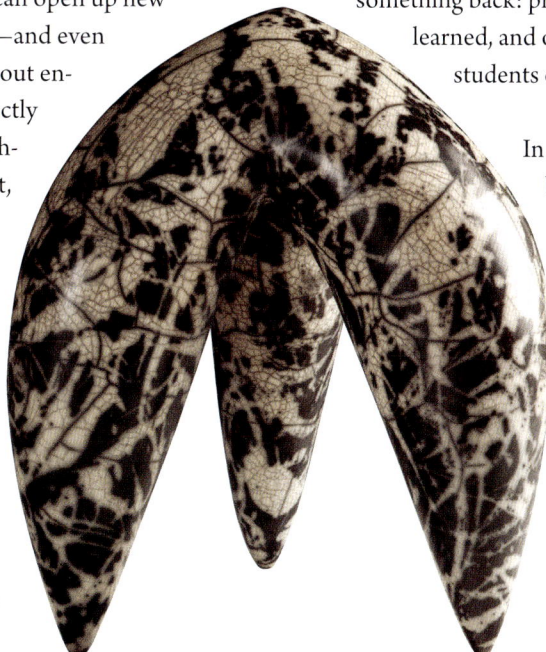

Gallery

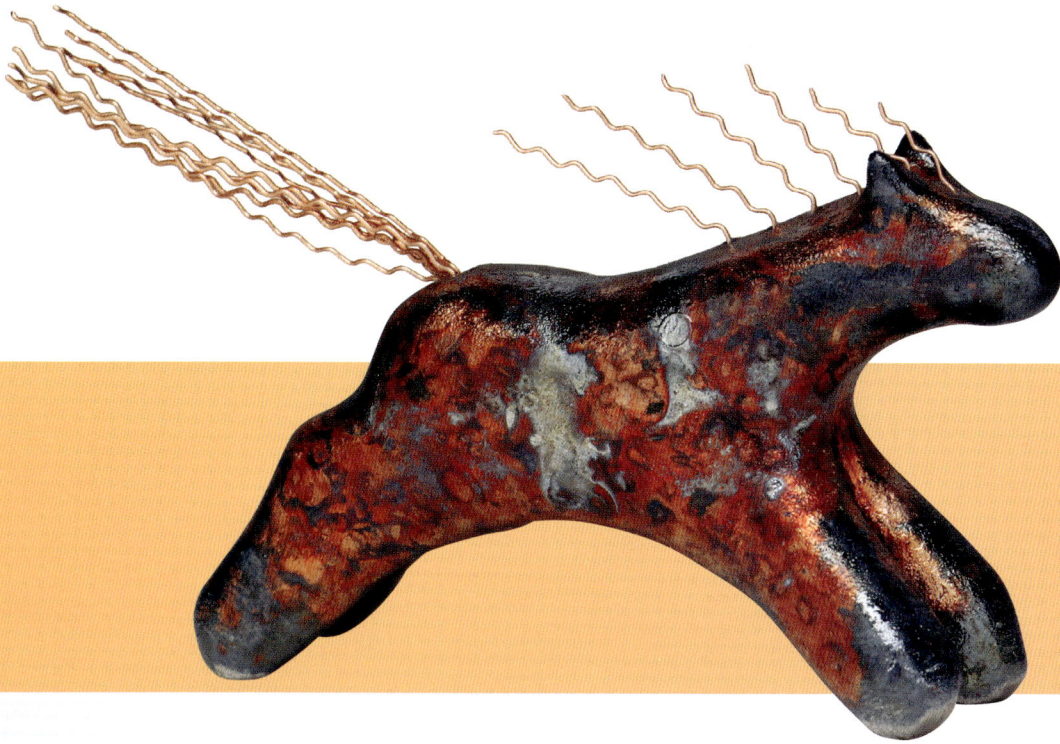

This page:

top:
RUTH APTER
Running Horse, 2004
5 x 3 x 1¼ inches (12.7 x 7.6 x 3.2 cm)
Press molded and hand built SPS Raku II;
brushed glaze; electric fired; smoking for
reduction, quick cooling in water
Photo by Frank Ross

bottom:
CATHERINE WEIR
Shadow Crackle Bowl, 2008
6 x 8 inches (15.2 x 20.3 cm)
Wheel thrown Sheba Raku; brushed and
poured glaze, tape resist; raku fired in
propane kiln; controlled cooling, smoking
for reduction; cone 08
Photo by Christie Gruppe

Opposite page:

DAVID JONES
Clustered 3, 2007
5½ x 8⅝ x 10⅝ inches
(14 x 22 x 27 cm)
Thrown T material and porcelain;
sprayed glaze; gas fired
Photo by Rod Dorling

wandless

Opposite page:

PAUL ANDREW WANDLESS
Tools of the Trade #4, 2008
13½ x 10 x 1 inches
(34.3 x 25.4 x 2.5 cm)
Clay monoprint earthenware; linocut
prints; underglaze brushwork, water
color underglazes; raku fired in electric
kiln; 1850°F
Photo by artist

This page:

top:
COLETTE BEARDALL
Charlie, 2008
6 x 5 x 4 inches
(15.2 x 12.7 x 10.2 cm)
Hand built Tucker's white sculpture clay;
brushed glaze; oxide wash; propane
fired; quick smoking
Photo by Anne Chambers

bottom:
LEO VAN DER HEYDEN
Jelly Fish Bowl, 2007
2¾ x 11 inches (7 x 28 cm)
Hand built and wheel thrown
Westerwald Clay; sprayed glaze;
gas fired; quick cooling, smoking for
reduction
Photo by artist

Opposite page:

top left:
GAIL PIEPENBURG
Roberge, 2007
21 x 9 x 4 inches (53.3 x 22.9 x 10.2 cm)
Hand built and slab built Hawthorn
Bonding and Kyanite; brushed glaze,
sprayed luster glaze; drawing, tearing,
layering clay sheets; raku fired in electric
kiln; smoking for reduction; cone 06
Photo by artist

bottom left:
MICHAEL HOUGH
Raku Vessel, 2007
21 x 10 x 6 inches
(53.3 x 25.4 x 15.2 cm)
Hand built and slab built High Waters
Desert Buff; brushed glaze; stamped,
sgraffito, underglaze brushwork; gas fired;
quick cooling, smoking for reduction
Photo by Ellen Martin

right:
IRENE POULTON
Pagoda
25⅝ x 7⅛ x 7⅛ inches
(65 x 18 x 18 cm)
Hand built Feeney's raku clay; copper matte
glaze, gold luster; raku fired; shredded
newspaper and sawdust reduction
Photo by artist

This page:

HARVEY SADOW
Winter Path, *Elkhorn Vessels*, 1977
10 x 6 x 6 inches (25.4 x 15.2 x 15.2 cm)
Wheel thrown personal clay; brushed
and dipped glaze; sgraffito, oxide wash;
raku fired in gas kiln; controlled cooling,
smoking for reduction
Photo by artist

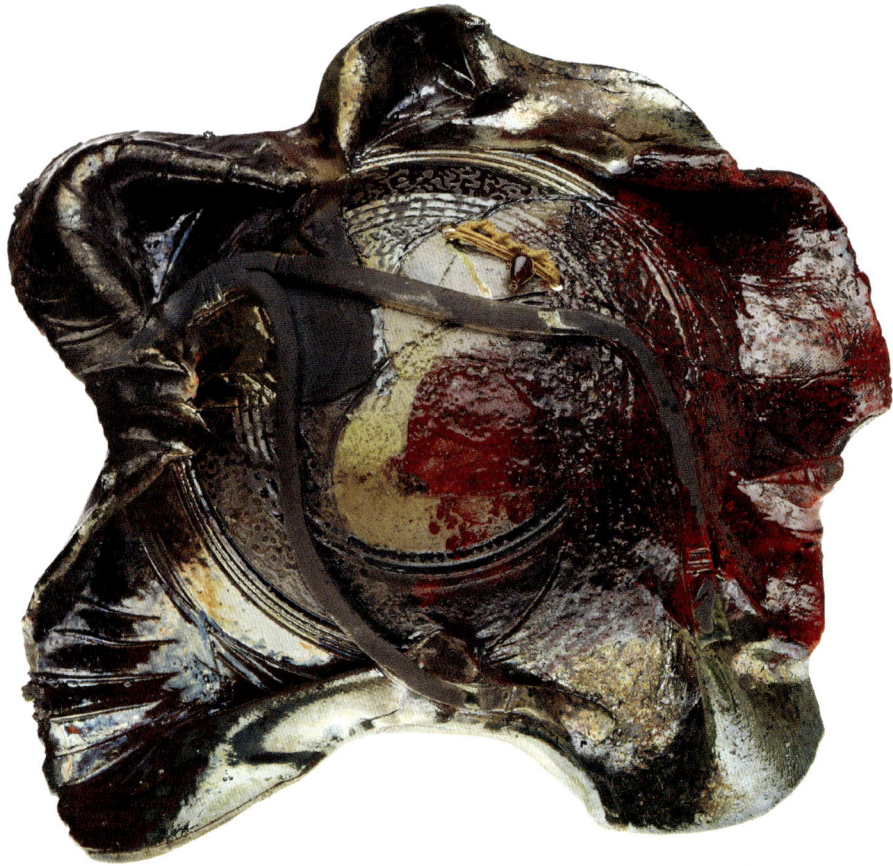

Opposite page:

top:
MARK LUSARDI
Sunset, 2008
17 x 17 inches (43.2 x 43.2 cm)
Hand built Continental raku clay;
brushed, dipped, and poured glaze;
electric and gas fired; heavy reduction
Photo by Mike Jensen

bottom left:
JAMES C. WATKINS
Double-Walled Platter, 2007
7 x 25 inches (17.8 x 63.5 cm)
Hand built and wheel thrown personal
clay; brushed glaze; gas fired; smoking for
reduction; cone 04
Photo by Jon Thompson

bottom right:
TIM ANDREWS
Tapering Form, 2008
16 x 10 x 10 inches
(40.6 x 25.4 x 25.4 cm)
Wheel thrown T Material and porcelain
mix; dipped glaze, glaze resist; smoked
lines on burnished surface; gas fired;
selective smoking for reduction
Photo by D. Garner

This page:

top:
NATHAN ANDERSON
Glasku Blue Hazel, 2009
8 x 6 inches (20.3 x 15.2 cm)
Wheel thrown raku clay; poured glaze;
electric and gas fired; smoking for
reduction
Photo by Peter Lee

bottom:
BOB GREEN
Melon Shape Globe, 2002
14 x 16 x 16 inches
(35.6 x 40.6 x 40.6 cm)
Wheel thrown Sheffield S-14 clay,
sprayed glaze; gas fired; reduction in
damp hardwood chips; cone 06
Photo by Ken Burris

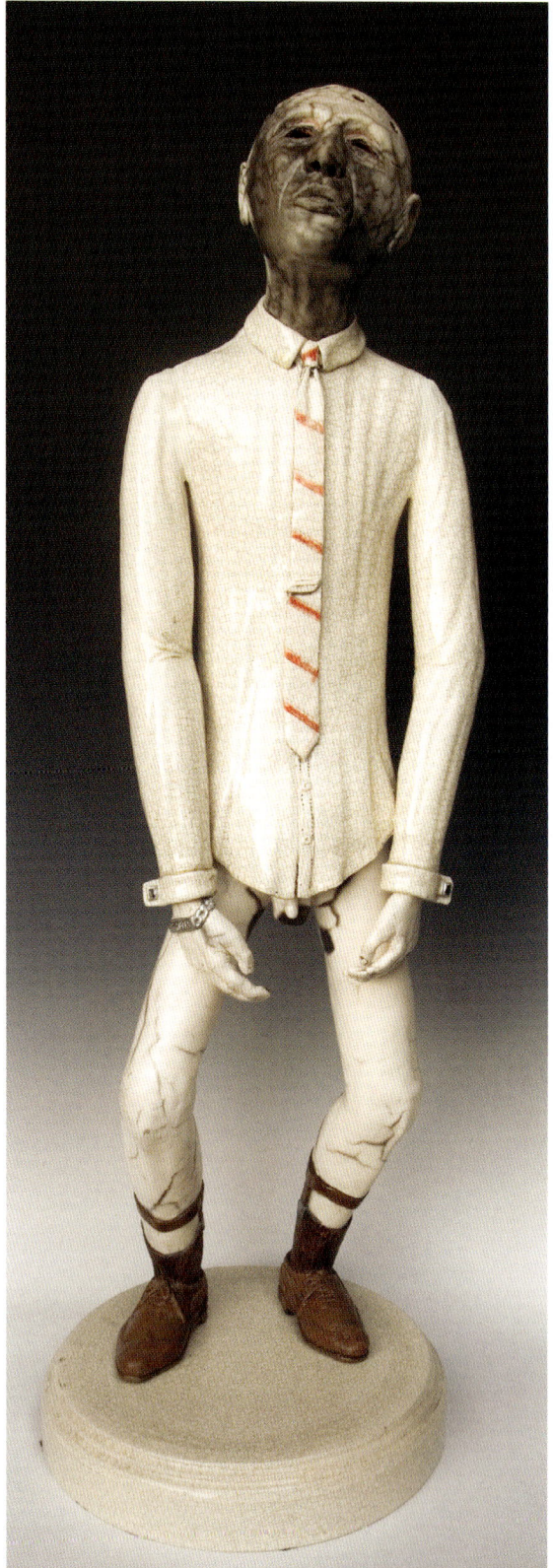

Opposite page:

top left:
KATE JACOBSON
WILL JACOBSON
Pear Song, 2008
18 x 8 x 8 inches (45.7 x 20.3 x 20.3 cm)
Press molded, hand built, and wheel
thrown Laguna Clay, Amador; brushed
and poured glaze; carved, paint/non-
ceramic/non-fired, burnish porcelain slips;
gas fired; smoking for reduction, sacrificial
glaze, naked raku
Photo by artist

right:
AMBER AGUIRRE
Daddy, 2008
26½ x 8½ x 8½ inches
(67.3 x 21.6 x 21.6 cm)
Hand built B-Mix Clay with grog (wheel
thrown base); brushed glaze; Mason
stains, acrylic; electric and gas fired;
smoking for reduction
Photo by artist

bottom left:
JOHN H. DORSEY
Raku Vase, 2008
5 x 4 inches (12.7 x 10.2 cm)
Wheel thrown Miller B-Mix Clay; dipped
glaze; copper wire; gas fired; smoking for
reduction
Photo by artist

This page:

top:
JÖRG BAUMÖLLER
Raku Craquele Vase, 2006
7 x 5⅞ inches (18 x 15 cm)
Wheel thrown Gres Collet PRAI-E Clay;
sprayed glaze; gas fired; smoking for
reduction
Photo by artist

bottom:
DAPHNE CORREGAN
Twins, 2005
22¼ x 16⅛ x 11 inches
(56.5 x 41 x 28 cm)
Hand built Solargil Clay; brushwork
(slips); gas fired; controlled cooling,
smoking for reduction
Photo by artist

Appendices

I've provided the creators of these recipes when known. My apologies to anyone I might have missed. (United Kingdom equivalents are provided in parentheses.)

STEVEN BRANFMAN
Tea Bowl, 2008
3½ x 4 inches (8.9 x 10.2 cm)
Brushed multi layered commercial low
fire glaze; pressed surface texture

Appendix A: Commercial Clay Bodies for Raku

Laguna Raku WC-636, #250. This is the clay body I use. Very plastic and smooth, with only medium grog. Excellent refractory qualities and a firing color that's slightly off-white. Available only on the East Coast of the United States.

Laguna Raku WC-635, #200. Similar to #250, but not quite as plastic and much more coarse.

Laguna Raku-K White, EM-345. Very similar to #250. Available only on the West Coast of the United States.

Standard Ceramics Moist Clay Body, 239. Very plastic; moderate in texture. Contains sand for its thermal qualities and fires to a yellowish white.

Standard Ceramics Moist Clay Body, 295. Similar to #239, but includes kyanite for added strength.

Highwater Clays Raku, #EC-R1 (C-06). A reasonably smooth, plastic, white-firing body, with kyanite for added refractory characteristics.

Amherst Potters Supply Raku. Good for throwing; a reasonably white body with good thermal qualities.

Dakota Potters Supply Raku. A very plastic, white throwing body with excellent thermal qualities. Slightly coarse texture.

Continental Clay Company Raku. Good plasticity and excellent thermal qualities. Smooth textured and white firing.

Great Lakes Clay, MCL-324, Raku II Porcelain. A very white porcelain-base clay body that contains no grog. Formulated for raku and good for pit firing as well.

Pottery Supply House (Ontario, Canada), #C575S, White, Sheba. A smooth, white-firing clay virtually identical in throwing properties to Laguna #250.

Potclays 1161 T-Material. An excellent all-purpose raku clay. Slightly off-white, plastic, with a medium texture. Provides outstanding refractory properties.

Glazes—and to a lesser extent clay bodies—often originate as base recipes in which each primary ingredient is listed as a percentage (by weight), with the total amount equaling 100 percent. When additional ingredients such as oxides are listed, the amounts required are given as percentages of the total weight of the prepared batch. In other recipes, these additional ingredients are included in the base recipe, with the total sometimes adding up to more than 100 percent. Over years of use, sharing, and experimentation, alterations and adjustments are made to recipes, and recalculations to 100 are rarely needed or desired. In fact, recalculation can alter a recipe in subtle ways that can change its results.

When a recipe calls for additional materials, always calculate that percentage based on the weight of the prepared base batch. Sometimes a glaze is mixed by volume and not by weight. In these cases, use any convenient but consistent measuring device, such as a spoon or cup.

The best way to prepare glazes is to sift your dry material into water. Allow the mixture to slake for an hour or so. Then mix with a spatula, or a drill and power-mixing attachment. Wet-screen all glazes before use. Unless otherwise indicated, a 60-mesh screen is fine for raku glazes.

Handle all raw materials with safety in mind. Those with a high risk of toxic exposure are indicated by a ☢.

Appendix B: Clay Recipes

Clay Recipes for Raku

In some of the recipes that follow, the maximum cone (vitrification) is included, but this is for your information only and should not be confused with whether or not a clay is suitable for raku firing. With the exception of clay bodies high in talc, most of these clays are cone 6–10 bodies as a result of the fireclay and stoneware clay in them and should be bisque fired to cone 08.

A few recipes include specific bisque instructions provided by their originators. These should be taken as suggestions only; they represent the firing styles and methods of those individual potters and may not apply to your approach.

Gray Throwing (cone 6–10)

AP.Green Fireclay (Potclays Fireclay 1275-3)	35
Cedar Heights Goldart (Potclays Buff Stoneware)	40
Tennessee Ball Clay (HVAR Ball Clay)	20
Custer feldspar (potash feldspar)	4
Grog	10

This recipe comes from John Jessiman, my first pottery teacher. It's an excellent throwing body, also suitable for salt firing.

Raku #1

AP Green Fireclay (Potclays Fireclay 1275-3)	100
Cedar Heights Goldart (Potclays Buff Stoneware)	100
Talc	20
Bentonite	4

This is a reasonably plastic, very versatile body.

Soldner Raku

AP Green Fireclay (Potclays Fireclay 1275-3)	100
Tennessee Ball Clay (HVAR Ball Clay)	30
Talc	30
Grog	10

This is a well-known recipe from Paul Soldner. It's very tough to throw, though.

Bryan's Raku

Hawthorne Fireclay	50%
OM-4 Ball Clay or XX Saggar Clay (AT Ball Clay)	20%
48-mesh grog	20%
Spodumene	10%
	100%

This recipe comes from my friend Bryan McGrath. A white-firing stoneware body with moderate tooth and texture that isn't too rough on your fingers, it's a very plastic and excellent throwing body.

RISD Raku (cone 10)

AP Green Fireclay (Potclays Fireclay 1275-3)	50
Cedar Heights Goldart (Potclays Buff Stoneware	150
Custer feldspar (potash feldspar)	10
Grog	15

This is the standard raku body from my student days at the Rhode Island School of Design.

Higby White Raku Clay (bisque cone 08–05)

Missouri Fireclay	100
OM-4 Ball Clay (AT Ball Clay)	30
Talc	30
Silica sand	1%

Wayne Higby is an icon of American raku. This is his usual white raku clay, developed many years ago.

Higby Red Raku Clay (bisque cone 08–06)

PBX Fireclay (Potclays Fireclay #6)	50
Cedar Heights Goldart (Potclays Buff Stoneware)	20
Redart (Fremington Clay or add 15% potash feldspar to Etruria Marl)	25
Talc	5
Silica sand	10
Macaloid	1%

This is Wayne Higby's usual red raku clay.

Kemenyffy Raku (bisque cone 06)

35-mesh Virginia kyanite	30
Cedar Heights Goldart (Potclays Buff Stoneware)	33
Frederick Fireclay	33

Steven Kemenyffy developed this clay body after much research. The use of kyanite as opposed to silica sand or grog is what allows him and his wife Susan to create such massive sculptures with little breakage.

Clark White Salt/Saggar Body (cone 010–04)

Talc	15%
Wollastonite	5%
AP Green Fireclay (Potclays Fireclay 1275-3)	40%
Tennessee Ball Clay (HVAR Ball Clay)	25%
Fine grog	7.5%
Medium grog	7.5%
	100%

This is a throwing body that gives excellent results when used in saggar and raku salt firing.

Clay Recipes for Saggars

Despite their specialized recipes, these clay bodies for saggars eventually crack from thermal shock, so keep several saggars on hand.

Brisson Saggar Formula

Fireclay	75%
Grog	20%
Talc	5%
	100%

Bisque fire this clay to cone 09.

Behren's Saggar Formula

Plastic fireclay	40%
Calcined fireclay	30%
Grog	28%
Bentonite	2%
	100%

Bisque fire this clay to cone 08.

NESRIN DURING
Untitled
Hand built Westerwald Clay; wood fired;
smoking for reduction
Photo by Stefan During

Appendix C: A Gerstley Borate Substitute

Cardew Saggar Formula		(Hindes's Variation)
Grog	50%	40%
China clay	40%	20%
Bonding clay	10%	
Ball clay		20%
Talc		20%
	100%	100%

Bisque fire this clay to cone 08.

Hindes's Saggar Formula	
Fireclay	2
Ball clay	1
Ground, coarse soft brick	1
Coarse sawdust	2

Bisque fire this clay to cone 08.

Tom Buck's Synthetic Gerstley Borate for Raku	
Pemco frit 2201 or Fusion frit F309	490
Whiting	280
Talc	125
Feldspar (any)	65
Unwashed, well-screened wood ash	40
Red iron oxide ☢	2
Titanium dioxide	1

Dry-mix the ingredients, and then use the mixture in your raku glazes in the same proportions as gerstley borate. Keep the mixture well stirred; it settles fairly quickly.

Appendix D: Glaze Recipes

All of the following glazes mature within an acceptable range, and all have been tested. You may substitute GB for cole-manite in them (see page 39–40).

Two very informative books on glaze formulation and color development in glazes of all firing ranges, including low-fire and raku, are *The Ceramic Spectrum: A Simplified Approach to Glaze & Color Development* by Robin Hopper (American Ceramic Society, 2001, 2nd ed.), and *Revealing Glazes: Using the Grid Method* by Ian Currie (Bootstrap Press, 2000). In addition, *Clay Times* and *Ceramics Monthly* publish more glaze recipes than could ever be used in a lifetime.

Recipes from My Regular Palette

Del Favero Luster	
Gerstley borate	80%
Cornwall stone	20%
	100%
Copper carbonate ☢	2%

This turquoise glaze turns to a rich, copper-penny luster under strong post-firing reduction. I got the recipe from Robert Piepenburg.

KEVIN NIERMAN
Untitled, 2007
Largest: 11 x 7 x 7 inches (27.9 x 17.8 x 17.8 cm)
Smallest: 6 x 5 x 5 inches (15.2 x 12.7 x 12.7 cm)
Sculpture 412 Clay; brushed glaze; propane fired; cone 09
Photo by Dave Larson

Yellow Crackle

Gerstley borate	80%
Cornwall stone	20%
100%	
Vanadium stain ☢	3–6%

The color of this yellow glaze depends on the type and amount of vanadium you use. You can also add 5% tin oxide ☢ for increased brightness.

New Rogers Black

Gerstley borate	80%
Custer feldspar	20%
	100%
Red iron oxide ☢	10%
Cobalt carbonate ☢	10%
Black copper oxide ☢	10%

This dark blue glaze develops a nice copper luster in strong post-firing reduction

Gold Raku

Gerstley borate	80%
Cornwall stone	20%
	100%
Tin oxide ☢	1%
Silver nitrate ☢ ☢	2%

This is a very reliable silver-gold glaze from Robert Piepenburg. (See page 50 for information on how to handle silver nitrate.)

Piepenburg Oil Luster

Frit 3134	50%
Gerstley borate	50%
	100%
Black copper oxide ☢	2.5%
Manganese dioxide ☢	1%

If you use it in moderation, this glaze produces the effect of an oil-spot glaze. It comes from Robert Piepenburg.

Erica's Aqua

Gerstley borate	80%
Cornwall stone	20%
	100%
Tin oxide ☢	5%
Cobalt carbonate ☢	2%
Copper carbonate ☢	3%

With light post-firing reduction, this lovely medium-blue glaze shows copper flashes and color variations. Heavy reduction results in an overall copper luster. It was developed by Erica Cashman, a student of mine at Thayer Academy.

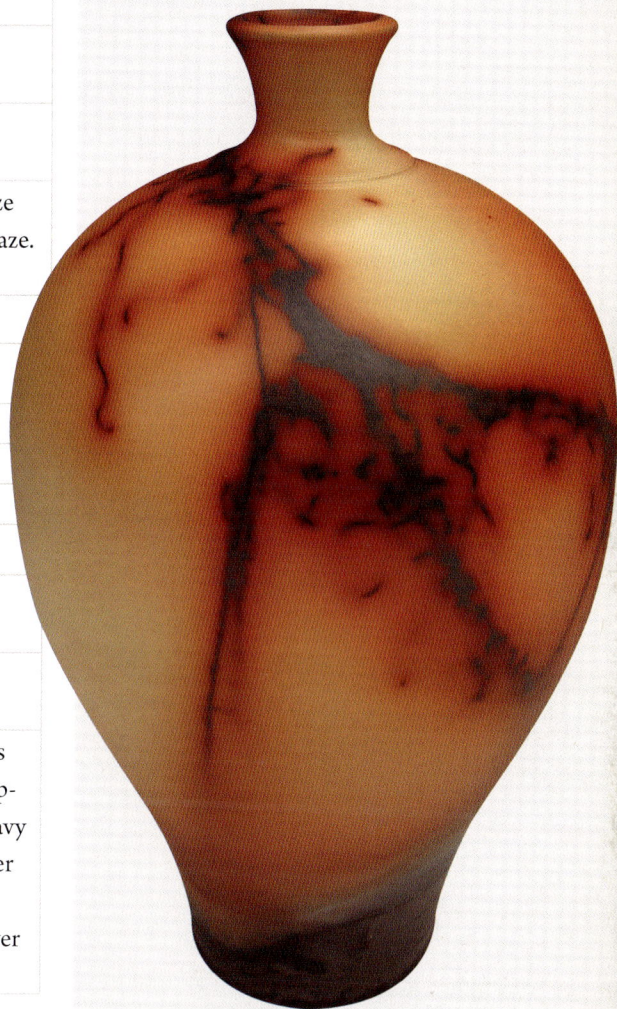

CHARLES RIGGS
LINDA RIGGS
Saggar-fired Bottle, 2008
10 x 5½ x 5½ inches
(25.4 x 14 x 14 cm)
Wheel thrown stoneware; sprayed terra sigillata, polished, bisqued; drapped in steel wool; raku gas fired in a clay saggar with sawdust, copper carb, salt and steel wool; 1650°F
Photo by artist

Basic White Crackle

Gerstley borate	65%
Tennessee Ball Clay	5%
Nepheline syenite	15%
Tin oxide ☢	10%
Flint	5%
	100%

This is my regular white glaze. Apply it thickly for a bright, opaque white. It also makes a good base glaze with which to experiment; add colorants or alter percentages of the basic ingredients to modify its glossiness or opacity.

Roger's White

Spodumene	35%
Gerstley borate	60%
Tennessee Ball Clay	5%
	100%

This is a truly clear glaze; when used on white clay, it's white! Apply it thickly.

For a gray-blue glaze, add:

Red iron oxide ☢	1%
Cobalt carbonate ☢	0.5%

For a purple glaze, add:

Manganese carbonate ☢	3%
Tin oxide ☢	5%

Piepenburg 50/50 Red Bronze Luster

Frit 3134	50%
Gerstley borate	60%
	100%
Tin oxide ☢	3%
Black copper oxide ☢	2.5%

Here's a beautiful copper luster glaze from Robert Piepenburg. Under reducing atmosphere conditions, the result is a blood red. In strong post-firing reduction, a bronze-like copper luster results.

Other Reliable Glaze Recipes

Higby 1-2-3 Base

Silica	1
EPK	2
Gerstley borate	3

This is a good clear base with which to experiment.

Higby Water Blue

Frit 3110	70
Gerstley borate	5
Silica	5
Soda ash	10
EPK	5
Copper carbonate ☢	3–6%

For a lime-green color, increase the copper carbonate to 8%.

This beautiful, blue-turquoise-aqua glaze tends toward red when you apply it thinly and fire it in reduction. It yields copper flashes in post-firing reduction.

Higby Green

Frit 3110	70
Colemanite	5
Flint	12
Soda ash	5
EPK	5
Copper carbonate ☢	8
Red iron oxide ☢	1

This is a multi-colored glaze, showing greens, blues, and reds. Fire it to a high gloss for best results.

Kemenyffy Opaque White

Both this glaze and the one that follows are fired to cone 5$\frac{1}{2}$—significantly higher than the other recipes in this appendix. The Calgon acts as a deflocculant to keep the ingredients suspended and smooth without having to add too much water.

Gerstley borate	30%
Frit 3110	30%
Custer feldspar	25%
EPK	5%
Barium carbonate ☢	5%
Tin oxide ☢	1%
Hommel frit 373	4%
	100%

Kemenyffy Gold Luster

To Kemenyffy Opaque White (above), add:

Silver nitrate ☢	1.5%
Yellow ochre ☢	1%
Soda bicarbonate	2%
Calgon Water Softener	0.5%

Fat White

Frit 3134	100
Flint	6
EPK	10
Bentonite	2
Tin oxide ☢	10

This very bright glaze develops excellent crackle.

Hal's Purple

Borax	38
Boric acid ☢	62
Talc	13
Flint	6
Copper carbonate ☢	6

This is one of Hal Riegger's signature glazes, which he gave to me.

Tutti Frutti

Gerstley borate	80%
Nepheline syenite	10%
Talc	10%
	100%
Copper carbonate ☢	A handful

This popular glaze appears in many variations all over the United States. Results include variegated color, copper flashes, and interesting surfaces.

Rick's Turquoise

Gerstley borate	1488
Nepheline syenite	750
Lithium carbonate ☢	780
Superpax	723
Copper carbonate ☢	98

This is Rick Berman's signature glaze. A spectrum of colors is possible through combinations of reduction and oxidation firing, as well as various degrees of post-firing reduction and smoking. Rick fires this to cone 04–02, but it can be fired to lower temperatures for different effects.

Stable Glaze Recipes from Tom Buck

Red Lustre #8

Gerstley borate	38%
Frit 3134	31%
Frit 3195	31%
	100%
Red copper oxide ☢	10%
Red iron oxide ☢	10%

This is a semi-matte luster; when it's fired at approximately cone 08, it yields reds and blues. If it's fired a bit higher, a gloss results.

LYNNE GIRRELL
BRUCE GIRRELL
Nature's Fury, 2001
10½ x 8¾ x 8¾ inches
(26.7 x 22.2 x 22.2 cm)
Coiled and thrown Great Lakes Clay White Stoneware; hand burnished; propane gas fired; no reduction air cooling; horsehair, ferric chloride, multiple firings
Photo by artist

JOHN MATHIESON
Untitled, 2008
Pot: 4⅛ inches (10.5 cm) tall
Bottle: 6½ inches (16.5 cm) tall
Thrown T-Material and Harry Fraser Porcelain; bisque fired, 1000°C; dipped glaze;
stamped, black slip pours, splash lines; propane fired, 900°C on pyrometer; air
cooling, reduction in mixed sawdust
Photo by artist

Copper Sand #2

Copper Sand #2	
Gerstley borate	56%
Flint	21%
Bone ash	14%
Grolleg	9%
	100%
Copper carbonate ☢	5%
Cobalt oxide ☢	2.5%

This is a textured surface glaze. Colors, degree of luster, and gloss depend on the firing temperature and post-firing technique.

Patina Glaze Recipes

Hines Patina	
Gerstley borate	7
Bone ash	3
Nepheline syenite	2
Cornwall stone	1
Copper carbonate ☢	1

For a rougher surface, add 5% 35-mesh alumina hydrate.
This is the patina glaze I use often. This dry, matte glaze has a variety of colors and surface effects. When fired high, it smoothes out to a satin surface.

Dry Alligator	
Gerstley borate	52.5%
Nepheline syenite	12%
Bone ash	23.5%
Copper carbonate ☢	12%
	100%

This dry, matte, textured glaze offers a rainbow of colors.

Copper 80/20 #1	
Colemanite	65
Nepheline syenite	16
Flint	15
Copper carbonate ☢	10
Red copper oxide ☢	5
Red iron oxide ☢	10%

This is a standard copper luster glaze. The addition of iron oxide offers some subtlety and variation.

Copper 80/20 #6	
Gerstley borate	67%
Frit 3195	17%
Flint	10%
EPK	6%
	100%
Copper carbonate ☢	10%
Red iron oxide ☢	5%

This is a copper luster with a broad melting range, and it's less runny than most.

Lizard Skin

Borax	10
Lithium carbonate ☢	15
Gerstley borate	70
Nepheline syenite	20
Magnesium carbonate ☢	40
Chrome oxide ☢	0.4
Copper carbonate ☢	5

This is a dry, multi-colored, crater-like glaze.

Jeff's Patina

Copper carbonate ☢	1
Red iron oxide ☢	1/8
Bone ash	1
Gerstley borate	5
Nepheline syenite	1

This dry matte glaze offers a variety of effects, depending on application, firing temperature, atmosphere, and post-firing method.

Stoneware Glaze Recipes

This section contains Mark Lancet's raku/stoneware glaze variations. Blue Mosque and White Earth are stoneware glazes for conventional use. For the raku variation, wet-mix a quantity of either glaze, by volume, with an 80 gerstley borate/20 nepheline syenite glaze (proportions are indicated after each recipe) or with any standard raku gloss glaze. Apply the glaze slightly thicker than usual.

Mark raku fires to cone 06, using a cone to determine maturity. As is the case with most raku glazes, a wide range of color variations is possible depending on your post-firing technique. Experiment, as Mark has done, to achieve your own unique results.

Blue Mosque (cone 5)

Barium carbonate ☢	4
Nepheline syenite	79
Ball clay	8
Flint	10
Copper carbonate ☢	10
Lithium carbonate ☢	4

For a matte surface, mix with 7 parts Blue Mosque and 3 parts 80/20. For a sugary matte surface, mix with 3 parts Blue Mosque and 2 parts 80/20. For a semigloss surface, mix with 1 part Blue Mosque and 1 part 80/20.

PAUL SOLDNER
Tea Bowl, 2003
6 x 6 x 3½ inches (15.2 x 15.2 x 8.9 cm)
Wheel thrown; dipped glaze;
smoking for reduction
Photo by Nicole Frazier
Courtesy of David Armstrong

RONDA M. LISKEY
Tee Pee Bowl, 2004
3 x 16 inches (7.6 x 40.6 cm)
Wheel thrown and thrown and altered
raku; brushed glaze; overglaze luster;
propane gas fired;
smoking for reduction
Photo by Raymond Kopen

White Earth (cone 5–7)

Talc	36
Kona F4 Spar	22
EPK	11
Flint	11
Magnesium carbonate ☢	11
Gerstley borate	7
Dolomite	4
Bentonite	1

For a matte crawl surface (dry riverbed-like effect), mix with 7 parts White Earth and 3 parts gloss glaze.

For a wet crawl surface (water-on-wax-paper effect), mix with 3 parts White Earth and 2 parts gloss glaze.

Appendix E: Slip Recipes

RISD Engobe (for bone-dry ware)

Cornwall stone	40%
EPK (kaolin)	40%
Frit 3124	15%
Borax	5%
	100%
Superpax (commercial opacifier)	10%

You may substitute tin oxide ☢ for Superpax, but use only half as much.

Higby Haystack Slip #5 (for leather-hard to dry ware)

EPK (kaolin)	25%
Ball clay	25%
Silica	20%
Frit 3304	30%
	100%

This recipe makes a good base for added colorants.

Kemenyffy White Slip (for leather-hard ware)

EPK (kaolin)	25%
Kentucky ball clay	25%
Custer feldspar (potash feldspar)	25%
Frit 3110	20%
Barium carbonate ☢	5%
	100%

Because their work is so large and therefore requires a very refractory clay that isn't as white as they'd like, the Kemenyffys often use this slip to highlight and brighten their glaze effects.

Appendix F: Terra Sigillata Recipes

Charlie Riggs's No-Frills Terra Sigillata for First-Timers

Water	3½ gallons (13.2 L)
XX Saggar Clay or Tennessee ball clay	15 pounds (6.8 kg)
Sodium silicate	1½ tablespoons (22.2 ml)
Soda ash	1½ tablespoons (22.2 ml)

Stir the sodium silicate and/or the soda ash into the water. (Use either or both.) Sift in the saggar or ball clay, and let the mixture sit overnight undisturbed. Pour or siphon off the top 1½ gallons (5.7 L) for use.

Robert Compton's White Terra Sigillata

EPK	1170 g
Ball clay	270 g
Bentonite	60 g
Calgon Water Softener	8 g
Water	14 cups (3.3 L)

For red, substitute Redart Clay for the EPK.

Mix the ingredients well, adding the clay to the water. Let stand for several days. Siphon off the top layer of water to expose the middle layer of fine slip. Siphon it off for use, and discard the sludgy bottom layer. Fire no higher than cone 06.

Red Terra Sigillata (cone 08–04)

Redart clay	400 g
Sodium silicate	3–7 drops
Water	3 cups (710 ml)

Add the Redart to the water, let the mixture slake for an hour, and then stir well. Add the sodium silicate a drop at a time until you notice the mixture thinning as you stir. If you add too much, the mixture thickens instead. Continue to stir until thoroughly mixed. Let stand and siphon, as in the preceding recipe.

Appendix G: Kiln Wash Recipe

Kiln Wash

EPK (Kaolin)	2
Flint	2
Alumina hydrate	1

This recipe is one that I've used throughout my career. Mix to a creamy consistency, and apply two coats with a wide brush.

Appendix H: Copper Matte, Fuming, and Halo Recipes

Copper Matte Recipes

Strozier Copper Matte

Frit 3110	25%
Copper carbonate ☣	75%
	100%
Red iron oxide ☣	10%
Cobalt carbonate ☣	5%

Mark's Copper Matte

Frit 3110	10%
Copper carbonate ☣	90%
	100%
Iron oxide	5%

Rick's Copper Matte

Frit 3110	20%
Copper carbonate ☣	80%
	100%
Red iron oxide ☣	5%

Jeremy's Copper Matte

Frit 3110	20%
Copper carbonate ☣	40%
Black copper oxide ☣	40%
	100%

Bob Green Copper Matte Base

Copper carbonate ☣	90%
Frit 3110	10%
	100%
Lithium carbonate ☣	5%

Variation #1: Add 2% cobalt carbonate ☣ (include the lithium as well).

Variation #2: Add 2% rutile (include the lithium as well).

LYNNE GIRRELL
BRUCE GIRRELL
Lightning Storm, 2005
9½ x 4½ x 4½ inches
(24.1 x 11.4 x 11.4 cm)
Wheel thrown Great Lakes Clay Smooth Porcelain Raku; hand burnished; propane gas fired; no reduction air cooling, horsehair, ferric chloride, multiple firings
Photo by artist

PAUL SOLDNER
Wall Plaque, 1982
18 x 24 x ¾ inches (45.7 x 61 x 1.9 cm)
Slab built; stamped glaze; smoking for reduction
Photo by Nicole Frazier
Courtesy of David Armstrong

Lehman Copper Matte Stain

Barium carbonate ☢	4.17%
Borax	4.17%
Copper carbonate ☢	62.5%
Lithium carbonate ☢	12.5%
Ferro frit 3134	16.66%
	100%

Put this glaze (including the borax) through an 80-mesh screen.

Fuming Recipes

The following recipes work well over raku glazed surfaces.

Biz's Peacock Blue

Stannous chloride	7
Strontium nitrate	1
Barium chloride	2

Biz's Ruby Red

Stannous chloride	8.25
Strontium nitrate	1.25
Barium chloride	0.5

Biz's Opal

Stannous chloride	7
Bismuth nitrate	3

Halo Recipes

Soldner Halo Base Slip

Gerstley borate	17%
EPK	33%
Flint	50%
	100%

Soldner Halo Wash

Copper carbonate ☢	50%
Red iron oxide ☢	50%
	100%

Appendix I: Naked Raku Slip and Glaze Recipes

To alter the tendency of any slip to peel, experiment with the percentage of alumina (more of it results in less peeling), the type of fireclay, and the thickness of application. Slips peel more easily from polished and burnished surfaces and are more difficult to remove from rough ones.

Hutchen's Raku Slip Resist

Measure by volume:

Cedar Heights Fireclay	50
EPK	20
Alumina hydrate	20

This recipe comes from Charlie and Linda Riggs.

Brett's Variation

Measure by weight:

Cedar Heights Fireclay	60
EPK	3
Alumina hydrate	1

Riggs's Resist Slip

Measure by volume:

Hawthorne Fireclay	5
EPK	3
Alumina hydrate	2

Mix to a thick sludge and apply by dipping. For candy raku, begin your experiments by adding 2 parts sugar.

Jacobson Resist Slip

Measure by weight:

Lincoln 60 Fireclay	40%
#6 tile clay	30%
Grog	20%
Custer feldspar	10%
	100%

Asselbergh's Slip Mixtures

Measure by weight:

Clay (see below)	50%
EPK	30%
Flint	20%
	100%

You may use Highwater Phoenix Stoneware, Highwater Raku Clay, or Laguna #52 Clay as the base. Dry the clay completely and pulverize it. Mix all ingredients in 185 ml of water, mix well, and let stand overnight. Mix again, and screen through an 80-mesh screen to remove the sand and grog from the clay.

Jacobson Clear Glaze for Slip Resist

Measure by weight:

Frit 3110	65%
Gerstley borate	35%
	100%

Middlebrook's Crackle White

Measure by weight:

Gerstley borate	40%
Potash feldspar	34%
Barium carbonate ☢	15%
Flint	11%
	100%

Contributing Artists

Bill Abright
San Anselmo, California
pages 18, 49

Daniel Achermann
Basel, Switzerland
pages 140, 146

Amber Aguirre
Kailua-Kona, Hawaii
page 156

Nathan Anderson
Shoreview, Minnesota
page 155

Tim Andrews
Exeter, Devon, UK
page 154

Ruth Apter
Port Townsend, Washington
pages 143, 149

Wally Asselberghs
Schoten, Belgium
pages 13, 147

Edge Barnes
Raleigh, North Carolina
page 133

Jörg Baumöller
Vallromanes, Spain
page 157

Colette Beardall
Metcalfe, Ontario, Canada
page 151

Rick Berman
Atlanta, Georgia
pages 43, 64

Doris Boschung-Johner
Kerzers, Switzerland
pages 64, 146

Steven Branfman
Newton, Massachusetts
pages 6, 8, 9, 10, 22, 29, 36, 52, 66, 90, 116, 128, 137, 142, 158

Ramon Camarillo II
Vienna, Virginia
pages 120, 124, 127

Robert Compton
Bristol, Vermont
pages 28, 87

Jim Connell
Rock Hill, South Carolina
page 140

Daphne Corregan
Draguignan, France
pages 24, 157

Patrick Crabb
Tustin, California
pages 12, 35

Andrew M. Denney
St. Louis, Missouri
page 56

John H. Dorsey
Dedham, Massachusetts
page 156

Nesrin During
Oosterand, Netherlands
pages 67, 70, 161

Mark Einhorn
North Haven, Connecticut
page 33

Don Ellis
Farmington, New Mexico
page 63

Rick Foris
Amherst Junction, Wisconsin
page 41

Lynne Girrell
Bruce Girrell
Traverse City, Michigan
pages 165, 169

Bob Green
Conway, Massachusetts
page 155

Domi Gruszecka
Belsele, Belgium
page 104

Wayne Higby
Alfred Station, New York
pages 31, 39, 40

Richard Hirsch
Churchville, New York
pages 17, 65

Michael Hough
Bridgewater, Virginia
pages 68, 152

Kate Jacobson
Will Jacobson
Kailua-Kona, Hawaii
pages 131, 156

David Jones
Leamington Spa, Warwickshire, UK
pages 26, 148

Eduardo Lazo
Belmont, California
pages 38, 121

Ronda M. Liskey
Laingsburg, Michigan
pages 138, 139, 168

Mark Lusardi
New Richmond, Wisconsin
page 154

Karen Mahoney
Newton, Massachusetts
page 125

John Mathieson
Weston Favell, Northampton, UK
pages 11, 30, 166

Steve Mattison
Colwyn Bay, Wales, UK
pages 35, 114

Kevin Nierman
Berkeley, California
pages 37, 162

Geoffrey Pagen
Portland, Oregon
pages 32, 113

Gail Piepenburg
Ann Arbor, Michigan
page 152

Irene Poulton
Beldon, Australia
page 152

Hal Riegger
page 15

Charles Riggs
Linda Riggs
Carthage, North Carolina
pages 129, 132, 163

David Roberts
Holmfirth, Yorkshire, UK
page 23

Jim Romberg
Abiquiu, New Mexico
pages 100, 111

Andreas Ruhrnschopf
Kandern-Holzen, Germany
page 145

Harvey Sadow
Paducah, Kentucky
pages 51, 117, 119, 153

Marcia Selsor
Brownsville, Texas
pages 27, 115

Michael Sheba
Toronto, Ontario, Canada
page 110

Lou Smedts
Boom, Belgium
page 88

Paul Soldner
Claremont, California
pages 16, 122, 167, 169

Marvin Sweet
Merrimac, Massachusetts
pages 34, 38

Kathi Tighe
Cambridge, Massachusetts
pages 53, 120

Leo Van der heyden
Belselle, Belgium
pages 91, 151

Paul Andrew Wandless
Upland, Pennsylvania
page 150

James C. Watkins
Lubbock, Texas
pages 14, 119, 154

Catherine Weir
Hamilton, Ontario, Canada
pages 144, 149

Patty Wouters
Antwerp, Belgium
page 123

Dedication

Jared Branfman was an extraordinary person. He accomplished more things and touched the lives of more people in his 23 years than most of us could ever hope to do. His curiosity was never satisfied, his intellect was always keen, his soul kind, and his smile contagious. Jared woke each morning with a plan: to do something that day that he had never done before. He never failed.

This book and my life's work are dedicated to the memory and legacy of my son: Be kind, be gentle, be helpful, and be compassionate. Make things better and make them beautiful.

Acknowledgments

Writing a book is the result of a lifelong collection of experiences and events. My parents encouraged my interest in and study of art. My high school art teacher, Pat Buzawa, first showed me how art could be both serious and fun. My sculpture professor, the late Gerry DiGuisto, took a young, naïve art student under his wing and, through his advice, wisdom, and warmth, opened my eyes to the value and meaning of art and the artist. John Jessiman was the first to whet my appetite for clay; I thank him for that and for our enduring friendship.

At the Rhode Island School of Design, David Manzella helped make it possible for me to study pottery and education, and Norm Shulman awakened a sense of criticism and objectivity in me toward my own art; to this day, I look to him for inspiration. Thayer Academy, where Bill Searle and I have taught side by side since 1978, has been an unfailing source of encouragement and support. Bill's insights into my work have been invaluable. To my many students over the years: the challenges you posed for me have kept me alert to the value of teaching and my love for it.

Many thanks to the following people for helping me with this book:
• Rick Hirsch and Morgan Pitelka, for helping me to understand the culture and history of raku;
• My dear friend Dan Levinson, for his insightful critique of the manuscript;
• Jeff Zamek, for his expert help with technical matters;
• Nicki Pardo, for her enthusiasm, patience, and long hours on location as my personal photographer;
• Everyone who graciously contributed images of their work, methods, kilns, and equipment; shared their recipes, experience, and knowledge; and offered their encouragement and help;
• Suzanne Tourtillott, for her confidence in me; my editor Chris Rich, for her immense help; Larry Shea for his expert final proofing and editing; Carol Morse for her beautiful design and layout; and everyone else at Lark Books who had a hand in the realization of *Mastering Raku*.

And finally, thanks to my son, Adam, who shows his pride in me (and mine in him) in more ways than he realizes; and to my dear wife, Ellen, who has been at my side every step of our lives together—with support, encouragement, patience, pride, and love.

About the Author

Steven Branfman credits a rich cultural childhood in New York City as the influence that led him to an art career. He has been a studio potter since 1975 and enjoys an international reputation as a potter, writer, teacher, and businessman. In 1977, he founded as his studio The Potters Shop and School, which has become a nationally known school, gallery, bookstore, and artist's workspace. His raku ware has appeared in more than 150 group and individual exhibitions in galleries and museums throughout the United States and abroad. It has found a place in the permanent collections of the American Museum of Ceramic Art; Museum of Art, Rhode Island School of Design; Schein-Joseph International Museum of Ceramic Art; Frederick R. Weisman Art Museum; and the Everson Museum of Art, among others.

Steven is the author of *Raku: A Practical Approach* and *The Potter's Professional Handbook*. He writes frequently for international craft and pottery magazines as well—articles by or about him have appeared in *Ceramics Monthly, The Crafts Report, Clay Times,* the *Boston Globe, Studio Potter*, and *Pottery Making Illustrated*, among others. His clayworking techniques, examples of his work, and personal profiles appear in many books on pottery and ceramics as well as *Who's Who in American Art* and *Who's Who Among America's Teachers.*

Steven currently teaches at Thayer Academy in Braintree, Massachusetts, having taught in several public school systems and at the college level. He is a popular workshop presenter and has done demonstrations and given lectures about his pottery forming, glazing, and firing techniques all over the United States as well as Canada, Mexico, and Europe. Steven lives in Newton, Massachusetts, with his wife, Ellen, and dog, Bruno.

Index

Credits

page 55 (photo 3): Courtesy of Hal Riegger

page 65 (photo 12): Courtesy of Bracker's Good Earth Clays, Inc.

page 65 (photo 13): Courtesy of Zen Pottery Equipment

page 68 (photo 1): Courtesy of Michael Hough

page 69 (photo 2): Courtesy of the Northern Clay Center, Minneapolis, Minnesota

page 76 (photo 17): Courtesy of Tom Clarke and Dakota Potters Supply

page 77 (photo 21): Courtesy of Steven Branfman

page 78 (photo 23): Courtesy of Harold Takayesu

page 81 (photo 37): Courtesy of Nathaniel Dubbs

page 83 (photo 40): Courtesy of Edge Barnes

pages 83 (photo 41) and 84 (photo 42): Courtesy of Steven Branfman

page 85 (photos 43 and 44): Courtesy of Nesrin During

page 89 (photo 52): Courtesy of Ronda M. Liskey

page 97 (photo 14): Courtesy of Robert Compton

page 111 (photos 38 and 39): Courtesy of Doug Johnson

pages 130 and 131 (photos 2–10): Courtesy of Kate Jacobson

page 133 (photo 13): Courtesy of Edge Barnes

pages 133 and 134 (photos 14–16): Courtesy of Charles Riggs

page 134 (photos 17–18): Courtesy of Maria Martinez

It's all on www.larkbooks.com

Can't find the materials you need to create a project?
Search our database for craft suppliers & sources for hard-to-find materials.

Got an idea for a book?
Read our book proposal guidelines and contact us.

Want to show off your work?
Browse current calls for entries.

Want to know what new and exciting books we're working on?
Sign up for our free e-newsletter.

Feeling crafty?
Find free, downloadable project directions on the site.

Interested in learning more about the authors, designers & editors who create Lark books?